REDEEMING GENDER

Redeeming Gender

ADRIAN THATCHER

OXFORD
UNIVERSITY PRESS

OXFORD

UNIVERSITY PRESS

Great Clarendon Street, Oxford, OX2 6DP,
United Kingdom

Oxford University Press is a department of the University of Oxford.
It furthers the University's objective of excellence in research, scholarship,
and education by publishing worldwide. Oxford is a registered trade mark of
Oxford University Press in the UK and in certain other countries

Published in the United States of America by Oxford University Press
198 Madison Avenue, New York, NY 10016, United States of America

British Library Cataloguing in Publication Data

Data available

Library of Congress Control Number: 2015956607

ISBN 978–0–19–874475–7

Printed in Great Britain by
Clays Ltd, St Ives plc

Contents

Introduction

This book is offered as a contribution to the Christian theology of gender. In this introduction I describe how and why it came to be written, and where the arguments go.

In 2009 (mainly on a sun bed in Majorca) I read Thomas Laqueur's *Making Sex: Body and Gender from the Greeks to Freud* (1990). This work is the primary source for the hypothesis, initially alarming and counterintuitive, that until the eighteenth century people in the West (doctors, philosophers, theologians, the common people) assumed there was a single sex, 'man'. Women belonged to this sex as inferior versions of men, as lesser or 'failed males'. There were only men, demonstrating greater or lesser degrees of perfection. I knew *Making Sex* was receiving much close attention from classicists and historians, and little attention from theologians. I was writing an undergraduate theology textbook, *God, Sex and Gender*, at the time (Thatcher 2011). I found that many of the issues that such a book would be expected to discuss were illuminated by this 'one-sex theory'. I resolved to read more widely about the theory and this present work is the result.

It is widely known that the New Testament contains difficult teaching about the relations between women and men. Many theologians from Tertullian to Barth, through Augustine, Aquinas, and Luther, are now rightly castigated for their teachings about gender (as we now say). But what if, until well into the modern period, there was general unanimity that there was only one sex? Would that not help to explain (and perhaps to mitigate to some extent) what appears as prejudice, gender bias, sexism, gynophobia, and misogyny in the Christian tradition? What if the universal acceptance of two sexes, that unquestionable binary of male and female, is shown to be a modern invention? What if modern theologians and writers of interminable reports on sexuality were wrongly writing two sexes into the scriptures, finding there only what they sought and expected? What if feminists, justly critical of sexism in the tradition, were mistakenly uncritical of the modern notion that there are two sexes? What if even the apparent proscription of homosexuality in the Bible were explicable by means of the one-sex theory (because penetrated men were treated, and treated themselves, as lesser versions of themselves, as women)? What if . . . ?

When I taught the philosophy of religion I sometimes discussed 'what if?' arguments in relation to the existence of God. There is a particular type of thinking called 'abductive inference' (formalized by C. S. Peirce). This kind of thinking moves from the existence of a surprising fact to an explanation of that fact that makes it less surprising. It is sometimes used in a cosmological argument for the existence of God, which runs like this. Take the surprising fact that there is a world. How might that be explained? A Cosmos-Explaining-Being would make the surprising existence of the world less surprising, and would be more likely than rival hypotheses (Shepherd 1975). The argument is unsuccessful, of course, as an argument (the existence of a Cosmos-Explaining-Being can always be challenged), but as a way of thinking, as a demand for the explanation of something inexplicable, it is a great incentive to the search for plausibility. The surprising fact I want to explain is the existence of so much sexism in Christian traditions, still poisoning the well of living water (John 5) from which all Christians drink. Why does the New Testament send mixed messages about the full value of women in the Body of Christ? Why does the tradition still regard women as second-class Christians? Why does the very community which exists to embody the values of unconditional love, acceptance, and respect for persons still allow its thinking about human relations to be emasculated by long-abandoned cultural assumptions?

The hypothesis I began to form was that the 'one-sex theory' would explain much of the bias against women in Christendom, from the Household Codes of the New Testament to the present day. It is of course a large claim which, if validated, could potentially make a distinctive contribution to contemporary discussions of gender. It would explain why so many Christians the world over are not at all surprised by sexism in their traditions: indeed they take it for granted and need to have it explained to them why women and sexual minorities have become so clamorous for fair treatment. It would explain why that transformation of relationships which Christians call 'salvation' was impeded and retarded in the course of Christian history. It would require careful enunciation, testing, attention to its classical sources, to the assessment given by medical and social historians, and to its use by the theologians who would have found no reason to question it. It would also require a difficult sifting of divine revelation from the historical conditions in which the revelation was given.

But there was a further range of surprising questions which the one-sex theory could also help to answer. The theory assumes that the transition to two sexes, arriving in the eighteenth century, led to an incommensurable polarity between the sexes, which (at least initially) was as bad for women as the one-sex theory it replaced. This modern transition is studied by a separate group of historians and is recognized by a different name—'the seventeenth- and eighteenth-century sexuality hypothesis' (McKeon 2012). Towards the end of the twentieth century, such was the confidence in the two-sex theory that, now understood as 'complementarity', it became a new means of normalizing heterosexuality, proscribing same-sex love, and marginalizing intersex and transgender people still further. But what if conservative and feminist theologians alike had read the two-sex theory into scripture and tradition, and had failed to realize its recent and problematic invention? What if the exposure of the historical and cultural assumptions of modern theories of sex and sexuality could lead to a 'clearing', to a 'theological space' where sex and gender negativity could be banished, and where a rejoicing in the fullness of the Gospel, as it transforms gender, could begin? This book details my answers to these questions.

There are several compelling reasons why the one-sex theory must be pulled out from the recesses of theological memory. First, no satisfactory understanding of biblical and traditional views about sex and gender can be achieved without recourse to it. It already shapes and dominates them, and its frame of reference can *never* legitimize the full equality of women with men, or facilitate genuine mutuality between them. However much the modern values of equality, mutuality, and gender justice may be read back into scripture and tradition, they will be superimposed upon a different world view which is unable to authenticate them. What is required is, rather, a transformation of human relations, on which the Christian faith actually insists. The parallels between relations between men and women, and masters and slaves (to which St Paul drew attention in Gal. 3:28) is instructive. Slavery is endorsed by scripture and tradition. Only in modernity was the appeal successfully made to beliefs and values at the very heart of faith, to subvert the iniquitous practice of people owning and trading in people. Sexism throughout the world causes incalculable oppression. Sexism in the churches, manifesting itself in recondite arguments about ordination and episcopacy, constitutes unfinished business. It is the product of a flawed theology, captivated instead of inspired by its heritage.

Second, the emerging belief that there are two distinct and 'opposite' sexes, still contested even at the beginning of the eighteenth century, may also be inadequate. Manufactured by (male) European philosophers, good arguments are available which indicate it was designed to maintain the inferiority of women (see section 3.1). The claim will be made that it oversimplifies human sexuality to the point of misrepresentation, and it assumes a version of scientific knowledge that is unfit for the social purpose of characterizing human relations. It creates 'opposite' sexes. There are no 'opposites' without opposition. On its terrain the outcome of any 'battle of the sexes' is predetermined. While popular versions of Christian faith sanction two opposite sexes within a framework of male ontological priority, a critical but spiritually sensitive theology of gender adduces theological, anthropological, and moral reasons for envisioning a common humanity with many differences, but without gender hierarchy or opposition.

Third, viewed through the lens of the one-sex theory, several Christian doctrines look different. The assumed masculinity of the Father God, the importance attached to the maleness of the incarnate Christ and of the Twelve, the lesser imaging of God by women in relation to men, and so on, are all rendered more explicable once the prism of ancient gendered assumptions through which these doctrines were formulated, and have been received and viewed, are removed from our eyes. The one-sex theory does not render these assumptions believable or acceptable; but it renders them more intelligible. Once they are better understood, they are more easily transformable. The absurdity (to us) of the one-sex theory enables us to jettison the cultural and ideological filters which come with it, and which assume that men are more perfect than women, and their perfection is warranted by the supremely perfect male God.

Fourth, the understanding of human conditions, or sexual norms, to which modern Europeans have ascribed adjectives like 'heterosexual' or 'homosexual', look very different outside the modern binary of two opposite sexes. Once the incapacitating weight of assumptions about opposite sexes is lifted from real relations between women and men, the ground is cleared for giving proper consideration to sexual *similarity* alongside sexual difference, along with many other human similarities and differences (see chapter 7), and giving thanks for them within a theological account of human salvation.

Fifth, the theology of sexuality and gender as it is found among the male giants of the genre (for example, Barth, von Balthasar) and among the sober admonitions of church reports, discussion documents and encyclical letters, can readily be shown to bypass the awkwardness of history. Authors tend to plunge directly into the well of scripture, woefully unmindful of two intervening millennia, and find themselves able to tell us that God made two distinct sexes at the very beginning of time. These mistakes are pervasive and self-enforcing. The recovery of more traditional ways of thinking about sexuality and gender should make it more difficult for theology and church to confuse ancient gender prejudice with God's full redemption of women and men in Christ.

The 'seventeenth- and eighteenth-century sexuality hypothesis' which gave rise to the modern treatment of sexuality raises important questions about how Christians are able to treat and incorporate tradition, reason, and experience as sources of theology. In those churches that value tradition, there remains a strong tendency to counterpose tradition to most or all proposals for doctrinal and moral development. But a likely lesson to be learned from tradition is that the default position of resistance to change is itself an unfaithful way of receiving it. In those churches that continue to value reason (at least as it is practised by the sciences and philosophy), there remains a tendency to allow modern vocabularies to supplant or even obliterate the proper articulation of theological wisdom. However, a paradox will soon emerge. It will be shown that conservative churches and writers have adopted modern vocabularies of sex uncritically and then read them back into the Bible and tradition (see chapter 4). Those churches most resistant to change might have been expected to be more circumspect in their handling of modern vocabularies.

Gender is a term conveying many meanings (see e.g. Bradley 2007: 3–7; Rahman and Jackson 2010: 4–5; Connell and Pearse 2015: 1–12). Harriet Bradley remarks, 'Very generally, gender refers to the relations between women and men' (Bradley 2007: 1). That is the primary meaning assumed in the chapters that follow. When I speak of gender and the need for gender to be redeemed, I think first of the relations between women and men blighted by long-term patriarchy, androcentrism, and sexism in church and world, but next of the exciting possibility that these same relations might be remade with the aid of God's Spirit as Christians discover the fullness of the redemption from these structural sins by the grace of Jesus Christ. That gender is about relationships will provide the key to the Trinitarian understanding of it later (see section 7.2).

THE AIMS OF THE BOOK

These are all good reasons why the one-sex theory and its two-sex successor deserve a full theological discussion and appraisal. The one-sex theory or one-sex model (Laqueur uses both terms) continues to be a major influence on, and a major part of, Christian thinking about sex and gender, even if it is largely unacknowledged. Its residue remains an inhibiting and distorting factor in the attempt to transform unjust gendered practices by Gospel graces. It conveniently relativizes the near impregnable cultural notion that there are two sexes (a notion which instantly delegitimizes intersex, transgender, and third-sex people). The very pervasiveness of the one-sex theory in history proves that attempts to locate its two-sex replacement in scripture and tradition are the consequences of poor hermeneutics. The recovery of traditional (and inadequate) meanings of sex and gender provides a powerful and motivating impetus in the moral development of that same tradition, while the cultural specificities of the two-sex theory require a strong degree of prophetic critique. While the book begins with an examination of both theories, the purpose of the book, to contribute to a much-needed Christian theology of gender, is considerably broader. Specifically, the aims of the book are to:

1. uncover the one-sex theory and its assumptions, and indicate its presence in early Christian thought;
2. describe what happened in our social, intellectual, and theological history, which leaves us thinking that there are two sexes;

3. expose the reliance of much church and theological teaching about sex and gender either on biblical proof texts or upon the language and nomenclature of late modernity, rather than upon considerations of theology and Christology;

4. indicate how theology and Christology, in the area of gender, envision the redemption of human relationships.

The book is in two parts. Part I, 'Retrievals', explains the legacy of both the one-sex and two-sex theories, and fulfils the first two aims. Part II, 'Transformations', contributes to an emerging theology of gender in which women and men are fully and equally valued, and in which sexual difference (insofar as it exists at all) is capable of transformation into joyful communion, reflecting (however finitely) the very life of God the Holy Trinity. Part II fulfils aims 3 and 4. Detailed synopses of the chapters can be found at the beginning of each chapter.

I gladly acknowledge the help of several people in writing the book. I thank Tom Perridge of Oxford University Press for his advice, support, and encouragement while the project was being proposed and prepared. I thank the two anonymous readers for their belief in the project at an early stage, and for their critical advice. I thank Eugene Rogers, Jr, Professor of Religious Studies at the University of North Carolina at Greensboro, for trialling several of the chapters among his students, and for forwarding to me his, and their, detailed responses. I thank my superb colleagues in the Department of Theology and Religion at the University of Exeter for their continued friendship and interest, for granting and renewing my honorary professorship among them, for inviting me to present research seminars and guest lectures at the university, and to attend both formal and more convivial occasions. As a retired academic, my freedom to use the library and online resources of the university has been invaluable. Once again I also thank Caroline Major for her constant encouragement, interest, and patience during the writing of many books, and now for yet another one.

Part I

Retrievals

1

Two Seeds, One Sex?

Chapter 1 begins the first aim of the book—to uncover the one-sex theory and its assumptions, and to indicate its presence in early Christian thought. It introduces the one-sex theory and the elements, qualities, and humours associated with it. It shows that no theory of sex can be derived solely from alleged facts about bodies—an entry point for theological discussion. Three classical theories of sex and reproduction are analysed—those of Hippocrates, Aristotle, and Galen—and the differences between 'one-seed' and 'two-seed' theories are noted. Classical views of gender are next discussed, together with their presence in and influence on the New Testament. Evidence of a new and countercultural understanding of gender in the New Testament is also found. The chapter closes with a short reflection on biblical interpretation in the book.

1.1. THE ONE-SEX THEORY

Early on in *Making Sex*, Laqueur explains, 'For thousands of years it had been a common place that women had the same genitals as men except that, as Nemesius, bishop of Emesa in the fourth century, put it: "theirs are inside the body and not outside it"' (Laqueur 1990: 4). Galen (*c.*130–*c.*210 CE), he continues, 'demonstrated at length that women were essentially men in whom a lack of vital heat—of perfection—had resulted in the retention, inside, of structures that in the male are visible without'. Men and women constitute a single sex with similar reproductive equipment: 'the vagina is imagined as an interior penis, the labia as foreskin, the uterus as scrotum, and the ovaries as testicles'. Until well into the eighteenth century, Laqueur claims, it was believed the orgasms of men and women were both required for the work of conception to be achieved: indeed, 'women, whose desires knew no bounds in the old scheme of things, and whose reason offered so little resistance to passion, became in some accounts creatures whose whole reproductive life might be spent anesthetized to the pleasures of the flesh' (Laqueur 1990: 4). After the two-sex theory had replaced its predecessor, a whole new understanding of sexuality emerged which began to exert a pervasive influence on the discussion of, and the experience of, sex.

The one-sex theory was almost unknown in modern theological and sexual ethics at least until recently. There were, however, notable exceptions (e.g. Martin 2006: 83–4; Farley 2006; Shaw 2007: 222–4; Ellison 2012: 19), while classical scholars have been discussing it for more than two decades. Laqueur thinks that around 1800 (we will need to revisit the date and the specificity of this claim—see section 2.3) sexed bodies begin to be viewed in a radically different way: 'writers of all sorts were determined to base what they insisted were fundamental differences between the male and female sexes, and thus between man and woman, on discoverable biological distinctions and to express these in a radically different rhetoric' (Laqueur 1990: 5). That men and women were two different sexes was a modern, startling idea. Modern medicine, pursued by modern philosophy, verified the change and ensured its permanence.

> Thus the old model, in which men and women were arrayed according to their *degree of metaphysical perfection*, their vital *heat*, along an *axis* whose *telos* was male, gave way by the late eighteenth century to a new model of radical *dimorphism*, of biological divergence. An anatomy and physiology of *incommensurability* replaced a metaphysics of hierarchy in the representation of woman in relation to man.   (Laqueur 1990: 5–6, emphases added)

I have italicized some of the terms in this passage because they operate like key words for Laqueur's entire thesis. So, in the classical way of thinking, *metaphysical* principles and cultural assumptions precede the observation of actual empirical differences, and were invoked to account for the differences which were to hand. The most obvious of these assumptions was *perfection*. Men were more perfect because of their greater *heat*, their bodies more attuned to fire, to summer, to the sun. Women were less perfect because of their lesser heat, their bodies more attuned to cold, to winter, to the moon.

While men and women were thought to share a biological common-ality, their differences were always a matter of *degree*, not a matter of kind. The axis was a single continuum. It included 'manly women' and 'womanish men'. It was always thought more perfect to be male than to be female, and that the direction or telos of the continuum was oriented to the masculine. The idea that humanity exists in two distinct forms (*radical dimorphism*) is an invention of the modern period. Only in the eighteenth century are men and women thought to inhabit opposite and irreconcilable (*incommensurable*) sexes. As we will see (chapter 3) the idea of complementarity was needed (and invented) to bring them back together.

Classical scholars and historians have been discussing the one-sex model for over twenty-five years, and as a result there is now a large collection of secondary literature critiquing it. So, at a time when theologians are waking up to the insights the one-sex model can offer for an evolving understanding of sex in the history of Christianity, classicists are drawing attention to its flaws and offering post-Laqueurian narratives both of the one-sex model and its two-sex 'replacement'. An examination of these criticisms must be postponed to section 2.3.

1.1.1. Elements and Qualities, Humours, and Heat

The one-sex theory is not just a historical theory about human sexual difference (or the lack of it). All bodies, inanimate and animate, animal and human, were thought to be composed of elements; all elements have qualities; and in the human case, the qualities are humours. The arrangements of these qualities are what make a being male or female. To be sexed is not simply a characteristic of a living species. Everything is deemed masculine or feminine. Every-thing in the terrestrial sphere was thought to consist, to differing degrees, of the four basic ontological *elements*, fire, air, water, and earth. Helkiah Brooke, court physician to James I of England, explained in his *Mikrokosmographia* (1615) the long-held view that each element possessed a *quality*: fire was hot and dry; air was hot and moist; water was cold and moist; and earth, cold and dry (Schiebinger 1989: 161). The body had four chief fluids, corresponding to the elements, called *cardinal humours* or simply *humours* ('humors' in US English). The four humours were blood, phlegm, yellow bile, and black bile. Blood was reckoned to be hot and wet. It heated the body and kept it moist. Phlegm (like water) was reckoned to be cold and wet, 'and provided for cold, moist organs and parts of the body, including the brain' (Crawford 2007: 103). Too much phlegm made a person 'dull in temperament'. Yellow bile, manufactured by the liver, caused excretion. Like fire, it was hot and dry. The cause of hair loss in bald men was an excess of yellow bile, while 'a deficiency of yellow bile meant women had long hair (as it did not burn off)'. Black bile (like earth) was cold and dry. It produced appetite, including sexual appetite. It was 'associated with the spleen, seen as the source of melancholy, and considered the cause of a depressive personality' (Crawford 2007: 103). The health of a person consisted of a balance of the four humours, and the balance was called *complexion*.

The elements linked human bodies to other bodies in an overall cosmic scheme. According to the theory biological difference just is the arrangement of these qualities and humours. Men are hotter and drier than women. The bodies of men and women are instances of a balance of qualities and elements, but so are the bodies of everything else. The sun is the body with the greatest heat. The sun is associated with the direction of its rising, and the season of its highest temperature. The sun is masculine. Its counterpart is the moon. The moon is cold and is associated with the coldest season of the year. The moon is feminine. Spring and autumn provide a more or less equal balance of hot and cold, wet and dry.

In the case of human bodies, sexual temperament (it would be misleading to call this 'sexuality') was also a combination of humours. The whole ontological picture seemed to explain the known condition of what we call intersex ('hermaphrodite'), and also the bodies and temperaments of men who displayed 'feminine' traits and women who displayed 'masculine' traits. In theory there could be perfect men and perfect women. But since it was always more perfect to be male than to be female, women could never reach the ideal of (masculine) perfection. The line between masculine and feminine could however easily be crossed. The humours and fluids of the body were 'fungible', that is, they could change from one state to another, and so their balance was always precarious. 'Endless mutations, a cacophonous ringing of changes, become possible where modern physiology would see distinct and often sexually specific entities' (Laqueur 1990: 35).

1.1.2. The Need for Ontology

Before we investigate in more detail the classical authors and their influence on biblical writers, a further advantage to Christian theology of the resurrection of this strange, almost mythical, single-sex theory should be noted. The claim is made that the theory, and its two-sex successor, exceeds the facts; or, put slightly differently, that 'no set of facts ever entails any particular account of [sexual] difference' (Laqueur 1990: 19). An example of the subsumption of apparent facts by theories is the clear mistake made by 'the giants of Renaissance anatomy' who 'persisted in seeing the vagina as an internal version of the penis' after the differences had become obvious. That they could stubbornly continue to do so, accuses Laqueur, 'suggests that almost any sign of difference is dependent on an underlying theory of, or context for, deciding what counts and what does not count as evidence' (Laqueur 1990: 21). An immediate consequence of the claim, if true, is that 'values' are required to complete the picture. Appeals to heat and perfection were also appeals to values. However, those values have long lost any explanatory or justificatory power they once might have had. But that does not render values redundant. It renders the search for values that make sense of sexual difference more urgent. Christian faith, despite its ambiguous record of teaching about human bodies, can still make audacious contributions to the search.

This lacuna in the field of sexual values is deeply significant. Laqueur qua historian makes no attempt to fill it; rather he lays it bare. He tries to persuade his readers 'that there is no "correct" representation of women in relation to men and that the whole science of difference is thus misconceived' (Laqueur 1990: 21). It is possible to imagine that St Paul had a similar purpose when he proclaimed the disassembly of 'male and female' to the Christians of Galatia (Gal. 3:28). The thought that the modern hiatus in sexual values represents an opportunity for theology is a positive one, provided that an appropriate excavation of the depths of Christian thought is undertaken. Laqueur said his 'goal' in writing *Making Sex* was

> to show how a biology of hierarchy in which there is only one sex, a biology of incommensurability between two sexes, and the claim that there is no publicly relevant sexual difference at all, or no sex, have constrained the interpretation of bodies and the strategies of sexual politics for some two thousand years. (Laqueur 1990: 23)

Here then is deconstruction at its finest. Three approaches to gender are all found wanting, because the problem of gender cannot be reduced to the problem of sex or the self-authenticating descriptions of science or sexology. It is easy for twenty-first-century people to reject the one-sex theory. It is far less easy for us to realize that the two-sex theory is historically contingent and carries with it inconsistencies, polarities, and values which are not supplied by medical science at all. Much theology is stuck in this two-sex theory. It gratefully reads it back into the Bible, and congratulates itself for finding it there. The third alternative, which would ride roughshod over obvious differences between men and women or issue ideological denials of them, is subject to the same criticisms that it aims at opposing views: it too cannot be established by 'the facts'. The impasse represents an entry point for theology, for theology has rich stories to tell about bodies, their origin, meaning, and end; about their vulnerability, connectivity, and frailty; about how they are diminished and restored. Here then, is a 'values vacuum' waiting to be filled.

It is not at all obvious, outside of a purely biological examination, who or what a man or a woman might be, and sometimes even biology itself yields baffling results. One becomes an adult within a particular context where norms of masculinity and femininity exercise formidable power. That is the case in any human society at all, and especially in those social groups where male and female are frequently separated or women are excluded. Christian theologians have several reasons for engaging with ontological questions. First, the question 'what is a man or a woman?' has come to the fore, not least because intersex, transgender, and 'third-sex' people are increasingly visible and are challenging the usual male/female binary (see section 4.2.2). What now calls itself 'theological anthropology' (the doctrine of human being) has scarcely begun to respond to this challenge. Second, because ontology is about being, it links human beings with non-human beings and with God, the Author of all beings whatsoever. To speak of human *being* may be thought to avoid temporarily the inevitable male/female binary, but that is not the principal reason for advocating ontology. Under God all beings share the status of creatureliness. Faith has a vision of God as the Source of all being, the mysterious and gracious One who bestows the grace of being on all beings, so that no being at all can be without sharing, in some minimal sense, the enabling being of God.

Third, and most important, Christians think Jesus Christ is the author of a new beginning for humanity. More than this, he initiates a new humanity (see section 7.2.1), as the Letters to Ephesus and Colossae affirm, and all churches attest. It is necessary to ask how this new humanity is constituted and how the relations between women and men within it are to be envisaged and performed. And fourth, the need to rethink gender comes at a time in the evolution of the humanities where the end of metaphysics has been announced, along with the impossibility of grand narratives and universal truth claims, the need to avoid colonial arrogance and 'totalizing discourses', and so on. This chastened cultural impasse is an invitation to theology to tell its own story, to proclaim a dimension of being which late modernity has marginalized and overlooked. That story contains massive androcentric and sexist assumptions, but the retelling of it can be jolted into freshness by attention to the very criticisms that have led to its large-scale abandonment.

1.2. THREE CLASSICAL VIEWS OF SEX

With these preliminaries in mind, we can now explore how three of the most influential authors in the West—Hippocrates (*c.*460–*c.*370 BCE), Aristotle (384–322 BCE), and Galen *c.*130–*c.*210 CE)—understood biological sex, and how they shaped Western attitudes to male/female relations. These authors provided Laqueur with his earliest historical evidence. Hippocrates and Galen believed both men and women emitted seed (*duogenesis*): Aristotle believed only men emitted seed (*monogenesis*). We shall see that all of them believed there was one sex. The title of the present chapter ('Two Seeds, One Sex?') is drawn from these theories. They provided alternative pathways to similar misogynistic conclusions.

1.2.1. Hippocrates

Perhaps the oldest conception theory in the West is the 'furrowed field theory' (Boylan 1984: 85). It is a 'one-seed' theory. In the *Eumenides*, a play written by Aeschylus in 458 BCE, Apollo says,

Not the true parent is the woman's womb
That bears the child; she doth but nurse the seed
New-sown: the male is parent; she for him,
As stranger for a stranger, hoards the germ
Of life, unless the god its promise blight.

I have heard this theory from the lips of contemporary Christians and Muslims, adept at the trick of transforming ancient biology into modern sexist metaphor. The man sows his seed in the woman's garden. 'Sowing wild oats' is a modern trope for male promiscuous behaviour which perpetuates the idea. The male is the true parent. 'She bore him a son.' But as Michael Boylan points out (1984: 86), ancient philosophers and physicians were already grappling with two difficulties posed by furrowed field theory. If men provide the source of life, why do some boys and men look like their mothers? More radically, why do women come to be at all? The assumption of the four qualities (hot, cold, wet, dry) helped to 'explain' the difficulties. The male was hot and dry: the female cold and moist. The determination of the sex of the child was provided by the temperature of the environment and other chance biological factors:

> The sex of the baby was not determined at all by the parent (father), but was the result of the environment of the seed in the womb. This environment might be affected by the winds (cold or warm), the right or left testicle from which the seed came, or the right or left side of the womb in which the infant was said to be generated. (Boylan 1984: 86)

This environmental qualification could 'explain' why a girl might resemble her father. It could *not* explain why a boy might resemble his mother. The solution of that conundrum lay in various two-seed theories, which persisted until the modern period. One of these is found in the writings attributed to Hippocrates. There are two seeds that fuse together to form a foetus. The observed fact that both men and women potentially experience pleasure when having sex was evidence that both of them emitted seed. Semen comes not simply from the testicles but from the whole body (in a theory known as *pangenesis*). Exhaustion after sex was thought to be evidence that the seed had come from the entire body. The problem of sex determination was therefore eased by the thought that men and women both ejaculate sperm. It was further eased by the addition that men ejaculate male and female sperm, and so do women. Yes, Hippocrates stated that

> In the male there is female sperm and male sperm; in the same way in the woman. The male sperm is stronger than the female. For of necessity the male develops from the stronger sperm. And here is another point. If the sperm that comes from both is strong, a male is born; if weak, a female is born. Whichever prevails [in quantity] that is which is born.   (*On Seed*, ch. 6. In Boylan 1984: 89)

Even though women have male sperm, male sperm is 'stronger'. A child is conceived by the mingling of two sets of male and two sets of female sperms. The sex of the child is determined by the quantity of male sperm present. Aside from the complications that arise from the mixing of so many sperms, a new question arises: given that women can produce male and female sperm, what is the point of having a male at all?

1.2.2. Aristotle

Aristotle tries to answer this question. He lays out his understanding of 'male' and 'female', and their respective roles in reproduction, in his *On the Generation of Animals*. 'Male' and 'female' are 'principles of generation'. The male is the efficient cause of offspring: the female is the material cause. These principles belong to a wider 'hierarchy of value' which is prior to any facts about real male and female bodies, however they may be understood. So, human beings are unities of soul and body (*hylomorphism*); 'soul is better than body', and the efficient cause 'is better and more divine in its nature than the material on which it works'. The male principle is superior, and 'it is better that the superior principle should be separated from the inferior ... For the first principle of the movement, or efficient cause, whereby that which comes into being is male, is better and more divine than the material whereby it is female' (Aristotle 2013: Book 2.1). The male provides the soul of the embryo. If an animal lives it has 'soul'. 'No soul will exist', Aristotle averred, 'in anything except that of which it is soul; it is plain therefore that semen both has soul, and is soul, potentially.'

Semen, continues Aristotle, 'is a compound of spirit (*pneuma*) and water, and the former is hot air (*aerh*); hence semen is liquid in its nature because it is made of water'. It 'is thick and white because it is mixed with spirit', but when it cools it resembles only water. It is white because it is 'foam'. Foam is evidence of heat. Sperm conveys spirit into the female. What is left of the semen 'dissolves and evaporates because it has a liquid and watery nature' (Aristotle 2013: Book 3). The spirit or soul is the 'vital heat', observable in the foam of the semen. Semen comes, fungibly, from blood. Blood comes from nutrition. The blood of women is less pure than the blood of men. And women, crucially, lack the heat to concoct from their blood the semen which conveys the soul. These deficiencies are responsible for Aristotle's infamous remark that the female 'is, as it were, a mutilated male, and the catamenia are semen, only not pure; for there is only one thing they have not in them, the principle of soul' (Aristotle 2013: Book 2.3, see section 2.2.2 below).

Once again lack of heat constitutes the weakness of women. Fertile men, because of their greater heat, concoct sperm, but the very nature of women is to be colder than men. So is their blood. Women have an excess supply of unconcocted blood, which in males becomes sperm. In women, the excess causes a 'sort of haemorrhage'. These 'tend to occur' in cooler times, or when the moon is waning or absent. Because nature is not wasteful, semen mingles with blood. The meaning of male and female is, then, to be the efficient or the material cause of offspring; to be the active or passive partner in reproduction, for

> the female always provides the material, the male that which fashions it, for this is the power that we say they each possess, and *this is what is meant by calling them male and female* . . . While the body is from the female, it is the soul that is from the male, for the soul is the reality of a particular body. (Aristotle 2013: Book 4, emphasis added)

Male and female are principles, not sexes. 'Sexual difference is a matter of degree and not kind, and thus a woman is an undercooked or parboiled man' (Kraemer 2011: 16, citing Levinson 2000). In Laqueur's judgement Aristotle held that 'All of the male organs . . . are similar in the female except that she has a womb, which presumably the male does not' (Laqueur 1990: 33). Men can produce seed and women can't. That is sexual difference. Both men and women have 'ungendered blood'. Only one sex can convert its blood into semen: '*sperma* and *katamenia* refer to greater or lesser refinements of an ungendered blood'. This is of course a metaphysical, not an empirical, description of alleged facts, for

What one sees, or could ever see, does not really matter except insofar as the thicker, white, frothier quality of the male semen is a hint that it is more powerful, more likely to act as an efficient cause, than the thinner, less pristinely white, and more watery female ejaculate or the still red, even less concocted, menstrua. Like reproductive organs, reproductive fluids turn out to be versions of each other; they are the biological articulation, in the language of a one-sex body, of the politics of two genders and ultimately of engendering.   (Laqueur 1990: 38–9)

Modern readers are likely to classify these early accounts of sexual difference as 'social constructions' or 'ideologous prejudices', while overlooking the possibility that modern accounts may not be entirely free from similar contaminants. It is easy to see how, once a world view is established which takes polarities such as active/passive, hot/cold, form/matter, and soul/body for granted, men and women are sufficiently pliable to be made to fit within them, and even to confirm them. Semen bears the immaterial reason which the woman receives, and reason (for Aristotle) is divine. 'Vital heat' makes the semen productive: it works through it. It is 'analogous to the element of the stars' (Aristotle 2013: Book 2.3). The man's vital heat connects him to God or the gods, to perfection (women lack heat so are imperfect), and to the heavens. In an Aristotelian framework women are constituted by a series of deficiencies, embarrassing to recall. Because they lack sperm and heat, they lack divinity, perfection, and reason. Women are less perfect, not just because of their lack of heat in relation to men, but also because they cannot produce that special substance which conveys the immaterial soul of a person. This was a further reason why men were associated with spirit, women with flesh.

1.2.3. Galen

More than half a millennium later, Galen returned to a two-seed theory which, he thought, overcame certain difficulties in Aristotle's account of conception. In his *On Seed* he developed two sorts of related objection to Aristotle's theory: philosophical and biological. Aristotle had taught that the male sperm, or at least the spiritual part of it, was the efficient cause of the embryo, the 'trigger' (Boylan 1984: 103) which initiated the processes of change in the womb but without contributing anything to the embryo materially. Its work was done once it had set off the process of conception. Galen could make no sense of this. In the case of offspring resembling their mothers, at the very least, Galen thought that mothers must provide the source of movement of the embryo as well as its material cause. He believed

> that female seed is expelled from the ovaries at the time of coition in such manner that both seeds meet in the womb, mix, and form a membrane; the female seed serves as food for the semen in its development, then the development follows, with *pneuma* bringing about the development of Galen's three major organs, liver, heart, and brain. (Preus 1977: 83. See also Cadden 1995: 32–5)

Male semen does not, on this account, evaporate as Aristotle taught. In any case, on Aristotle's view it mingles with menstrual blood, and being mixed, it cannot be unmixed in order to be evacuated. While Galen sometimes confuses *katamenia* and female seed as the object that male sperm mixes with, his position is that the *katamenia* provides nourishment for the foetus, while the female seed contributes to its efficient cause. However, the hierarchy of value which presets Aristotle's theory is not entirely overcome. There is strong seed and weak seed. The usual familiar ontological qualities (male: hot and dry; female: cold and wet) become the explanation for weaker seed: 'The female's moistness is used to aid in nourishment and the cold is a given which (following Aristotle) makes the female "weaker" than the male' (Boylan 1984: 101). According to Galenic and humoral theory, 'genital anatomy was differentiated along a hierarchical continuum that reflected the superiority of men and the inferiority of women. By this way of thinking, women have less body heat than men do, and therefore women's sex organs are morphologically underdeveloped, an inverted and internalized version of men's' (McKeon 2012: 792).

We have considered two two-seed theories and one one-seed theory. In the two-seed theories, the male sperm is stronger, or more profuse. Men are stronger and hotter. In the one-seed theory, women produce *katamenia* only, because they lack the heat to convert it into sperm. Indeed, women represent a range of lacks—sperm, heat, divinity, perfection, reason, and so on. Both theories reinforce later misogyny. These remarkable prejudices belong to a broader prior ontology. Men and women are made to fit into it. They provide its chief exemplification. But reproductive theories alone are not responsible for the alleged deficiencies of women. These 'deficiencies' work their way into the descriptions. They are located in ancient cultures, and classical scholars have brought them to the attention of theologians.

1.3. CLASSICAL VIEWS OF GENDER

It should be well apparent by now that biological sexual differences provide only a single strand in any discussion of gender. That is because gender intersects with many other categories and strands of inquiry, making its extraction from these difficult, if not impossible (see Warnke 2011: 92–9). Pamela Sue Anderson explains: '"Intersectionality" is a current term for the inescapably interrelated categories in the construction of gender. Gender is inescapably formed by, and recognized where it intersects with, a range of social and material categories, including race, religion, ethnicity, class, age and sexual orientation' (Anderson 2012: xii). Tina Beattie adds ability and disability, postcolonial perspectives, and cultural affiliations to the open list of categories with which gender intersects (Beattie 2015). Classicists too incorporate many of these categories when analysing gender in the ancient world.

Roman men, for example, were expected to display 'hardness' (*duritia, robur*), which, while apparently rooted in the body, shaded over into the moral and social realms. Hardness, writes Mathew Kuefler, 'referred to the muscularity of the ideal male body; it also symbolized the moral uprightness and self-discipline that men were presumed to embody' (Kuefler 2001: 21). The opposite quality assigned to women was 'softness' or 'delicateness' (*mollitia*) which 'represented not only their delicate bodies, but also their love of luxury, the languor of their minds, the ease with which they gave themselves to their emotions, and their dissolute morals' (Kuefler 2001: 21). Once again we find the illicit move made from certain assumed biological facts about men to certain moral conclusions, this time about the active and passive sexual roles of men and women:

> The hardness of men marked not only their moral austerity but also their role as sexual penetrators and sexual aggressors. In a complimentary [*sic*] way, the *mollitia* or softness of women denoted their role as sexually penetrated, and beyond that, the passive role they were expected to play not only in sexual relations but also in society generally. (Kuefler 2001: 22)

The ancients, writes Diana Swancutt, did not think of people as 'two genetically differentiated sexes, male, and female' (how could they?). Rather, they 'constructed the human physique on a one-body, multi-gendered model with the perfect body deemed "male/man"' (Swancutt 2003: 197). But what is construable as a bland biomedical matter is seen to extend into every nook and cranny of personal and social life. Greek and Roman men 'were described with cultural superlatives that reflected their perfect "natural" state: physical and political strength, rationality, spirituality, superiority, activity, dryness, and penetration'. Women, conversely, were thought to embody the negative qualities of 'physical and political weakness, irrationality, fleshliness, inferiority, passivity, wetness, and being penetrated' (Swancutt 2003: 197–8). Swancutt stresses that these 'opposite' qualities do not at all reflect two opposite sexes. Rather,

> because all bodies were thought to contain more- (masculine) and less-perfect (feminine) elements that required constant maintenance to produce the perfect male/masculine body, females/women and the other gendered beings (e.g., androgynes, *kinaidoi* [effeminates], and *tribades* [dominatrices]) were deemed differently imperfect versions of the male body, versions whose imperfections (e.g., breasts, fat, menstruation, weak sperm, inverted internal penises) were manifestations of their impaired physiological health.   (Swancutt 2003: 198)

Elite men, Swancutt says, were defined as 'hard, rational penetrators' at the top of the social ladder, while 'Women occupied its lowest rungs because they were soft, leaky, and wild—the least perfect male-bodies, their vaginas deemed undescended penises' (Swancutt 2006: 71). Heat, hardness, reason, spirituality, and so on—in short, perfection—were key marks of elite masculinity.

There is a wide range of classical studies which, since Laqueur's *Making Sex* in 1990, have become available to New Testament scholars. They confirm the one-sex theory. One of these summarizes the 'ground rules of Greco-Roman masculinity' as follows:

> 1) Mastery is the basic criterion of masculinity. Being fully gendered as a man, as opposed to merely having the physical features held to signify a male, means being on top in relation to non-men (women, slaves, children, barbarians) and being able to control one's own passions and desires. 2) Manliness is an achievement and has to be constantly proven in competition with other men. Masculinity is always under construction. 3) Manliness is a moral quality . . . Being manly is always a

positive value, even when applied to a woman. By contrast, being effeminate or soft is morally reprehensible. (Ivarsson 2006:165–6; and see Stowers 1997)

Colleen Conway confirms the one-sex theory and its seepage into the social body. Greeks and Romans ranked higher than other people of other nationalities; men were ranked higher than women, and women belonged with slaves, foreigners, and animals in the requirement of submission to male authority:

> slaves, too, were like animals, women, and foreigners insofar as they lived lives of submission. In short, understanding what it meant to be a man in the Greco-Roman world meant understanding one's place in a rationally ordered cosmos in which free men were placed at the top and what fell beneath could all be classified as 'unmen'. (Conway 2008: 15)

Aristotle is cited for the assumption that men are more 'godlike' than women because, being active, their activity 'was linked to the creative activity of the gods' (Conway 2008: 22, 36). Aristotle and Galen together 'operated on the basis of a vertical hierarchy with elite free males at the top, and less perfect versions of the male sex populating the space below (freed men, women, slaves, barbarians)' (Conway 2015: 222). Conway reissues a warning which in this book has been taken very much to heart: 'Because it showed the fundamentally different way that ancient thinkers "constructed" the male and female bodies, Laqueur's work highlighted the dangers of importing contemporary ideas of sexual difference onto these ancient texts, including the New Testament' (Conway 2015: 222). It will be shown later in these pages that these dangers have been almost entirely ignored.

1.4. GENDER IN THE NEW TESTAMENT

Readers may be patiently wondering what these descriptions of sex and gender in the classical world have to do with the New Testament. The answer is that the New Testament world *belongs to* the classical world, with the obvious qualification that the Jesus movement was born within the Palestinian Jewish faith, identity, and practice, and more obviously influenced by these. The big questions for a theology of gender are the extent to which relations of gender in, and prescribed by, the New Testament are already governed by the prior ontology, and the extent to which the divine revelation recorded there has been able to begin to transform them. The New Testament provides evidence for the one-sex theory and the gender hierarchy that accompanies it. And it also provides evidence for the beginnings of the transformation of the gendered relations embedded in it (see chapter 5). Given that the promise of the New Testament is nothing less than a 'new creation' (2 Cor. 5:17 NRSV; the New Revised Standard Version of the Bible is used for all biblical quotations, unless otherwise stated), it would be pointless living the faith now if lives were not at least partially transformed by it. Equally, since the incarnation of God in Christ happened in 'flesh', it happened in time and in history, and its situatedness in both cannot be bypassed.

There may be a reference in the New Testament to a two-seed theory. William Loader certainly thinks so (2010: 43; 2013: 59; see also van der Horst 1990). The author of Hebrews explains that 'Through faith also Sara herself received strength to conceive seed' (Heb. 11:11 KJV). All the modern translations I have consulted make a mess of this verse. The King James Version accurately and literally renders the Greek text (*pistei kai autè Sarra dunamin eis katabolèn spermatos elaben*). When the translators of the KJV (published in 1611) were at work, the European medical profession and probably everyone else still held to a one-sex, two-seed theory, so when the translators were confronted with an obvious Greek text which stated that Sarah received strength to conceive seed, they did not think to question it. A straightforward literal translation posed no interpretative difficulty. The narrative records the miraculous birth of Isaac according to the same medical orthodoxy known both to the author of Hebrews and to the British translators of the Bible in the early seventeenth century. The Talmud too assumes a two-seed theory (Irshai 2015: 425–6).

1.4.1. Household Codes

But the focus of our interest is not on the familiarity of New Testament writers with reproductive theory. It is with the influence on the New Testament of the one-sex theory and its incorporation into a larger, totalizing world view that we are concerned. The hierarchical view is at its most obvious in the Household Codes of the New Testament (Col. 3:18–4:1; Eph. 5:22–6:9; 1 Tim. 2:8–15, 6:1–2; Titus

2:1–10). Wives are to submit to their husbands; children are to obey their parents; and slaves are to obey their masters. The structure of the household confirms what was already familiar to readers of, for example, Aristotle's *Politics* (n/d Book 1.5). Aristotle assumed 'the male is by nature superior, and the female inferior; and the one rules, and the other is ruled; this principle, of necessity, extends to all mankind' (n/d Book 1.5). Indeed, the code in Ephesians (5.21–6.9) confines marital love to husbands only. Husbands are thrice told to love their wives. Wives are thrice told to submit to their husbands. We are a long historical distance away from modern egalitarian marriage.

It is well known that the gender hierarchy extends into churches. 'Women should be silent in the churches. For they are not permitted to speak, but should be subordinate, as the law also says' (1 Cor. 14:34 NRSV). There is no such law in Jewish scripture that silences women in the synagogue, and earlier in the same letter women are allowed to pray and prophesy as long as their heads are veiled (1 Cor. 11:5). Paul deploys a theological argument confirming what he already 'knew' about male superiority from his citizenship in the wider culture. He gives the man/woman hierarchy explicit Christological endorsement—'But I want you to understand that Christ is the head of every man, and the husband is the head of his wife, and God is the head of Christ' (1 Cor. 11:3). He then utilizes Genesis 2 in order to endorse the veiling of women in church:

> [7]For a man ought not to have his head veiled, since he is the image and reflection of God; but woman is the reflection of man. [8]Indeed, man was not made from woman, but woman from man. [9]Neither was man created for the sake of woman, but woman for the sake of man. [10]For this reason a woman ought to have a symbol of authority on her head, because of the angels. [11]Nevertheless, in the Lord woman is not independent of man or man independent of woman. [12]For just as woman came from man, so man comes through woman; but all things come from God.

Any appeal to the special circumstances possibly prevailing in Corinth cannot mitigate the impact of the clear theological message. Alarmingly, the argument, intended to establish a settled liturgical practice, draws in evolving doctrines of God, of Christ, and of the image of God, differently 'reflected' in men and women. And that is not all. The argument assumes an even broader ontology. Drawing on a creation narrative, the ontology even encompasses angels and 'all things'. Everyone knew in Paul's day that a man is more perfect than a woman. Paul finds scriptural warrant for this assumption. He could, like many modern writers, have appealed directly to Genesis 1:27, where there is a well-known reference to the image of God being shared between men and women (and no suggestion of subordination, however much it was subsequently read into the text). This verse has become a proof text in the last fifty years, deployed to support the late modern doctrine of complementarity (see section 6.2). Paul had no such thought when he wrote his letter to the church at Corinth. He went straight to Genesis 2 where the *chronological* priority of the man over the woman in the order of creation ('man was not made from woman, but woman from man') became the basis for the *ontological* priority of the man in all areas of life ('Neither was man created for the sake of woman, but woman for the sake of man').

The account of creation in Genesis 2 is made to authorize a dress code for women in church. Later in the New Testament a similar argument from Genesis 2 compels women's silence in church altogether (1 Tim. 2:11–12) and authorizes further strictures on what women are allowed to wear in church (1 Tim. 2:9–10). The author of 1 Peter extends the dress code beyond the assembly and makes it a general rule (1 Pet. 3:1–6). The chronological priority of Adam over Eve in the order of creation again becomes the reason for the ontological priority of Adam over Eve in the orders of church and world. Adam is first in the order of creation; Eve is first in the order of deception: 'For Adam was formed first, then Eve; and Adam was not deceived, but the woman was deceived and became a transgressor' (1 Tim. 2:13–14). Forever after Eve is scapegoated as the temptress of Adam, the woman as the temptress of the man. Her role lies in childbearing, and her salvation depends conditionally on the acceptance of that position: 'Yet she will be saved through childbearing, provided they continue in faith and love and holiness, with modesty' (1 Tim. 2:15). The broader theology is utilized to endorse the wider social order and to replicate that order in the local church.

It is often said that the maleness of Jesus and the twelve disciples constitutes the reason why women cannot represent Christ as priests (Congregation for the Doctrine of the Faith 1976), but attention is less often paid to the live and influential cultural presumption that it is better—more perfect—to be male than to be female. Men are 'naturally' leaders in this ancient milieu. Since men are more perfect than women, women, according to Paul, cannot share the image of God in the same way that men can (1 Cor. 11:7). The inevitable sharp question arises whether the ground for the exclusion of women from priesthood confuses Gospel with culture. The 'natural' and cultural priority of men over women, in every respect, provides the background which helps to explain the resort of New Testament writers to what we rightly diagnose as androcentrism.

1.4.2. Transformative Elements

But these bleak, oppressive elements of biblical thought thankfully tell only part of the story. There are transformative elements too. While the Household Codes provide evidence for the hierarchical ordering of households, including slaves—rightly distressing for modern readers—they also provide evidence for the beginning of Christian reflection on life within these households and subsequent alteration of practices. Elsewhere I have called this 'the trajectory hypothesis', that is, 'the idea that there existed a trajectory in early Christianity toward equality of the sexes and equal regard marriages . . . with the proviso . . . that the development was unfortunately (and very early) interrupted' (Thatcher 2007: 39; and see Thatcher 2015a: 601). The codes can no longer be used as guides to household life (because they take slavery and the inferiority of women for granted), but they may well be used to illustrate the beginnings of a 'trajectory' towards the full equality of persons which, two millennia later, has still not been fully achieved. Wives must be subject to their husbands, but this subjection must be 'in the Lord' (Col. 3:18). Husbands are to love their wives. That is remarkable enough, but their required love is to be measured by a most exacting standard—the love of Christ for the church (Eph. 5:25). The new faith places exacting demands on the slaves and their owners. Perhaps it is remarkable that slaves are *directly addressed* at all (Roberts 2007). They have their place in the 'household of faith' as well as in the household. They are enjoined to serve their masters as if they were serving Christ (Col. 3:23–4), and even to endure suffering from them following the example of Christ who suffered for them (1 Pet. 2:18–23). While the uses of these texts over time have been scandalous, validating slavery and enforcing cruel compliance, they may also be read as an attempt to enable slaves to think theologically about their wretched condition, and find the presence of Christ in the midst of it. Slave owners are enjoined to 'treat your slaves justly and fairly', in the knowledge that their 'Master in heaven' (Col. 4:1) relativizes their authority, and requires their subjection to a different understanding of personal and social power.

But the text of any of the scriptures is most useful when it generates theological thinking about the significance of Jesus Christ. The codes do this, as does Paul in the notorious 1 Cor. 11 passage. It is possible to see a theological method in the passage. His advice to the Corinthians begins in Christology ('I want you to understand that Christ is the head of every man'). It moves to the doctrine of God ('God is the head of Christ'). It is based in scripture, in fact in the 'theological anthropology' found there (the reference to Genesis 2), and it moves from these to practical implications for worship and Christian practice. I adopt a similar 'Pauline method' in this book but come to very different, non-hierarchical conclusions about the relations between women and men in the church and the world. But the method remains. Scripture remains foundational for the understanding of God and of ourselves. Jesus Christ is who and what changes everything. He is to be understood as the revelation of the Triune God, and from meditation on what God has revealed and done, ethical and practical conclusions follow. The argument of this book will demonstrate that it is possible to arrive at conclusions very different from the subordinationism of 1 Cor. 11, while based on the methodology and principles that Paul himself used. A similar methodology is used in the Household Code of Ephesians 5 (Thatcher 2007: 34). Suzanne Henderson adopts a similar reading of, and detects similar principles in, the Colossian Household Code (Henderson 2006). These texts cry out for redemption from patriarchal voices using them to author and to 'author-ize' exclusionary and oppressive practices.

1.4.3. A Note on Biblical Interpretation

Readers who have survived thus far will already have a good idea of the theological method and assumptions that are used in the book. The use of the Bible is consistent with my detailed account of what the Bible is and the hermeneutical principles required for its use in an earlier work, *The Savage Text* (Thatcher 2008a). I argued there that belief in the primacy of the Bible as a theological source should not be allowed to compromise the finality of Jesus as the revealed Word of God (John 1), and that the application of the honorific title 'Word of God' to the Bible frequently elevates it to a position that ought to be reserved only for the One to whom the Bible bears witness. Once this mistake is made, the Bible is understood as a guidebook which is quarried for guidance about moral and spiritual matters, often with contradictory, undecidable, and morally disastrous results, as historical arguments about race, slavery, witchcraft, the end of the world, the corporal punishment of children, the persecution of Jews, and—currently—sexuality and gender, well attest. I called this use of the Bible in Christian ethics the 'circle of futility' (Thatcher 2008a: 160). Gender will not be knowingly exposed to the circle of futility in this volume.

This author is an Anglican Christian. Discussions of this unfortunate and limited kind are continuing among Anglicans about sexuality (by which is usually meant 'homosexuality'). Leaving aside the contention that questions about sexuality may be reducible to questions about gender, it is easy to see a similarly unfortunate and parallel discussion of gender gathering pace. This discussion alights all too quickly on a limited number of biblical texts. The most prominent of these is Paul's assertion, in Galatians 3:28, that 'There is no longer Jew or Greek, there is no longer slave or free, there is no longer male and female; for all of you are one in Christ Jesus.' It is a verse offering a vision, unique in the New Testament, which indicates that 'male and female' require transformation, and that God in Christ has accomplished it. Two sets of problems are then likely to arise: the first about how 'male and female' and 'one in Christ Jesus' are to be understood within the letter to the Galatians as a whole; the second about how this verse can be reconciled with several lengthy passages in the New Testament which indicate that relationships between men and women are required to be conducted, in churches, marriages, and households, along the lines of male dominance and female submission (see Martin 2006: 77–90). The stalemate between these alternative views is likely then to be resolved by regarding Galatians 3:28 either as an aberration, or by allowing its transformative potential to disappear under the weight of texts which appear to contradict it (see Kartzow 2010). As the philosopher Antony Flew once wrote (in the context of the failure of theodicies to convince sceptics), 'a fine brash hypothesis may thus be killed by inches, the death by a thousand qualifications' (Flew 1955: 97).

Contemporary interpreters of the Bible often follow a threefold ordering of their inquiries, into what is 'behind the text', 'in the text', and 'in front of the text' (Turner 2000: 44–70; House of Bishops' Group on *Issues in Human Sexuality* 2003: 45–7; Green 2010). But these simple spatial prepositions can be misleading. Used ordinarily, they describe the limits of our visual field as, in this case, we sit with an open Bible in front of us. They can induce cosy expectations of immediate familiarity with the thought worlds of the Bible, with the 'meaning' of these texts and their relevance for modern-day Christian practice or discipleship available to inquiring readers. But overfamiliarity with the Bible is what produces the circle of futility. Peter Brown, at the beginning of his magisterial opus *The Body and Society*, warned those of his readers for whom sexuality had come to wear a 'comfortable face' 'that they must not sink into the cosy, even arch, familiarity with which a modern person often feels entitled to approach the sexual concerns of men and women in a distant age' (Brown 1988: xvii–xviii). What may be needed instead is a recovery of the sheer strangeness of the biblical world and much of the world 'behind', 'within', and 'in front of' it. A 'defamiliarization' of ourselves from many of the biblical texts ostensibly about gender (and much else) has become a requirement for a fresh reading of them, for (as Alan Wall writes) the aim of defamiliarization

> is to set the mind in a state of radical unpreparedness; to cultivate the willing suspension of disbelief. We see and hear things as if for the first time. We see through the eyes, as Blake put it, instead of with them. In other words, the conventionality of our perceptions is put into question. We see the world afresh. This requires effort.   (Wall 2009: 20)

There may be some understandable misgiving about any suggestion of defamiliarization. Isn't familiarity with the Christian heritage already too weak in most of the churches and the world at large? Isn't the assumption, common enough in the humanities disciplines, that 'Discontinuity rather than continuity is the postmodern watchword' (Vanhoozer 2003: 11) too unsettling to introduce to the churches and their teachings? There are several types of answer to these questions. First, 'the conventionality of our perceptions' may be a barrier to our understanding. There are many instances in Bible and tradition where a changed perception of things leads to flashes of insight. Barriers can fall away. The use of imagination, the ability to envisage the familiar differently, may be the key to renewed understanding. Second, Christians don't have to worry about discontinuity. The Christian church actually *provides* the vital thread of continuity between the times of Jesus and our own times. 'She' has survived, surpassed, and interpreted many thought worlds other than the one in which she was born. Her 'rule of faith', later to become her creeds, provides the required threads of continuity when combined with a generous latitude of interpretation. All thought worlds since the time of Jesus, especially our own, are relativized by the presence of the church in history. And third, there is the real possibility of divine assistance in the effort to engage with the unbelieving world, for 'the Spirit of truth', Jesus taught, 'will guide you into all the truth' (John 16:13). The evidence of much disagreement in the churches would appear to falsify that promise. But the promise may suggest a subtler nuance: if we are to be guided 'into all the truth', we cannot already have it. We need fresh guidance, and for that to happen our imaginations may need to be broken open, and the strangeness of our traditions fully owned.

2

One Seed, Two Sexes?

Chapter 2 continues the first aim of the book and begins the second aim—to describe what happened in our social, intellectual, and theological history, which leaves us thinking that there are two sexes. It begins by noting the persistence of the one-sex theory in some seventeenth-century medical literature. It then observes the beginnings of the transition to an understanding of two sexes. Having established the persistence of the one-sex theory into modernity, a path of continuity in the theological understanding of sex from the first century on is traced, with Tertullian and Aquinas exciting particular interest. Because of the weight of emphasis in the book on the one-sex theory, the chapter concludes with an examination of some of its critics, concluding that the theory is sound. The way is thus prepared for the analysis of the arrival of two sexes in chapter 3.

2.1. STILL TWO SEEDS

I looked for lingering evidence of the one-sex theory in my local Plymouth Medical Society Discovery Library Collection of rare books on medical history. This is located in the Plymouth University Peninsula College of Medicine and Dentistry at Derriford Hospital, Plymouth, UK. I discovered a second edition of a rare tome by a French doctor, François Mauriceau (1637–1709), *The Diseases of Women with Child, and in Child-Bed*. The first edition was published in 1668, the second edition in 1683. These dates will prove to be significant. The first chapter describes and illustrates 'The Parts of a Woman Destin'd to Generation'.

The work lends the full authority of the emerging science of anatomy to the standard belief that women, being men, have testicles; it describes what female testicles do; why these testicles are inferior to men's (no surprise there); and why women need to have an orgasm (or orgasms) to conceive. In 1668 the two-seed theory is alive and well in the medical schools of Europe. 'Every Woman', declares Mauriceau, '*hath two Teſticles as well as Men, being alſo for the ſame uſe, which is to convert into fruitful Seed the Blood that is brought to them by the Preparing Veſſels . . . but they differ from thoſe of Men in ſeituation, figure, magnitude, ſubſtance, temperature, and compoſition*' (1683: 8).

Testicles in men and women receive refined blood and convert it into sperm. This blood is made ready by the work of special blood vessels, called '*Preparing*' or '*Spermatick Vessels*': '*The Spermatick Veſſels in Women, called Preparing, becauſe they prepare and convey to the Teſticles, the Blood, of which Seed is engendred, differ not from thoſe in Men, either in number, rife, or uſe, but only in their inſertion, and manner of their diſtribution*' (1683: 7). Yes, women have two testicles. They do what men's testicles do. I take *rife* to mean 'to become active', or 'to produce or give rise to': *inſertion* is about their location in male and female bodies; and *diſtribution* is about where the sperm goes after its manufacture. Women's spermatic vessels don't just prepare blood for semen-making. They carry away menstrual blood as well. (A pregnant woman, of course, is nurturing her child with the same blood (1683: 8).)

Several further details are important. First, women's testicles are located where they are because women are *cold*: '*the temperament of Women is much more cold and moiſt than of Men, for the heat of their Teſticles is weaker*' (1683: 9). This is a medical fact, apparently beyond question. Galen's belief that women lack the heat to propel their genitals outside their bodies remains intact. The lesser heat of women belongs to Aristotelian physics and is based on assumptions about the four elements of which all material things consist, and the four humours, based on the four elements, which comprise human bodies (see section 1.1.1). The internal location of women's testicles addresses this problem, but only partly. Second, a consequence of women being cold is that their seed is '*much more wateriſh than Mens*'. Third, the process of sperm-making begun in the spermatic vessels is completed and '*perfected*' by the testicles themselves. The testicles provide the sperm's '*prolifick virtue*'.

Fourth, women need to ejaculate, as the name of the alleged equipment for that purpose ('ejaculatory vessels') suggests. Fifth, they do it by having an orgasm (or orgasms). Sixth, the longer the 'ejaculatory vessels', the greater the pleasure the woman has. Mauriceau observes (following Laurentius), '*big-bellied Women find more pleafure in Coition, than others, becaufe the Seed is then difcharged by a longer Paffage*' (1683: 11). Finally he compares the womb to a field where seed is sown, but his analogy is not the one we might expect (the 'furrowed field theory', which we met in chapter 1). No, following Hippocrates, what is sown there is provided by male and female seeds sown together:

> *We may, with good reafon, compare the Womb to a fruitful Field . . . for*
> *. . . the Seed of Men and Women (tho potentially containing in them the*
> *Form and Idea of all the parts of a Child to be engendred out of it) would*
> *never produce fo admirable an effect, if they were not poured into the*
> *fruitful Field of Nature, to wit, the Womb, which having received both,*
> *embraceth them clofely, and by its heat and particular properties, making*
> *ufe of the Spirits, with which the Seed abounds, immediately feparates the*
> *Chaos, and afterwards delineates and traceth forth all the parts of the*
> *Body of an Infant, which it perfects, nourifheth, and preferves to the full*
> *time of Labour.*   (1683: 14)

Let us consider two further examples of the continuing belief that women and men possess the same reproductive equipment. One of these is provided by André Du Laurens, in 1639:

> The opinion of the Ancients, confirmed by the authority of learned men and the writings of nearly all the Anatomists is that the parts of women which serve in generation do not differ from those of men except in location, because the parts of women are hidden inside on account of their natural debility and their colder temperature. Those of men are outside and hanging.   (Du Laurens 1639: 357; cited in Crawford 2007: 100)

A final example is the pseudonymous but widely read work *Aristotle's Master-Piece* (*c*.1680). The author, possibly a William Salmon, summarizes his description 'Of the Instruments of Generation in Men' in doggerel verse:

> And thus man's nobler parts we see,
> For such the parts of generation be;
> And they that carefully survey will find

> Each part is fitted for the use design'd.
> The purest blood, we find, if well we heed,
> Is in the testicles turn'd into seed.
> Which by most proper channels is transmitted
> Into the place by Nature for it fitted;
> With highest sense of pleasure to excite
> In amorous combatants the more delight.
> For Nature does in this work design
> Profit and pleasure in one act to join.
>
> (Pseudo-Aristotle 1680: I.1 [p.14])

A detailed, lurid description 'Of the secret Parts in Woman' follows, concluding in a matching doggerel verse:

> Thus the woman's secrets I have survey'd
> And let them see how curiously they're made.
> And that, though they of different sexes be,
> Yet in the whole they are the same as we.
> For those that have the strictest searchers been,
> Find women are but men turn'd outside in:
> And men, if they but cast their eyes about,
> May find they're women with their inside out.
>
> (Pseudo-Aristotle 1680: I.2 [p.18])

2.1.1. Two Seeds or One?

These three seventeenth-century examples of the continuity of the ancient belief in one sex and two seeds are remarkable. They show that the belief in similar genitals and two seeds persisted, even in the medical textbooks, well into the modern period. In a moment we will chart the course of these beliefs from the ancient to the modern world. But each of the three examples also provides evidence for the weakening of the ancient view, and for its modern replacement. All three works unwittingly indicate that they are in the throes of a far-reaching change of social and medical opinion. The second edition of Mauriceau's work contains a commentary by the editor, Hugh Chamberlen. This commentary is especially useful for understanding how, in the short period between the first and second edition, the earlier view was already being challenged. Chamberlen frankly disagrees with Mauriceau. 'Our Author', he chides, in a dissenting footnote, is '*lying under a Miftake*'. Women, he proclaims (in 1683), don't have testicles at all. They have *Ovaria*. They don't make seed. There aren't any spermatic vessels for conveying it to the womb. Women have eggs which get impregnated by the sperms of men:

> We find that the Tefticles of a Woman are no more than, as it were, two clufters of Eggs, which lie there to be impregnated by the fpirituous Particles, or animating Effluviums, conveyed out of the Womb through the two Tubes, called by our Author Deferent Veffels. And as he is miftaken in the Tefticles, fo is he likewife in an Error in his acceptation of the Woman's Seed: For indeed there is none fent forth by the Ejaculatory Veffels (by us called Fallopius's Tubes) in coition, there being no Seed in the Ovaria, or Tefticles: But fome days after the impregnation of the Egg, or Eggs, as in Twins, they decide [sic] through thofe two Tubes into the Womb, where being placed, the Embrio takes up its quarters.
>
> (Mauriceau 1683: 9)

Chamberlen's interjection into the text is especially instructive, for it indicates the anatomical upheaval that was going on in the seventeenth century, and the dates 1668 and 1683 enable us to date it fairly precisely. Mauriceau's text is otherwise allowed to remain intact. There is no modification of the ancient theories of humours and heat. Chamberlen lapses into an Aristotelian mode of understanding sperm: it is produced only by men, and its '*spirituous Particles*' alone are the bearers of life or spirit. Yet one of the reasons for the persistence of the belief in the generation of women's sperm was women's orgasm(s): similitude in the peaks of pleasure was thought to be proof of similitude of ejaculation. The growing recognition that neither women's seed nor women's orgasm was necessary for procreation to occur (and so for the whole purpose of sex, on theological accounts, to be fulfilled) eventually made a profound difference to women's experience of sexual intercourse (as Laqueur reports). Ancient prejudices about female passivity were rejuvenated by the advance in the study of anatomy.

The assumed, joint, physiological basis for the 'highest sense of pleasure to excite / In amorous combatants the more delight' was disappearing in the second half of the seventeenth century. But a harmful prejudice, engendered by the old physiology, regarding the victims of rape existed for three centuries more. The prejudice is that a victim of rape who becomes pregnant must have consented to having sex, so the act of rape was not rape. 'The common presumption that conception was impossible without orgasm added a further horrific twist to the fate of women who had been forcibly impregnated' (Dabhoiwala 2013: 145). The prejudice is of course despicable. But it is also readily explicable, and the two-seed theory explains it fully. According to the theory a woman cannot conceive without orgasm and ejaculation, similar to those experienced by men. If she conceived, she must have climaxed, and a climax could not (it was thought) be involuntary. Once orgasm for women became disassociated from conception, it became superfluous to the purpose of making babies. By the nineteenth century the medical and clerical professions 'took the absence of pleasure a step further, maintaining that sexual pleasure was incompatible with proper feminine delicacy and purity. Sexual pleasure for women became a matter of damned if you do (have an orgasm) and damned to frustration if you don't' (Crawford 2007: 123).

Katherine Crawford has noticed that when Du Laurens speaks of 'the Ancients' he is beginning to distance himself from the ancient view, while retaining 'the idea that men were hotter and dryer, and women were colder and moister, as explanations for their anatomical differences' (Crawford 2007: 100). *Aristotle's Master-Piece* provides clear evidence of an attempt to conflate, unsuccessfully, the ancient and modern views of conception. It does so by what it says about the clitoris, the womb, and women's testicles. The author describes the clitoris as

> a sinewy and hard part of the womb, replete with spongy and black matter within, *in the same manner as the side ligaments of the yard [= penis]; and indeed [it] resembles it in form, suffers erection and falling in the same manner,* and both stirs up lust, and gives delight in copulation; for without this, the fair sex neither desire nuptial embraces, nor have pleasure in them, nor conceive by them; and according to the greatness or smallness of this part, they are more or less fond of men's embraces; so that it may properly be styled the seat of lust. (Pseudo-Aristotle 1680: 1.II, pp. 14–15, emphasis added)

The one-sex theory had consistently identified the womb as an inverted penis. Now the comparison is made, not between the womb and the penis, but between the *clitoris* and the penis. Katherine Park and others have used the phrase 'the discovery (or the rediscovery) of the clitoris' to describe the new comparison. Initially this is a puzzling phrase, for it absurdly implies that for years, or perhaps for several centuries, women had forgotten that they had one until, one day in 1559, the male anatomist Realdo Columbo reminded them. Certainly Columbo made this claim. In his discussion of women's genitalia in *De re anatomica* (1559), Book 11, he speaks of a

> certain small part, which is elevated on the apex vaginae above the foramen from which urine exits. And this dearest reader is that, it is the principal seat of women's enjoyment in intercourse; so that if you not only rub it with your penis, but even touch it with your little finger, the pleasure causes their seed to flow forth in all directions, swifter than the wind, even if they don't want it to.   (cited in Stringer and Becker 2010: 131)

Arrogantly he claims this 'discovery' for himself:

> Since no one else has discerned these processes and their working; if it is permissible to give a name to things discovered by me, it should be called the love or sweetness of Venus. It cannot be said how much I am astonished by so many remarkable anatomists, that they not even have detected [it] on account of so great advantage this so beautiful thing formed by so great art.   (cited in Stringer and Becker 2010: 131–2)

The claim is nonsense, but it may be too dismissive to conclude (with Stringer and Becker) that 'In Renaissance Europe, the clitoris was not newly discovered, only newly legitimised as an anatomical entity by male anatomists competing for reputation and priority'. It only makes sense to suggest that the clitoris is 'discovered' at all, without a long period of time when discussion of it had fallen out of use and it had made no appearance in the medical literature. That was probably because of the strength of the one-sex theory in the medical and the social 'imaginaries' which took the penis/vagina homology for granted. The clitoris, Crawford explains, 'represented a problem for the one-sex model . . . Its existence meant that women had two homologies to the penis: the inverted, interior vagina and the small, exterior, decidedly erectile clitoris' (Crawford 2007: 109). The one-sex model was giving way in the face of anatomical complexity.

Even the doggerel verses from *Aristotle's Master-Piece* hint at the arrival of a one-seed, two-sex theory. A woman, compared to a man, is now an object of male curiosity, 'curiously' made. She belongs to a different sex ('they of different sexes be'). The similarity with men in the one-sex theory is qualified ('Yet *in the whole* they are the same as we'). While the older view persists, the author is clear that women do not ejaculate seed, and their 'stones' (testicles) differ from those of men in several ways:

> Some indeed will have their use [women's testicles] to be the same as in men, but that is for want of judgment; for Aristotle and Scotus both affirm that this women [*sic*] have no seed, and that their stones differ also in their use from those of men; their use being, as I have already said, to contain the egg which is to be impregnated by the seed of man. (Pseudo-Aristotle 1680: 1.II, p.18)

The verses may not have lost their power to amuse, and perhaps to titillate, in 1680, but their power to explain was expiring fast.

Enough has been said to establish the persistence of the one-sex theory into the modern period. It will be argued in chapter 3 that, against the one-sex theory, the modern two-sex theory is an innovation (which proves as problematic as the one it replaced). But the innovative impact of two sexes can only be maintained if it can be shown to replace a settled orthodoxy. It is necessary, then, to have an overview of the intervening years and to test the one-sex theory against the criticisms against it, before describing the innovative uses to which the replacement theory was put.

2.2. FROM THE FIRST TO THE SEVENTEENTH CENTURY

The brief overview will show that while the one-sex theory persisted, it encompassed one-seed and two-seed versions of itself. It accompanied and contributed to the gender hierarchy described in chapter 1 which helped to shape the behaviour of women and men in relation to each other. It reinforced the ontological assumptions about elements and humours, and about the masculinization and feminization of all things. That is why Peter Brown, discussing the second and third centuries CE, observes:

> The learned treatises of the age collaborated with ancient commonsense notions to endow the men and women of late antiquity with bodies totally unlike those of modern persons. Here were little fiery universes, through whose heart, brain, and veins there pulsed the same heat and vital spirit as glowed in the stars. To make love was to bring one's blood to the boil, as the fiery vital spirit swept through the veins, turning the

blood into the whitened foam of semen. It was a process in which the body as a whole—the brain cavity, the marrow of the backbone, the kidneys, and the lower bowel region—was brought into play, 'as in a mighty choir' [Galen, *On Seed*, 1.8]. The genital regions were mere points of passage. They were the outlets of a human Espresso machine. It was the body as a whole, and not merely the genitals, that made orgasm possible. (Brown 1988: 17)

The process Brown describes is an example of 'pangenesis', the idea that the whole body is the source of sperm. Neither is the description of pangenesis confined to men: 'Though a clammier creature, through whom damp mists swirled, even the wife must give all of herself if her seed was to be released into the womb so as to embrace that of her husband' (Brown 1988: 18).

2.2.1. Tertullian

It is clear that Tertullian (160–225 CE) held to the pangenetic view of the production of sperm by both men and women. His refutation of the idea that souls pre-existed bodies in his treatise *On the Soul* led him to insist that soul and body both begin at conception, a process which he then describes. He speaks of two seeds, but here a note of caution is necessary. The double seeds are not those of men and women, but those of body and soul: 'For although we shall allow that there are two kinds of seed—that of the body and that of the soul—we still declare that they are inseparable, and therefore contemporaneous and simultaneous in origin' (Tertullian n/d: ch. 27). Tertullian is somewhat bashful about the source of his contention, because it lies in the experience of sexual climax. He prepares his startled readership by reminding them that 'Nature should be to us an object of reverence, not of blushes. It is lust, not natural usage, which has brought shame on the intercourse of the sexes.' The experience of climax is then taken to be evidence of *the ejaculation of soul, accompanying the ejaculation of bodies*:

> We know that both the soul and the flesh discharge a duty together: the soul supplies desire, the flesh contributes the gratification of it; the soul furnishes the instigation, the flesh affords the realization. The entire man being excited by the one effort of both natures, his seminal substance is discharged, deriving its fluidity from the body, and its warmth from the soul. (Tertullian n/d: ch. 27)

Tertullian has a remarkably physical account of the soul which seems to be conceptually, but not actually, separate from bodies (whether his theory is that of 'conceptual dualism', 'substantive dualism', or even 'anomalous monism' [Thatcher 1990] need not delay us). Of greater interest is his insistence that, when having sex, a lot more than ejaculation happens:

> I cannot help asking, whether we do not, in that very heat of extreme gratification when the generative fluid is ejected, feel that somewhat of our soul has gone from us? And do we not experience a faintness and prostration along with a dimness of sight? This, then, must be the soul-producing seed, which arises at once from the out-drip of the soul, just as that fluid is the body-producing seed which proceeds from the drainage of the flesh.   (Tertullian n/d: ch. 27)

A two-seed theory is given a Judaeo-Christian gloss by references to Genesis 2. Tertullian notes that the first man was made from clay and the breath of life (Gen. 2:7). What is clay, he asks, but 'an excellent moisture, whence should spring the generating fluid? From the breath of God first came the soul. But what else is the breath of God than the vapour of the spirit, whence should spring that which we breathe out through the generative fluid?' (Tertullian n/d: ch. 27). The making of a man from the two substances of clay and breath becomes paradigmatic for the creation of all subsequent human beings:

> Forasmuch, therefore, as these two different and separate substances, the clay and the breath, combined at the first creation in forming the individual man, they then both amalgamated and mixed their proper seminal rudiments in one, and ever afterwards communicated to the human race the normal mode of its propagation, so that even now the two substances, although diverse from each other, flow forth simultaneously in a united channel; and finding their way together into their appointed seed-plot, they fertilize with their combined vigour the human fruit out of their respective natures.   (Tertullian n/d: ch. 27)

In the patristic period, the two-seed theories of Hippocrates and Galen and the one-seed theory of Aristotle existed together, but there was agreement among the medical writers that 'the generalised or "default" body was a male one, unless some accident in gestation turned it into a female one' (Kuefler 2015: 242; see Laqueur 1990: ch. 2). Mathew Kuefler follows Laqueur for an accurate analysis of the 'default body', observing that 'Christian writers echoed these opinions in their own discussions about whether males alone or females along with them were created in the image of God' (see also Conway 2015: 222). Augustine, commenting on St Paul's view that 'a man ought not to have his head veiled, since he is the image and reflection of God; but woman is the reflection of man' (1 Cor. 11:7), envisages the *imago dei* as active in all human beings ('men'), in the power of reason and contemplation of what is eternal. But male human beings have superior rational and spiritual powers. That is why the part of their bodies associated with thought may remain uncovered. Women, however, are preoccupied with lower, baser matters. They are not excluded from becoming 'new men' in Christ, or from the contemplation of eternal realities. But, specifies Augustine, because the woman

> differs from the man in bodily sex, it was possible rightly *to represent under her bodily covering* that part of the reason which is diverted to the government of temporal things; so that the image of God may remain on that side of the mind of man on which it cleaves to the beholding or the consulting of the eternal reasons of things.   (Augustine 1887: 7.12; emphasis added)

The assumption that women are deficient in powers of thought and spirituality is not dispersed, but rather invoked in order to account for women's deficiency as God's image-bearers. It is a case where doctrine endorses culture, instead of confronting it.

Vincent de Beauvais (1190–1264), in his encyclopaedic miscellany *The Mirror of Nature*, frequently repeats the traditional view 'that women were not only more lustful than men but more lustful than all female animals with the possible exception of the mare' (see Elliott 1999: 37). Vincent was quoting William of Conches, who about a century earlier maintained the historic view that women emit seed. Medieval historian Dyan Elliott links his contention 'with what Thomas Laqueur has dubbed the one-sex model', noting that William was attempting to deny the possibility of pregnancy after rape by affirming the victim's emission of seed and so her apparent consent to the sexual act. Contemporary readers may have noted an obvious contradiction among these uncomprehending male views of women's desire. On the one hand, from the earliest classical writers men are depicted as active, and women as passive: on the other hand, from the earliest times women are depicted as randier than men (the converse of the modern view). William had obviously given this conundrum some thought. Retaining the thought that men are hot and dry, and women are cold and wet, he invented the cunning metaphor of wet wood:

> Since, moreover, women are naturally frigid and humid, how does it happen that a woman is more fervent than a man in lust? I answer that it is harder to light a fire in wet wood, but it nevertheless burns longer and more intensely in it. Thus the heat of lust in a woman who is naturally more humid burns longer and more intensely. (Elliott 1999: 37)

The 'cold womb', Elliott explains, 'yearns for and delights in the man's hot seed . . . In contrast with the single pleasure of a man's ejaculation, woman enjoys a twofold pleasure in coitus, both expelling and receiving seed' (Elliott 1999: 38).

2.2.2. Aquinas

Elliott tentatively suggests that the thirteenth century marks the time 'when the Aristotelian one-seed theory of conception was possibly gaining over the Galenic two-seed' (Elliott 1999: 40). Ruth Karras puts the point more strongly: 'Medieval theories of reproduction, from the thirteenth century on, relied heavily on Aristotle, who, as they understood him, held that the man provided the seed for conception, and women the material' (Karras 2005: 66). But Karras also notes that 'Not everyone adhered to this view—many medical writers kept to the two-seed theory.' Aquinas is credited with having reintroduced Aristotelian science to theology, and with it the one-seed theory. In a moment we will need to query this assumption.

Aquinas discusses the creation of men and women in his *Summa theologica* at 1.91, 'The Production of the First Man's Body', and 1.92, 'The Production of the Woman' (Aquinas 1889). When he speaks inclusively of human beings (usually translated 'man') he uses the word *homo*. When he speaks of male human beings ('men'), he uses the word *vir*. He makes much of the detail that the first human being (*homo*) was made 'from the slime of the earth' (Gen. 2:7). 'Man' has 'a rational soul of the genus of spiritual substances'. He is comprised of the same elements that comprise the earth (slime) and everything else. There are 'higher' and 'lower' elements. 'The higher elements, fire and air, predominate in him by their power; for life is mostly found where there is heat, which is from fire; and where there is humor, which is of the air.' But the lower elements (earth and water) are also plentiful in the human being because we are said to be creatures of perfect elemental and humoral balance. That is why 'the body of man is said to have been formed from the slime of the earth; because earth and water mingled are called slime, and for this reason man is called "a little world", because all creatures of the world are in a way to be found in him'. There is continuity between humankind and all creatures by means of the elements, and continuity between humankind and the angels by means of the 'spiritual substance' which for Aquinas is the 'rational soul'.

Next Aquinas turns to the creation of 'woman' (*mulier*) and addresses the Aristotelian judgement that 'the female is a misbegotten male' (*femina est mas occasionatus*, 92.1; see Aquinas 1889 for the Latin text and Aquinas 1920 for the English text). He argues that she is, and she isn't. 'It was necessary for woman (*femina*) to be made, as the Scripture says, as a "helper" to man (*adiutorium viri*); not, indeed, as a helpmate in other works, as some say, since man can be more efficiently helped by another man in other works; but as a helper in the work of generation.' Woman, then, has a clear but limited purpose. The ambivalent answer to the question of the defectiveness of woman proceeds by way of two pairs of familiar opposites: active/ passive, and particular/universal:

> As regards the individual nature (*ad naturam particularem*), woman is defective and misbegotten (*femina est aliquid deficiens et occasionatum*), for the active force (*virtus activa*) in the male seed (*in semine maris*) tends to the production of a perfect likeness in the masculine sex (*masculinum sexum*); while the production of woman comes from defect in the active force or from some material indisposition, or even from some external influence; such as that of a south wind (*puta a ventis Australibus*), which is moist, as the Philosopher observes (De Gener. Animal. iv, 2). On the other hand, as regards human nature in general (*ad naturam universalem*), woman is not misbegotten, but is included in nature's intention as directed to the work of generation.   (Aquinas 1920: 92.1, reply 1)

There are several further matters to be investigated in this part of the *Summa*. The first is Aquinas's careful rationale for the subjection of women to men. The reader of the *Summa* is bombarded with binaries: active/passive, perfect/imperfect, higher/lower, particular/universal, hot/cold, and so on, and the male/female binary is mapped on to most of them. Subjection, understood as a general principle, is also a binary. It is 'twofold' (*duplex*). One form of it is slavery (*servilis*), and it belongs to the fallen world. But the other kind of subjection, which existed before the Fall, 'is called economic or civil, whereby the superior (*praesidens*) makes use of his subjects (*subiectis*) for their own benefit and good; and this kind of subjection existed even before sin'. The world in its perfect, created state, contained servility. Why? Because

> good order would have been wanting in the human family if some were not governed by others wiser than themselves. So by such a kind of subjection woman is naturally subject to man (*naturaliter femina subiecta est viro*), because in man (*in homine*) the discretion of reason predominates. Nor is inequality among men (*inaequalitas hominum*) excluded by the state of innocence... (Aquinas 1920: 92.1, reply 2)

The second matter is that of male dignity. Why was the man made from slime, while the woman was made from man? Why did the man and the woman have different origins since they belong to the same species? The man has to be made first, answers Aquinas, so he can affirm his primacy over woman, and so demonstrate his superior likeness to God which the woman lacks. 'First, in order thus to give the first man a certain dignity (*dignitas*) consisting in this, that as God is the principle (*principium*) of the whole universe, so the first man, in likeness to God, was the principle of the whole human race' (Aquinas 1920: 92.2). This male *principium* or 'principleship' is intended by God 'not only for generation, as with other animals, but also for the purpose of domestic life, in which each has his or her particular duty, and in which the man is the head of the woman. Wherefore it was suitable for the woman to be made out of man, as out of her principle.'

The third matter is the significance of the woman's creation from the man's rib. We have seen Augustine's defence of the veil on the heads of women. Now Aquinas too endows body parts with symbolic significance. She could not be made from the man's head, since the head is the organ of authority; 'nor was it right for her to be subject to man's contempt as his slave, and so she was not made from his feet'. The rib is the midpoint of the body (well, almost), and nicely confirms the free woman's social midpoint, beneath the freeman and above the slave. (It is interesting to note that Christine de Pizan (*c*.1405) reversed Aquinas's argument. She held that women's bodies were superior to men's since men's bodies were made from clay, while women's bodies were made from human flesh. See O'Neill 2011: 446.)

Finally, Aquinas deals with the question whether the first woman was made directly by God or through the mediation of angels. To answer the question, he appeals directly to the physiology of conception and affirms its material basis. Especially interesting is a secondary comment about what happens in generation:

> the natural generation of every species is from some determinate matter. Now the matter whence man is naturally begotten is *the human semen of man or woman* (*materia autem ex qua naturaliter generatur homo, est semen humanum viri vel feminae*). Wherefore from any other matter an individual of the human species cannot naturally be generated. (Aquinas 1920: 92.4, emphasis added)

But when God creates, God can operate 'outside the ordinary course of nature', and in the case of the first man and woman, that is what God does.

These chapters of the *Summa* are a rich resource for the development of several of the themes of this book. Yes, Aquinas can be credited with reintroducing Aristotelian philosophy into Catholic thought, along with Aristotle's one-seed theory of human conception. But it is clear from the previous paragraph that the two-seed understanding of conception still remains in evidence. Conception occurs by the 'human semen of man or woman'. The statement could hardly be clearer. If we were to judge Aquinas by that phrase alone, he is an obvious 'two-seeder'. Immediately, though, the judgement sounds misleading, for conception, following Aristotle, is due to 'the active force in the male seed'. The woman's role is passive and receptive. This passivity troubled Scotus a few years later. He 'mocks' it, says Marilyn Adams, claiming 'Aristotle's picture reduces mothers to containers of stuff out of which life is formed' (Adams 2015: 256–7). Exactly. Why are there women at all if they are defective even in their created state? Aquinas does not address the problem that girls and boys alike can, and often do, look like their mothers (a problem which Galen attempted to resolve over a thousand years earlier). Perhaps Aquinas relapses into the two-seed theory because he was aware of these difficulties?

Aquinas's theory retains classic assumptions about elements and humours. Men have the monopoly in the human species of the higher elements of fire and air. From these elements they have a monopoly of heat and spirit. In relation to these monopolies, women are deficient already. Men have the driving force of life, both of body and soul. The male 'active force' (*virtus activa*) seals together a range of meanings. While the noun *virtus* is feminine, the practice of it is 'manly' or masculine, as *vir-* clearly indicates. The *vir* is the *vir*tuous male person. He is the active one and nowhere is that more obvious than when his hot body is planting its life-giving and soul-producing seed in the cooler, passive body of the woman. Cold is feminine, like the shivering south winds (*ventis Australibus*) from Australia! A blast of cold air is dangerous enough to rob the male semen of its power to reproduce itself. It is to be feared, like cold air on a traumatized tooth. God ordains the male *principium*, nature teaches it, the elements express it, scripture confirms it, families enact it, and the church sacralizes it. Biology, ethics, theology, society, ecclesiology, and destiny are seamlessly brought together.

I think Elliott is right to say that in the thirteenth century the one-seed theory gained ground over the two-seed theory. While in theology the one-seed theory continued to gain ground, the same cannot be said for the growing medical tradition which resiliently followed Galen for at least another three hundred years (as the work of Mauriceau shows). Undoubtedly there are two sexes in Aquinas, the *masculinum sexum* and the *femininum sexum*. So is Aquinas really one of us 'moderns' where a two-sex theory is indelibly written across medical, popular, and ecclesial cultures alike? Hardly. The 'fact' of the defectiveness of the female body is enough to confirm Laqueur's thesis that the male body is the default body. The female sex consists of defective male bodies lacking heat and active power. But the division of sexes would soon become a way of men talking about women which would embed itself in any and every discussion of gender, and so provide a misleading and question-begging framework which merely compounded its difficulties.

2.3. THE PROBITY OF THE ONE-SEX THEORY

We are almost at the point of examining the independently named 'seventeenth- and eighteenth-century sexuality hypothesis' which replaces the one-sex model of humankind. There remains one further task: to examine and assess some of the criticisms of the one-sex model. This task accords with the first aim of the book, to uncover the one-sex theory *and its assumptions*. A quarter of a century has elapsed since the publication of *Making Sex*. Its importance has earned intensive and far-reaching scrutiny from different sets of scholars. While its influence on theological discussions of sexuality remains slight we should not be surprised if the extensive discussion it has received elsewhere leads to a revised appreciation of it. I am eager to take these developments seriously in order to proceed with a refined version of the model in the chapters that follow.

2.3.1. Criticisms

A principal criticism is that Laqueur's work is overly discursive. The broad sweep of his narrative succeeds only if complexity is reduced to simplicity (e.g. King 2013: xi). Some critics have pointed out that the experience of corporeality in the premodern world was simply different for women than for men, and that the differences cannot be accounted for by social organization or by medical orthodoxy (Park and Nye 1991: 53–7). Pregnancy, childbirth, and nursing are experiences men don't have. Karen Harvey pursues a similar criticism, augmenting it by an appeal to the vernacular language of the sixteenth century. This is a time when the one-sex theory was supposedly undisturbed, but which nonetheless reveals an assumption of sexual difference, at least as far as that topic was commonly thought and spoken about:

> evidence from court depositions from the period c. 1560–1640 reveal that ordinary men and women tended to stress sexual difference rather than similarity. The centrality of women's orgasm to conception was commonly adhered to, but the notion 'that female and male were two halves of the same sex, does not seem to have taken root in the popular imagination'. In everyday language quite different terms were used for male and female genitalia, and this was at a time when scientific and medical writings had not yet developed a distinct nomenclature for the female body. A colloquial language which distinguished these body parts suggested that male and female bodies were considered structurally, functionally, and morally distinct. Parts of the one-sex model could be articulated without people subscribing to the entire vision. (Harvey 2002: 913)

The very title of Mauriceau's work (*The Diseases of Women with Child, and in Child-Bed*; see section 2.1), while it acknowledges the common genitalia of women and men, might be thought also to recognize two sexes, since the diseases it describes do not occur in men.

Several critics think that the transition to two sexes began earlier. 'Any one-sex model' had its demise, not in the eighteenth, but in the sixteenth century (King 2013: 74). Yet other critics cite evidence for 'the persistence of humoral understandings of the body well into the nineteenth century and beyond, suggesting that in humoral terms the one-sex model was still current long after the turning point situated by Laqueur in the mid eighteenth century' (McClive n/d 4). Joan Cadden, Helen King, and others accuse Laqueur of ignoring evidence which complicates the one-sex model. In her study *Meanings of Sex Differences in the Middle Ages: Medicine, Science, and Culture*, Cadden says she 'differs . . . from Thomas Laqueur, whose recent work argues that before the eighteenth century male and female were in various ways regarded as manifestations of a unified substratum' (Cadden 1995: 3). While she agrees there is 'much evidence' in her study 'that fits his "one sex" model', she thinks medieval views on the status of the uterus and the opinions of medieval physiognomers about male and female traits suggest evidence of other models not reducible to Laqueur's:

> [T]he Aristotelian and Hippocratic traditions opened up very different paths for the expression of later misogyny. From Aristotle came the hierarchical formulation which represented females as consistently inferior and specifically cool, weak, and passive. From the Hippocratic writers—and no doubt the popular conceptions represented by Plato—came the womb-centered version, according to which females (still likely to be cool and weak) were subject to the erratic influence of a powerful and active organ that affected health and disposition and was the repository of a formidable sexual appetite. (Cadden 1995: 26; see also King 2013)

On Cadden's view, Laqueur omits some of the contrary evidence which might afford him some difficulty. King thinks his omission of the Hippocratic corpus is a principal weakness, especially its emphasis on the womb (see also Holmes 2012: 39). The homological equivalent, the scrotum, was never convincing. Galen, on whom Laqueur relies, can be read differently (King 2013).

Harvey complains that too many historians of sexuality are guilty of 'absorbing the Laqueurian narrative' (Harvey 2002: 910; see King 2013). Assumptions derived from *Making Sex* contaminate their reading of the evidence. Brooke Holmes and Helen King locate *Making Sex* in the academic and cultural milieu of the 1980s when the felt opposition between nature and culture was at its height. The criticism is that the troubling modern binary between sex and gender was *imposed on ancient understandings* as much as it was found there. The 'primacy of social construction over essentialism' was what people 'wanted to hear' (King 2012: 6) in the 1970s and 1980s. Laqueur's claims should be placed 'in the scholarly milieu where they developed, at the crossroads of feminism, the history of science and cultural studies' (Holmes 2012: 47). The transition from a one-sex to a two-sex body in the early modern or modern period is, so the criticism runs, an inversion. The ancient one-sex body, as Laqueur describes it, has an unstable idea of sex and a stable idea of gender. The modern two-sex body has a stable idea of sex and an unstable idea of gender, with the result, says Holmes, that 'a polarising opposition between the ancients and moderns . . . ends up underwriting the contemporary binary between sex and gender'. The ancient material 'doesn't confirm the oppositional logic that structures the modern sex/gender binary as much as it challenges that logic altogether' (Holmes 2012: 51). The question must arise, 'Why project our own rigid contrast between nature and culture onto the relationship in classical antiquity between the categories or principles "male" and "female" and sexed bodies?' (Holmes 2012: 53).

2.3.2. Responses

There is agreement that a transition took place. There is disagreement about precisely *when* it occurred and precisely *what* it was. The problems of embodiment and of gender awareness are eased by making a customary distinction between one's experience and one's interpretation of that experience. It could not have been doubted that only women could experience pregnancy, childbirth, and nursing (even though the idea of fungible bodily fluids rendered the development of male breasts, including lactating breasts, a hideous possibility). Birthing is something only women can do. But that does not prevent dominant discourses locating them as failed males, or at the lower end of a scale of perfection. The one-sex theory does not eliminate sexual difference. It assumes sexual difference is a difference of degree along a male/female continuum, not a difference of kind. Men do in fact give birth, because women are (inferior) men. Earlier vernacular language, often coarse, was sexually specific about body parts but it is not clear what follows from this. Again, difference is just as easily located as a difference in degree within a single sex as a difference in kind between two sexes. Harvey recognizes the belief in the necessity of women's orgasm for conception to happen, and that the commonality of men and women does not end with common ejaculation. Male and female are not in any case 'two halves of the same sex' on the Laqueurian one-sex theory. To think this is already to think of the one sex as two, and the two sexes as equal ('halves'). The theory assumes men and women are located along a single continuum.

The charge of the selective use of available evidence can be partially met by distinguishing between the different historical aims of different writers. King concedes the force of Laqueur's 'startling conclusion', in the preface to *Making Sex*, 'that a two-sex and a one-sex model had always been available to those who thought about difference' (King 2013: 8, citing Laqueur 1990: viii). Cadden admits she is pursuing a different end. She is not pursuing 'a grand synthetic scheme that captures the medieval concept of gender' or attempting 'the discovery of the essence of medieval views on sex difference'. Her aim is to describe 'a cluster of gender-related notions, sometimes competing, sometimes mutually re-inforcing . . . sometimes permissive, sometimes constraining' (Cadden 1995: 9). While there may be a polemical trace in her denials, she acknowledges Laqueur's aim is a different one, proposing a different case over a longer period.

In *Gender in English Society, 1650–1850* Robert Shoemaker accepts the transition from a one-sex to a two-sex model, with the important proviso (shared with several other critics) that the latter 'evolved over a long period, from the late seventeenth to the early nineteenth century' (Shoemaker 1998: 62). This, he reminds us, was the time when the term 'vagina' began to be used instead of 'the neck of the womb' and women's testicles were renamed 'ovaries' after their use was better understood. Other anatomical discoveries of the period, leading to the adoption of the two-sex model, included Regnier de Graaf's 'discovery of the ovarian follicle' and his argument that 'eggs were produced there', and the discovery in the same decade of 'active sperm in men's semen' (Shoemaker 1998: 62). A 'new language of sexual difference' arose, first uttered by anatomists to themselves before becoming more widely adopted.

The one-sex theory acknowledges both one-seed and two-seed understandings of conception. The combined influences of Aristotle and Galen are acknowledged together with their differences. In the two-seed theory there is a commonality in seed production, but the male seed is hotter, better, more perfect, and so on. In the one-seed theory, women are still inferior men, and their lack of seed is what constitutes their deficiency. In either case the male body remains the default body, and the unity of the one sex is not threatened by existing in two versions. It would be interesting to know how Laqueur might incorporate more recent research findings on medieval attitudes to the womb. It should also be noted, however, that both the one-seed and two-seed theories, despite their different constructions and historic pathways, lead (in Cadden's judgement) to the same misogynistic end.

Most critics think that the changes of which Laqueur speaks began earlier, in the sixteenth century. The worry that Laqueur's theory is having an undue, distorting influence is a worry about the possible bias of subsequent writings, and need serve only as a reminder to retain vigilance when interpreting the relevant evidence. Crawford thinks that 'Laqueur and his critics both have their merits . . . early modern ideas about bodies reflected both a fondness for the one-sex idea and resistance to it' (Crawford 2007: 106, 110). She speaks of an 'accumulation of an awareness of sexual difference' which 'contributed in time to the predominance of the idea of two incommensurate sexes that Laqueur identified'. The discovery of the male prostate, 'arterial arrangements that accommodated the female sex organs, and eventually skeletal discrepancies between men and women' are cited. So was Laqueur right? The answer is an appropriately qualified 'Yes, but.' Yes, 'But just as the one-sex model was never the only understanding of the sexed body, ambiguity and contestation continued to shape theorization of the sexual body. Homology and uniqueness, hierarchy and continuum jostled to guide understanding even as ancient knowledge fell by the wayside.' Crawford thinks Laqueur shrugs off some of the complexity of medieval understandings of the body. Yes, there is a transition from a one-sex idea to a two-sex idea, but the idea of one sex was already a simplification. Homology—the matching of sexual organs—and uniqueness—the distinct identities of men and women—were views of the body which did not readily coalesce, just as male superiority never coalesced with the idea of male and female gender polarities within the unity of a single sex.

Crawford's judgement is a strong reason for utilizing the one-sex theory in a theological account of sexuality which takes history and tradition seriously. It coincides with two further recent appraisals. In the eighteenth century the one-sex and two-sex models jostled with each other, interacted, and overlapped before the two-sex model prevailed. The bodies of men and women were believed to be both distinctive and commensurable, both the same and different (see Harvey 2004, chs 2–3). The title and the subtitle of Faramerz Dabhoiwala's recent *The Origins of Sex: A History of the First Sexual Revolution* both refer to the events and processes that occurred in the transition from one to two sexes. Laqueur's thesis is enthusiastically endorsed (Dabhoiwala 2013: 143), and the claim made that while 'Laqueur's argument has been much criticized, no alternative explanation has been advanced' (Dabhoiwala 2013: 408 n. 3). There is an important proviso. The shift in medical ideas in the eighteenth century was not caused by medical discoveries. The 'shifting balance of ideas' is bound up with 'other, more general ways of considering nature, culture, and society: in plays and novels, journalism, poetry, works of theology, philosophy, and moral commentary' (Dabhoiwala 2013: 144; and see section 3.1.2 below). (Laqueur too has his similar list of causal factors (Laqueur 2012: 805–6).)

Holmes's treatment of the one-sex theory does not lead her to reject the many insights it contains. The early medical writers were convinced that women 'are wetter than men'; that 'From the fourth century BCE on . . . the learned medical tradition increasingly emphasises the similarities between male and female bodies. It goes almost without saying', she continues, 'that the female remains a flawed specimen.' She acknowledges that 'the tendency of some physicians to assimilate female bodies to male bodies undoubtedly has an impact on the later Western medical tradition' (Holmes 2012: 35). Since male and female are principles and not sexes, 'Aristotle cannot see the difference between individual males and females as an *essential* difference.' What differences they have are 'contingent', and 'belong to a realm more fluid and accidental than that of essence and principles— namely, the realm of matter' (Holmes 2012: 43, original emphasis). Instead of 'radical difference' we should think of 'a sliding scale' or a 'continuum'. These themes from Aristotle are central to Laqueur's one-sex default body. The weakness of Laqueur's model, according to Holmes, is the failure to combine together 'both fixity and fluidity'. What we should think of instead is 'a continuum *within* material

bodies along which maleness and femaleness is more or less fixed'
(Holmes 2012: 53).

Discussion of the charge that Laqueur perpetuates the late modern
difference between sex and gender (or nature and nurture, or essentialism and constructionism) must be postponed to chapter 7. Suffice
it to say that I shall be speaking there more in terms of similarity
between men and women than of difference between them. Conservative theological thought responds vigorously to suggestions that
manhood and womanhood are constructed because God creates us as
men and women prior to any social or cultural formation. Constructionism does not win the day in chapter 7. What proves decisive is
Christology—the remaking of humanity in Christ, the full and complete image of God.

How safe, then, is the one-sex model after nearly three decades of
discussion among historians? King in particular has little time for it.
As if to anticipate some of King's criticisms, Laqueur, reflecting back
on the one-sex model twenty-two years after *Making Sex*, adopted a
more qualified tone. He does not say that there was *no* tradition of
two sexes prior to the eighteenth century, but that 'prior to the
eighteenth century the category of biologically distinct—what we
would call opposite—sexes was *radically underdeveloped*' (Laqueur
2012: 802, emphasis added; see also Laqueur 2003). He explains he
did not mean by this 'that corporeal differences were of no political
and social consequence . . . but rather that what we take to be self-
evident marks of opposition—penis and vagina, ovary and testicle,
female menstruation and the absence of monthly bleeding in men—
were not understood as such' (Laqueur 2012: 803). Rather,

> each element of these was understood as a version of the other in accord
> with a metaphysically given relationship: women were less perfect men
> whose respective anatomy and physiology reflected this order . . . Like-
> wise, various bodily fluids and substances—semen, milk, blood, fat—
> were construed as more or less fungible versions of one another,
> distributed between the sexes along a more fundamental distinction
> than mere biology. (Laqueur 2012: 803–4)

It was this 'configuration', he continues, that he called 'the "one-sex
model"' (Laqueur 2012: 804). He concedes 'the causes of the change
from the one-sex to the two-sex model and its relation to sexuality'
are 'far more exigent than I [thought] two decades ago' (Laqueur
2012: 805).

It would be surprising if Laqueur had learned nothing from the discussion of his work in over twenty years. I think the thesis, and especially the second part of it, now named the 'seventeenth- and eighteenth-century sexuality hypothesis', remains strong. But the novelty of the two-sex model, its impact and extent, makes sense only when the stark contrast with what preceded it is drawn out. However, what preceded it may well be more complicated than Laqueur initially allowed, both in the classical and the medieval periods. Historians of sex and of medicine work with empirical data, often confined to specific periods and places. My interest as a theologian lies in the beliefs and values that are brought to the data in all periods from biblical times to our own. If the Hippocratic emphasis on the womb (the most obvious organ of sexual difference) cannot be incorporated into an overarching one-sex view of human-kind, it is an additional route to misogyny (Cadden) *alongside* the one-sex theory. It is remarkable that historians of the Common Era interested in gender generally demonstrate little interest in what theologians have said about these matters, whereas scholars agree that religious traditions throughout the world display highly gen-dered attitudes to human bodies. In the next chapter we will observe how religious language assumes a one-sex theory to be still current.

I continue to speak of 'one-sex' for the light it throws on how some of the biblical writers and later theologians thought about the human body, and on the contingency of the two-sex view which became dominant in the Enlightenment. Laqueur has shown the impossibility of deriving judgements about people and their relationships from facts about their bodies. However, my interest, and presumably the interest of most of my readers, is not in medical and sexual history per se (there is a vast literature available to slake that particular thirst) but in how relations between women and men may be justly practised and performed throughout the world. The Christian faith decisively offers a new way forward, even as its practices are disfigured by ancient prejudices. But there are modern prejudices too which equally disfigure the face of gender. The next task is to examine the develop-ment of the social and cultural assumptions that there are two sexes, and to observe how these assumptions shaped modern, and especially theological, understandings of sexuality and gender.

3

The Arrival of Two Sexes

Chapter 2 concludes the first aim of the book, while the present chapter continues the second aim, 'to describe what happened in our social, intellectual and theological history, which leaves us thinking that there are two sexes'. It is suggested that the milieu of one sex still survives in much Christian worship, where it can be experienced directly. Modern social developments are described, and the growth of the idea that there are two sexes is traced through authors who insist that these sexes are equal or unequal. The authors are Poullain de la Barre, Rousseau, Kant, Hegel, and Mill. The chapter suggests why the churches found two sexes generally congenial to their aim of defending marriage and closes with comments about the ambiguous legacy of two-sex theory.

3.1. THE TRANSITION TO TWO SEXES

Diarmaid MacCulloch, in his magisterial tome on the Reformation, dismisses ancient and medieval Christian teaching about sexuality as 'ancient nonsense' (MacCulloch 2004: 611). While it possessed 'a lunatic coherence',

> eventually in the seventeenth century, medical discoveries showed up the ancient physiological theories for the nonsense they were, but old cliché and new discovery jostled uneasily side by side in discussions of gender, until a new framework of discussion, based on the new idea of the human nervous system, drove out older ideas. And even then, both ancient and revised theories worked towards one agenda: men were superior and women inferior.

Between 1500 and 1800 'the notions of maleness and femaleness had been redefined'. Society, he explains,

> once integrated by the cosmology of humours and by Galen's theories, *with gender a continuum*, was from around 1700 conceived in terms of *rigidly divided opposites*—especially gender. By 1800, men were told that they must exercise rigid self-control and never shed tears; women that, after all, they were not uncontrollable and lustful like Eve, just passive and gentle crybabies, to be shielded from life's brutality. (emphases added)

3.1.1. Still One Sex in Church

There is one obvious place, in fact a trio of linked discourses, where traces of the one-sex theory survive more or less intact down to the present day. These are the expressive practices of Christianity in liturgy, hymnody, and proclamation. Many theological students (and their teachers) in the 1970s and 1980s utilized the new and disparaging term 'sexism' to identify, remove, and replace terms such as 'man', 'men', 'mankind', etc., when these same terms were intended to include women and children, but without saying so. We railed against the masculine nomenclature at the basis of Christian God-language, and tried not to use 'He', 'Him', 'His', 'Himself' when preaching and hymn-singing. We completely failed to understand the origin of this masculinist language. Instead of condemning prejudice (which of course it was) we had yet to learn that masculinist language provided massive, primary evidence of the unaltered continuation of the one-sex theory into the twentieth century, and now well beyond it. Since women are men, it is obvious that to speak of 'men' is to speak of men and women. That is what the church has always done.

There is an irony in the fact that the theological liberals and radicals of the 1970s and 1980s were *against* inclusive language. 'Man' and 'men', unless they referred to male people individually or collectively, were already *inclusive* terms. Women were included, but their inclusion was silent and invisible. The moral problem of sexist language in worship came to be a problem just because Christians continued to use the same masculinist language long after the idea of two sexes had become established. The iniquity of sexism depended on a new and prior assumption, the arrival of a second, independent, female sex. To continue to speak of men and women as 'men', after the establishment of a second sex, was certain, eventually, to invite the charge of exclusion. The new demand for non-sexist languages of prayer, praise, and procreation altered the meaning of 'inclusive language'. Yes, women were to be included in this language, but explicitly as a second, equal, and independent sex.

The illustration of the continuation of the one-sex theory in Christian languages throughout the last five hundred years is beyond the remit of this book. Perhaps the service of Morning Prayer in the Book of Common Prayer and in later versions can be a good, but single, example. In the 1662 version, the first of the opening sentences that may be chosen by the minister is from Ezekiel 18:27—'When the wicked man turneth away from his wickedness that he hath committed, and doeth that which is lawful and right, he shall save his soul alive' (Book of Common Prayer 1662). Prior to praying the General Confession the minister addresses his congregation as 'Dearly beloved brethren'. The same greeting is used in the 1928 version of the service over 250 years later (Proposed Book of Common Prayer 1928). The Confession contains the phrase 'According to thy promises declared unto mankind in Christ Jesu our Lord'. The new Prayer of Confession in the Alternative Service Book of 1980 confesses to Almighty God that 'we have sinned against you and against our fellow men'. In Common Worship (2000) 'and against our fellow men' is removed, presumably less for theological reasons than for discomfort at the blatant sexism and the difficulty of replacing it.

Worshippers saying or singing the Te Deum in the 1662 and 1928 versions will come to 'When thou tookest upon thee to deliver man: thou didst not abhor the Virgin's womb.' Not only is there one sex here, there is a barely disguised patriarchal revulsion from the female body. To 'abhor' is to recoil in horror (Latin *abhorrere*, from *ab*- 'away from' + *horrere* 'to shudder'—Oxford Dictionaries Pro 2014). No, God does not recoil from the place of birth and new life: the same cannot be said for the patriarchs, for whom the thought of a fertile woman's body, even if the woman is the Virgin, is fraught with distaste and danger. It is hard to avoid singing 'Lo! He abhors not the Virgin's womb' at Christmas time. The 1980 Alternative Service Book removed the archaism but not the abhorrence ('you did not abhor the Virgin's womb'). Only at the turn of the new century was it replaced—'When you took our flesh to set us free, you humbly chose the Virgin's womb' (Common Worship 2000b). But the phrase of the

Nicene Creed referring to Christ's incarnation, 'and was made man', seems unrevisable (more on this in section 6.4). Carol sheets proclaim one sex: 'Pleased as Man with man to dwell'; 'Born that man no more may die, Born to raise the sons of earth'; 'Peace on the earth, goodwill to men'; 'And man at war with man hears not'; 'Glory to God and peace to men'; 'God rest ye merry, gentlemen', etc.

There is, then, a space and a discourse, a continuity preserved through the discontinuities of modernity, through which it is still possible to experience the old single gender continuum, and of course in most forms of Christianity, the exclusion of women from ministry. Nowhere else is the saying *lex orandi lex credendi* more appropriate than it is here. As the church worships, so it believes; as it believes, so it worships. The linguistic space of liturgy, hymnody, and proclamation is occupied by authorized males, authorized because their bodies are more perfect, more like God, more representative of the male Jesus, than their female counterparts.

3.1.2. New Foundations for Two Sexes

Mary Hawkesworth has drawn attention to the importance of sex as a *legal* category in ensuring the growing status of sexual dimorphism. She too notes that in the eighteenth century 'the one-sex model of embodiment that had dominated European political thought and practice for nearly two millennia gave way to a two-sex model that posited men and women as incommensurate opposites rather than as embodied souls ordered along a continuum on the basis of proximity to the divine' (Hawkesworth 2013: 33). If sex was once about 'embodiment' it became at this time a political and legal *category* 'that determines citizenship rights, educational and employment opportunities, levels of income and wealth, and access to prestige and power' (Hawkesworth 2013: 31). Sex was no longer just a 'biological or physical characteristic'. Babies were assigned a sex before they were given a name. Modern bureaucracies affixed sexual status 'to birth certificates, passports, drivers' licenses, draft cards, credit applications, marriage licenses, and death certificates', where it 'sculpts the contours of individual freedom and belonging in ways that ensure that domination and subordination are thoroughly corporeal'. Over the course of the nineteenth century, she explains, 'male lawmakers in nations across the globe replicated the republican

practice of using the law to bar women from politics and restrict them
to the private sphere'.

The terminology of 'oppositions and contrasts' regularly appears in
descriptions of the two sexes. 'Reproductive biology' was made to
serve a political end (Laqueur 1986: 1). By the 1840s it was clear that
bitches could ovulate without copulation and presumably without
orgasm (Laqueur 1986: 3, 26). It was immediately assumed that a
similar process occurred in other mammals, including women. Only
in 1930 was the existence of an unfertilized egg reported and verified,
the same decade as the discovery of the hormonal control of ovulation
by the ovary and the pituitary gland. Yet by the middle of the
nineteenth century, and in advance of the evidence, 'the ovaries
came to be regarded as largely autonomous control centers of reproduction in the female animal, and in humans they were thought to be
the essence of femininity itself'. Laqueur concludes:

> With these interpretations of spontaneous ovulation the old physiology
> of pleasure and the old anatomy of sexual homologies were definitively
> dead. The ovary, whose distinction from the male testes had only been
> recognized a century earlier, became the driving force of the whole
> female economy, with menstruation its awesome power. (Laqueur
> 1986: 27–8)

The female orgasm, once thought to be a sine qua non in the
achievement of conception, was by now biologically unnecessary, a
mere epiphenomenon (if it happened at all) early in the reproductive
process. Male writers preoccupied themselves with another female
bodily process, that of menstruation, believing it to be the counterpart
of female animals on heat. Many unfounded claims were based on the
disabling effect of this mysterious and explosive process, rendering
women 'unfit for education, a variety of jobs, and other activities that
demand large expenditures of the mental and physical energy that
was thought to be in such short supply' (Laqueur 1986: 32). A smaller
cerebellum than the one found in men was thought to be responsible
for women's reduced 'amativeness' (Laqueur 1990: 209–10).

Laqueur and the historians influenced by him frequently stress
the lack of causal connection between biological discoveries and
the arrival of the two sexes. Rather it is the case that European
politics needed a means of justification for the subordination of
women at a time when the idea of democracy was becoming more
influential, and the new biology provided it. The causes of some of the

astonishing changes to sexual behaviour in the later seventeenth and eighteenth centuries are analysed at length by Faramerz Dabhoiwala (Dabhoiwala 2013). These include the crises of authority brought about by 'the Civil War and the execution of Charles I in 1649, the revolution of 1688, the growth of religious division, the expansion of urban society'; the new 'principles of individual privacy, equality, and freedom' which 'remain distinctive to this day' (Dabhoiwala 2013: 3; and see Hitchcock 1996), together with many other factors like the decline of influence of the church courts, the declining authority of the Bible in the light of scientific knowledge and emerging biblical criticism, and the increasing authority of conscience. Laqueur too has his list, which includes:

> the rise of evangelical religion, Enlightenment political theory, the development of new sorts of public spaces in the eighteenth century, Lockean ideas of marriage as a contract, the cataclysmic possibilities for social change wrought by the French revolution, postrevolutionary conservatism, postrevolutionary feminism, the factory system with its restructuring of the sexual division of labor, the rise of a free market economy in services or commodities, the birth of classes, singly or in combination . . . (Laqueur 1990: 11)

None of these factors, he insists, '*caused* the making of a new sexed body. Instead, the remaking of the body is itself intrinsic to each of these developments' (original emphasis).

Before we leave biology, there is one more recent and important case, spanning the twentieth century, which may be traduced as a further example of culture shaping nature: Freud's myth of the vaginal orgasm. So convinced was Freud that the vagina (and not the clitoris) was the opposite of the penis, that he is said to have 'invented' the vaginal orgasm:

> After four hundred, perhaps even two thousand, years there was all of a sudden a second place from which women derived sexual pleasure. In 1905, for the first time, a doctor claimed that there were two kinds of orgasm, and that the vaginal sort was the expected norm among adult women. (Laqueur 1990: 233)

As Laqueur reads Freud, 'a great wave of amnesia descended on scientific circles around 1900'. Masters and Johnson's discovery in the 1950s 'that female orgasm is almost entirely clitoral would have been a commonplace to every seventeenth-century midwife' (Laqueur

1990: 234; and see Laqueur 2000). We explore in the next chapter how a similar wave of amnesia enveloped the churches and their theologians when they took and continue to take modern narratives of sexuality and heterosexuality as read, and validated by scripture. 'There is nothing in nature', says Laqueur, 'about how the clitoris is construed. It is not self-evidently a female penis, and it is not self-evidently in opposition to the vagina' (1990: 234). Freud's theory is understood to be an attempt to justify two sexes by naturalizing sexual pleasure in the supposedly complementary organs of each sex. Heavy cultural meanings are read onto bodies, in the guise of being read off them.

3.2. TWO EQUAL SEXES?

Several writers in early modern Europe had advanced the case for the equality of women with men, including Anne Thérèse de Lambert, Gabrielle Suchon, François Poullain de la Barre, and Marie de Gournay (see O'Neill 2011). This section opens with one of these, and contrasts the arguments of Poullain de la Barre that men and women are different but equal with the counterarguments of better known 'malestream' authors, Rousseau, Kant, and Hegel. It closes with an examination of John Stuart Mill's exasperated rejection of these arguments. The aim of the section is to show how the idea of two sexes broadened and developed in different ways, and came to influence future social, philosophical, and theological thought.

3.2.1. Different and Equal: Poullain de la Barre

Hobbes in *Leviathan* (1651) had asserted that 'men and women are relatively equal in both strength and wit' (see Hirschmann 2014). In 1673 François Poullain de la Barre, the Catholic priest and Cartesian philosopher who converted to Protestantism, wrote *The Woman as Good as the Man, or The Equallity [sic] of Both Sexes*. As a Cartesian he insisted on the principle of doubting everything that could not be certainly known. Assuming that 'we are filled with prejudices', that '*we muft abfolutely Renounce them*', and that some of them are 'as ancient as the World, of as great extent as the Earth, and as Univerfal as Mankind', he attacks the prejudice of the '*inequality [sic] of the two*

Sexes' (1673: A4). There are '*Natural Reafons*', he continues, '*which invincibly prove, that both Sexes are a like[sic], both as to Body, and Soul*' (1673: B3). Poullain de la Barre does not deny two sexes or differences between them. For example, he takes it as empirically established that in matters of child play '*The Girles fhow therein a more gentile air, more of Wit, and greater dexterity: And when fear or fhame does not ftifle their Humours, their Difcourfe, is more ingenious, and pleafant.*' '*In the cradle*', he opines, '*the more lovely* [sic] *gives alfo the faireft hopes,*' and he bemoans that

> *yet men take no notice thereof; Mafters and Teaching are only for the Men: Particular care is taken to instruct them in all which is thought proper, to form and improve the mind; whilft in the mean time, the Women are let languifh in Idlenefs, Softnefs, and Ignorance: Or, other-wife grovel in low, and bafe imployments.*   (1673: 27–8)

While there are real differences between the sexes, many of these are the product of '*Cuftom*' and '*Prejudice*', which the rational man must recognize and seek to eradicate.

But there is another important fact about Poullain de la Barre's starting point. The philosophy of Descartes, extremely popular and fashionable throughout much of Europe at the time, claimed to prove that the human person was essentially a 'thinking thing', a *res cogitans*, an immaterial mind or spirit, united to a body but essentially separate from it. But since the essence of the person has nothing to do with that person's body, biological sex has nothing to do with the soul or the identity of the person. On this basis, then, on the very bedrock of Cartesian rationalism, there is *no essential difference at all* between women and men. Conceptually there can be no barriers preventing the full equality between them. Why? Because 'The mind has no sex.' Londa Schiebinger wove this quotation from Poullain de la Barre into the title of her book *The Mind Has No Sex? Women in the Origins of Modern Science* (Schiebinger 1989). If there is no intellectual difference between men and women, why are women excluded from science, she asks. 'Enlightenment thinkers faced a dilemma: how was the continued subordination of women to be reconciled with the axiom that all men are by nature equal?' (Schiebinger 1989: 215; see also Schiebinger 1993). The answer to that question takes us to the heart of the political and philosophical thought of the Enlightenment. Any 'appeal to natural rights could be countered only by proof of natural inequalities'.

3.2.2. Different but not Equal

Rousseau

In 1762, a quarter of a century before the French Revolution, Jean-Jacques Rousseau wrote his influential treatise *Émile, or On Education*. An English translation followed a year later. His answer to the question of the equality of the two sexes was explicit: there isn't any. The treatise consisted of five books, four of them about the education of a fictitious pupil, Émile, and the fifth about the education of his fictitious girl companion Sophy. Many of the attitudes and assumptions found in Book 5 became highly influential in the next two centuries.

Book 5 begins with a quotation from Genesis 2:18, 'It is not good that the man should be alone.' Émile's 'helpmeet' is named Sophy, not Eve, but Sophy bears many of the burdens history has placed on 'the mother of all who live' (Gen. 3:20). Sophy is required to 'possess all those characters of her sex which are required to enable her to play her part in the physical and moral order'. Addressing the male reader, he asks, 'Let us inquire to begin with in what respects her sex differs from our own' (Rousseau n/d). The initial answer could have been given two centuries earlier: 'But for her sex, a woman is a man; she has the same organs, the same needs, the same faculties. The machine is the same in its construction; its parts, its working, and its appearance are similar. Regard it as you will the difference is only in degree.' The two sexes, then, do not exist in two kinds. They differ *only in degree*. Men and women are the same with regard to the 'characteristics of the species'; they are different with regard to 'the characteristics of sex'. With regard to biological sex, 'man and woman are unlike; each is the complement of the other'. Here we find the genesis of a modern idea, that of complementarity, which became surprisingly and uncritically central to Christian discussions of gender over two hundred years later (see chapter 4).

But the difference in degree between the sexes turns out to be massive, like its consequences. Rousseau pretends to grapple with the difficulty of deciding 'in either case, what is a matter of sex, and what is not'. Knowable or not, sexual differences serve to justify the social and political ranking of the sexes, and the different sort of education deemed suitable for each to pursue their different social roles. These differences, declares Rousseau without pausing for breath, 'must have an influence on the moral nature'. The leap from the biological to the moral is an 'obvious' inference, and it is 'confirmed by experience'. The differences between men and women are sufficient to show

> the vanity of the disputes as to the superiority or the equality of the sexes; as if each sex, pursuing the path marked out for it by nature, were not more perfect in that very divergence than if it more closely resembled the other. A perfect man and a perfect woman should no more be alike in mind than in face, and perfection admits of neither less nor more.

Each sex then, *is* different in kind, whatever Rousseau may have said earlier. On the one hand he thinks it makes no sense to claim that the male sex is 'superior' to the female sex because the two sexes do not have enough in common to admit of comparison. On the other hand, he is able, on the basis of (inscrutable) inference and (indubitable) experience that the male sex is superior. In the same way the question of the equality of the sexes is held to make no sense, for the basis of any comparison just isn't there. The sexes are complementary, yet incommensurable at the same time. 'Each alike contributes to the common end, but in different ways.'

Rousseau leaps from descriptions of sexual difference to the 'difference which may be observed between man and woman in their moral relations'. He returns to an ancient polarity, that of active/passive, which now becomes morally prescriptive: 'The man should be strong and active; the woman should be weak and passive; the one must have both the power and the will; it is enough that the other should offer little resistance.' From this point on, the 'argument' becomes both daft and dangerous. It follows, thinks Rousseau, anticipating the popular culture of the 1960s,

> that woman is specially made for man's delight. If man in his turn ought to be pleasing in her eyes, the necessity is less urgent, his virtue is in his strength, he pleases because he is strong. I grant you this is not the law of love, but it is the law of nature, which is older than love itself.

The strong, protecting male and the weak, passive female are bound together in a natural complementary union. Inasmuch as 'woman' is strong, 'her strength is in her charms'. Because she is 'made to please and to be in subjection to man, she ought to make herself pleasing in his eyes and not provoke him to anger'. By the exercise of feminine guile she is able to keep the masculine volcano from dangerous eruption. By pleasing her man,

> she should compel him to discover and use his strength. The surest way of arousing this strength is to make it necessary by resistance. Thus pride comes to the help of desire and each exults in the other's victory. This is the origin of attack and defence, of the boldness of one sex and the timidity of the other, and even of the shame and modesty with which nature has armed the weak for the conquest of the strong.

These lines are seriously disconcerting. They convey to contemporary readers a health warning about complementarity theory, and they may encourage cruelty and violence even as they appeal to nature and protest their innocence. Especially noticeable are the combative metaphors by which relations between these opposite and warring sexes are to be conducted. Here is a primary myth of the 'battle of the sexes', still a common phrase in the late modern vernacular. Opposites engage: strength/weakness; victory/defeat; attack/defence; boldness/timidity; and man/woman. Yes, this is how relations between women and men are to be conducted. A century later, the famous treatise of Richard Freiherr von Krafft-Ebing, *Psychopathia Sexualis* (1887), was to exaggerate still further the opposition of two sexes. Hugely influential and written for psychiatrists, lawyers, and doctors, the naturalness of opposite-sex desire was intended to pathologize the newly invented character, the 'homosexual' (see section 4.5). As Stephen Katz explains, Krafft-Ebing

> repeatedly refers to males and females as 'opposite'—anatomical, genital differences signify an all-encompassing, fundamental contrariety. Just as he conceives of homosexual desire as 'contrary sexual instinct,' so he conceives of women and men as 'contrary' sexes. Human males and females are not just different in some biological structures and functions, similar in others, depending on one's standard of evaluation. This doctor's two sexes are antithetical. This alleged opposition appears repeatedly in heterosexual history, inspiring various ingenious explanations of how such contrary sexes ever manage to get together.   (Katz 2007: 30–1)

Rousseau's 'man' and 'woman' engage in a phoney war. Always available to titillate when required, women must show their strength in the exercise of modesty. Men and women are equally randy, but while God 'has endowed man with boundless passions' and given him 'reason by which to control them', God has also 'endowed woman with boundless passions' and 'given her modesty to restrain them'.

But God did not ordain that boundless passions are always restrained, and the continuing flow of battlefield metaphors in the narrative, of attack and repulse, siege and besieged, violence and resistance, even victim and aggressor, suggests a different reality beneath the bourgeois veneer of charmed appearances. No, no real harm can come to women when relations between the sexes are conducted in this way. 'The freest and most delightful of activities does not permit of any real violence; reason and nature are alike against it,' claims Rousseau. The testimony of millions of abused women exposes any resurfacing of these sentiments as malicious and dangerous, indeed as patronizing, condescending, demeaning, and false.

Because nature 'has endowed woman with a power of stimulating man's passions in excess of man's power of satisfying those passions', nature 'has thus made him dependent on her goodwill, and compelled him in his turn to endeavour to please her, so that she may be willing to yield to his superior strength'. 'The woman's mind exactly resembles her body; far from being ashamed of her weakness, she is proud of it; her soft muscles offer no resistance, she professes that she cannot lift the lightest weight; she would be ashamed to be strong.' Rousseau cites Deuteronomy 22, which prescribes what is to happen if a betrothed woman is raped by a man. If it happens in a city, both of them are put to death. If it happens in the countryside, only the assailant is condemned 'because the engaged woman may have cried for help, but there was no one to rescue her' (Deut. 22:27). Rousseau calls her exoneration 'merciful', and draws the positive conclusion that 'From this merciful interpretation of the law, girls learnt not to let themselves be surprised in lonely places.' The corollary is plain. While men are free to roam, women are not. They must learn to constrain their freedom lest men molest them.

Mary Wollstonecraft's *A Vindication of the Rights of Woman* (1792) rebutted many of Rousseau's mannered observations. Her introduction lambasts Rousseau and others for 'considering females rather as women than human creatures' (Wollstonecraft 2004: 2). The terminology is interesting; for 'females' is neutral vis-à-vis status, 'women' is pejorative, while 'human creatures' is the preferred, non-gendered term that encompasses males and females together. There is more than a hint of the one-sex theory here, where to be a woman is to be an inferior version of a man. 'Ladies', she avers, would be a more accurate target term than 'women' for Rousseau's class-laden comments about females:

Women are told from their infancy, and taught by the example of their mothers, that a little knowledge of human weakness, justly termed cunning, softness of temper, *outward* obedience, and a scrupulous attention to a puerile kind of propriety, will obtain for them the protection of man . . .   (Wollstonecraft 2004: 9 original emphasis)

Kant

A year after the publication of *Émile*, Immanuel Kant produced his *Observations on the Feeling of the Beautiful and Sublime* (1763; see Mahowald 1978). Our interest in Kant's aesthetics must be confined to its role in differentiating still further between men and women in the middle of the eighteenth century. He does this by basing further distinctions between men and women on a prior aesthetic distinction (deriving from Burke), between the 'beautiful' and the 'sublime'. For the sake of clarity and brevity, let us say with Mary Mahowald that for Kant (at least in his earlier work):

The two attributes refer to the chief kinds of finer human feelings. The 'sublime' is that which arouses esteem and admiration; it is always great and simple. In contrast, the 'beautiful' arouses love and joy; it may be small or ornamented. The sublime may be terrifying, noble, or splendid; the beautiful may be merely pretty (outwardly only), or properly beautiful (internally and externally).   (Mahowald 1978: 116)

A section of Kant's *Observations* is entitled 'Of the Distinction of the Beautiful and Sublime in the Interrelations of the Two Sexes'. Addressing his male readers regarding the 'fair sex' he says 'certain specific traits lie especially in the personality of this sex which distinguish it clearly from ours and chiefly result in making her known by the mark of the beautiful'. Whereas men may not lack beauty and women may not lack nobility, 'among the masculine qualities the sublime clearly stands out as the criterion of his [men's] kind. All judgments of the two sexes must refer to these criteria' (Kant in Mahowald 1978: 117). As in Rousseau, the educational arrangements for each sex must reflect the basic difference between them.

Women are said to 'have a strong inborn feeling for all that is beautiful, elegant, and decorated'. They 'love pleasure and can be entertained by trivialities'. They have 'a modest manner'. They have 'many sympathetic sensations, good-heartedness, and compassion' and 'prefer the beautiful to the useful'. 'In short, they contain the chief cause in human nature for the contrast of the beautiful qualities with the noble.' By exposure to these feminine qualities the noble sex is itself refined. 'The fair sex', explains Kant, 'has just as much understanding as the male, but it is a beautiful understanding, whereas ours should be a deep understanding, an expression that signifies identity with the sublime.'

Several pairs of opposites are brought to the distinction, in order to prise it open further. One has just been noted: one sex is superficial; the other is deep. Women do things that are easy ('display facility') while 'strivings and surmounted difficulties arouse admiration and belong to the sublime'. The old irrational/rational pair of opposites reappears: women lack the capacity for thought because 'deep meditation and a long-sustained reflection are noble but difficult', whereas 'laborious learning or painful pondering, even if a woman should greatly succeed in it, destroy[s] the merits that are proper to her sex'. Intellectually astute women do themselves a disservice. Men will not be envious of them, and they 'will weaken the charms with which she exercises her great power over the other sex'. A woman with 'a head full of Greek', continues Kant, 'might as well even have a beard; for perhaps that would express more obviously the mien of profundity for which she strives'.

And so the dualities mount up. 'The beautiful understanding' [the minds of women] selects for its objects 'everything closely related to the finer feeling, and relinquishes to the diligent, fundamental, and deep understanding abstract speculations or branches of knowledge useful but dry' (Kant in Mahowald 1978: 117–18). Gender distributes knowledge, and limits comprehension. Women need men's assistance in cultivating their 'beautiful nature'. This is education. Women are bound to their senses, whereas men are capable of abstract thought, and so of moral reasoning. Morality means something different to each sex. Men understand the 'universal rules' of morality: women proceed 'by some judgment upon the conduct that they see about them'. Women can be taught to appreciate the arts, but should not be expected to contribute to them. The 'fair sex' 'do something because it pleases them'. They can't cope with abstract principles, but to compensate, 'Providence has put in their breast kind and benevolent sensations, a fine feeling for propriety, and a complaisant soul.' They can be manipulated. Reason is set against feeling; the pursuit of principles against the pursuit of pleasure; the tearful sex versus the tear-less sex: 'A man must never weep other than magnanimous tears.

Those he sheds in pain or over circumstances of fortune make him contemptible' (Kant in Mahowald 1978: 119). Real men don't cry. Kant next launches into painful discussions about the appropriate demeanour of women; about their 'merry wit', their 'devices of dress', and the various shades of coquettishness, haughtiness, and flirtatiousness that confound the male suitors who are confronted by them. Remarks about shades of 'prettiness' and 'charm', about appropriate facial expressions and the use of make-up, are provided. Men must moderate their sexist banter. They must avoid 'mischief in their jest, which make us call them loose or waggish' (Kant in Mahowald 1978: 120). Insofar as women are capable of the male virtue of nobility, it presents itself in modesty. Morality demands that men and women become perfect, but differently perfect, and the route to the perfection of women is through marriage:

> The principal object is that the man should become more perfect as a man, and the woman as a wife; that is, that the motives of the sexual inclination work according to the hint of nature, still more to ennoble the one and to beautify the qualities of the other. (Kant in Mahowald 1978: 124)

Kant's attribution of beauty to women is a backhanded compliment. It removes women from morality because it separates them from the abstract thought required of them. It anchors them in nature whereas men, as Pamela Sue Anderson observes, can 'distance themselves from nature and move closer to the divine' (Anderson 2012: 23). Women's beauty, she reminds us, became a liability because 'modern science and technology seek to dominate all of nature as unruly and threatening rather than orderly and nurturing'; worse still, 'theological accounts of divine greatness as the sublime give further substantial ground to privilege men over women'.

Hegel

Almost half a century later, Hegel emphasized still further the differences between the two unequal sexes. While Rousseau the romantic locates sexual difference within the moral relations between women and men, Hegel the idealist locates sexual difference in the relation of each sex to the abstract universal. (Feminist philosophers in the next century would dub the elevation of abstraction over other more practical forms of thought as itself a masculinist ploy.) Describing the 'ethical world' in the *Phenomenology of Mind*, written in 1807, Hegel begins with the primary notion of *Geist* ('Mind' or 'Spirit'), which manifests itself in the human spirit, or consciousness. In human self-consciousness, the divine Spirit also becomes conscious of itself. Spirit becomes 'a realised actual social order, immediately given as a historical fact, and present directly to the minds of the individuals composing it' (Hegel 1807: 438). But 'Spirit' is said to be unable to realize itself 'except through the union of opposing elements', which are part of all contingent social orders.

The 'ethical world' is a combination (in Hegel's terms an 'opposition') of divine and human. Hegel thinks they are inseparable, but they must be separable, at least for thought, for the distinction to be made at all. Divine law is known through its universality; human law is known through the forms of individuality. Universality and individuality interact at the levels of community or nation, and family, and at each level the two sexes, introduced as an established fact, have different relationships to the divine law, and so to everything else, including to each other. Nations consist of the families who comprise them, just as families are comprised of individual members. What makes a family an *ethical* entity is not the quality of the contingent relations between each particular member (maternal, filial, and so on), as they are in Rousseau, but between the relation of each member *to the universal*. The family, Hegel insists, is

> an ethical entity, but not so far as it is the natural relation of its component members, or so far as their connexion is one immediately holding between individual concrete beings. For the ethical element is intrinsically universal, and this relation established by nature is essentially just as much a spiritual fact, and is only ethical by being spiritual. (Hegel 1807: 443)

Hegel makes much of the abstract character of the ethical family. 'Because the ethical element is the intrinsically universal element, the ethical relation between the members of the family is not that of sentiment or the relationship of love.' Men and women in the ethical family conform to divine law, and this dictates that men, while belonging to families, also provide the main connection with wider society. Men are also 'citizens'. 'Because it is only as citizen that he is real and substantial, the individual, when not a citizen, and belonging to the family, is merely unreal insubstantial shadow' (Hegel 1807: 445).

'The feminine life' is attached to the home (or, as Hegel says, to 'household divinities (*Penates*)'), and the woman 'sees in them both her universal substance, and her particular individuality'. Within a household 'of the ethical kind, a woman's relationships are not based on a reference to this particular husband, this particular child, but to *a* husband, to children *in general*,—not to feeling, but to the universal' (Hegel 1807: 452). The husband 'possesses, as a citizen, the self-conscious power belonging to the universal life, the life of the social whole'. The defined roles played by husbands and wives await their sons and daughters. 'The brother is the member of the family in whom its spirit becomes individualised, and enabled thereby to turn towards another sphere, towards what is other than and external to itself, and pass over into consciousness of universality' (Hegel 1807: 453). The sister, however, 'becomes, or the wife remains, director of the home and the preserver of the divine law'.

Divine law decrees, and nature dictates, the confinement of the female sex to the household. 'Nature, not the accident of circumstances or choice, assigns one sex to one law, the other to the other law; or conversely both the ethical powers themselves establish their individual existence and actualization in the two sexes' (Hegel 1807: 461). The wider community is said to consist of 'insular independent families which are under the management of womankind' (Hegel 1807: 473). Hegel may have had Proverbs 31:10–21 in mind when he wrote this. The destiny of mankind as a whole is to move beyond domesticity to the realm of human law in its business of secular government, commerce, making money, making war, and so on. Using language certain to be regarded as inflammatory or downright misogynistic over two centuries later, 'womankind' is said to be 'the everlasting irony in the life of the community', because she

> changes by intrigue the universal purpose of government into a private end, transforms its universal activity into a work of this or that specific individual, and perverts the universal property of the state into a possession and ornament for the family. Woman in this way turns to ridicule the grave wisdom of maturity, which, being dead to all particular aims, to private pleasure, personal satisfaction, and actual activity as well, thinks of, and is concerned for, merely what is universal; she makes this wisdom the laughing-stock of raw and wanton youth, an object of derision and scorn, unworthy of their enthusiasm. (Hegel 1807: 474)

Hegel has no trouble in accepting two sexes. They already express the intention of nature and divine law. One sex is confined to domesticity, the other is allowed a free run over all the world. Gone are the attempts to base gender distinctions on heat or the balance of ancient elements and humours. The two sexes can be accepted as given by nature and God, along with their proper roles. Readers will have noted the passages we have considered are riddled with pairs of opposites—absolute/relative, abstract/concrete, general/particular, substance/shadow, ethical/spiritual, God/nature, universality/individuality. All these are manifestations of divine law/human law. Other pairs of opposites provide the defining tools of social life. The private/public pair provides the basis for sexual distinctions and opposites. To one side is assigned domesticity, household management, and insubstantiality or shadow: to the other side is assigned government, commerce, and real substance. Real differences between men and women are made to fit into a grand a priori dialectical scheme where biological differences can be taken as read. Only when the scheme of opposites is introduced, is up and running and given, is the male/female pair introduced. Nature has already expressed itself in two distinct sexes and in the unequal roles each plays in divine and human law.

3.2.3. Different and Equal: Mill

Perhaps the most unequivocal argument for the full equality of two sexes in the nineteenth century is provided by John Stuart Mill's 1869 work *The Subjection of Women*. The opening paragraph states directly his aim to demolish the legal framework which preserves the privileges of patriarchy. His thesis was:

> That the principle which regulates the existing social relations between the two sexes—the legal subordination of one sex to the other—is wrong in itself, and now one of the chief hindrances to human improvement; and that it ought to be replaced by a principle of perfect equality, admitting no power or privilege on the one side, nor disability on the other. (Mill 1869: 1)

Mill was painfully aware that he was taking on 'universal opinion', so firmly entrenched in the minds of both men and women and 'so strongly rooted in the feelings', that even to question it and to suggest an alternative seemed impossible. A similar sense of helplessness is felt by contemporary writers who seek to query the modern dogma that there are two opposite sexes. 'Where does the burden of proof lie?' he asks. Why not with those who are in favour of the present restrictions? Is there not an a priori assumption 'in favour of freedom and impartiality'? Appeals to 'the intention of Nature and the ordinance of God' conceal prejudice. The authority of men over women, assumed because of men's greater strength, has never been tested against any alternative arrangement, for no such arrangement exists. Reminiscent of John Rawls's 'original position' at the outset of his *A Theory of Justice* (Rawls 1973: 17–22), Mill asks rhetorically whether the present arrangements would be thought to maximize the happiness of men and women if they had been designed in advance to achieve it.

The subjection of women is held to be analogous to the subjection of slaves, and just as one apparatus is being demolished, so ought the other, he insists, to be torn down. His contemporaries are 'mostly so little aware how completely, during the greater part of the duration of our species, the law of force was the avowed rule of general conduct' (Mill 1869: 17). The 'government' of one sex by the other may appear to be a 'natural' state, but, asks Mill, 'was there any domination which did not appear natural to those who possessed it?' (Mill 1869: 21) That Aristotle once held such a view merely shows that the greatest of minds can be deceived. That 'there are different natures among mankind, free natures, and slave natures' was an assumption responsible for a great evil, and any similar assumption about male and female nature ought to be abandoned for similar reasons. Women who 'make no complaint' about their legal and social status would entertain aspirations of freedom 'were they not so strenuously taught to repress them as contrary to the proprieties of their sex' (Mill 1869: 27). In other words, like the women today who, in several countries, still advocate genital cutting in full knowledge of the terrible pain and disadvantage it causes, they are duped by the oppressive power of custom, and victims not merely of patriarchy but of false consciousness (Hudson et al. 2012). The complaint that the doctrine of the equality of the sexes rests only on theory elicits the riposte that the same is true of the status quo favouring men (Mill 1869: 37).

Mill's critique of separate education for women includes his disdain for the new custom of the two sexes being regarded as 'opposites'. Women, he observes, have been

> brought up from the very earliest years in the belief that their ideal of character is the very opposite to that of men; not self-will, and government by self-control, but submission, and yielding to the control of others. All the moralities tell them that it is the duty of women, and all the current sentimentalities that it is their nature, to live for others; to make complete abnegation of themselves and to have no life but in their affections.   (Mill 1869: 37)

The practices of living for others and of self-denial are, of course, highly valued in Christian faith, but Mill is not condemning these practices per se: only that, when demanded, they are demanded of women only. This position of abjection is deftly utilized to explain why women are obliged to present themselves as sexually attractive to men:

> When we put together three things—first, the natural attraction between opposite sexes; secondly, the wife's entire dependence on the husband, every privilege or pleasure she has being either his gift, or depending entirely on his will; and lastly, that the principal object of human pursuit, consideration, and all objects of social ambition, can in general be sought or obtained by her only through him, it would be a miracle if the object of being attractive to men had not become the polar star of feminine education and formation of character.   (Mill 1869: 29)

'I deny', says Mill, 'that any one knows, or can know, the nature of the two sexes, as long as they have only been seen in their present relation to one another' (Mill 1869: 39). Knowledge of either would have to be an observed, empirical matter, and the complete separation of the sexes which would be necessary to observe it is unachieved and unachievable. 'Hence, in regard to that most difficult question, what are the natural differences between the two sexes—a subject on which it is impossible in the present state of society to obtain complete and correct knowledge—while almost everybody dogmatizes upon it', Mill counsels waiting for the partial answers provided by the investigations of the newish science of psychology into 'the laws of the influence of circumstances on character' (Mill 1869: 41). Even then, thinks Mill, the 'profoundest knowledge of the laws of the formation of character' may not 'entitle any one to affirm even that there is any difference, much more what the difference is, between the two sexes considered as moral and rational beings'. He considers it only a 'presumption in any one to pretend to decide what women are or are not, can or cannot be, by natural constitution' (Mill 1869: 105).

It is unfortunate that Mill's criticisms of the subjection of women in marriage were taken to be a criticism of the institution of marriage itself, and not a criticism of the widening, unequal, and unjust roles socially assigned to each of the parties. Mary Lyndon Shanley has cogently argued that *The Subjection of Women* was about more than equal opportunity for modern women. It was 'about the corruption of male–female relationships and the hope of establishing friendship in marriage' (Shanley 1981: 229). 'The fundamental assertion of *The Subjection of Women*', she holds, 'was not that equal opportunity would ensure the liberation of women, but that male–female equality, however achieved, was essential to marital friendship and to the progression of human society.'

3.3. TWO SEXES AND THE CHURCHES

We have examined some examples of the widening differentiation of two sexes and also some criticisms. How does the story go of parallel or reciprocal developments in theological thought? Throughout the period the churches' priority lay in preserving marriage. Marriages were necessary for stable families, and stable families were necessary for stable nation states. States were expected to provide the social and legal frameworks which structured marital and family life. Analogies were drawn between the nation or commonwealth and the family (see Witte 1997, 2015). Just as monarchs reigned over their subjects, so fathers were expected to reign over their families. In each case the lines of authority and the recognition of dominance and submission were essential. Both were institutions of hierarchical government, and each reinforced the other. 'The man is the ruler of the family, and the head of the woman', taught Pius XI, as late as 1930 (Pope Pius XI 1930: no. 29), repeating a line of his predecessor's encyclical (Pope Leo XIII 1880) nearly fifty years before. While Protestant and Catholic Christians disagreed with each other about many matters, there was complete agreement that sexual relations should be confined to marriage. Marriage still controls the sexual teaching of the churches: the possible admission of same-sex couples to marriage merely re-emphasizes its continuing hegemony within the area of sexual relations.

There are many reasons for this. One explanation, that marriage was a form of control exercised by the churches (principally over a promiscuous laity in the high medieval period), is only partially correct. There were other theological reasons for affirming marriage as the exclusive context for the conduct of sexual relations. God had provided marriage as a way of containing lust, taught Luther (reading Paul), so Christians should avail themselves of God's provision (with few exceptions), and marry. The 1662 Book of Common Prayer taught that marriage was 'ordained', first, 'for the procreation of children', second, 'for a remedy against sin, and to avoid fornication', and third, 'for the mutual society, help, and comfort, that the one ought to have of the other, both in prosperity and adversity'. Although these purposes of marriage are not ranked, procreation was likely regarded as the most important of the three, and remained so into the twentieth century. Catholics were left in no doubt about the matter. Pius XI, again following his predecessor, derived 'the principal ends of marriage laid down in the beginning by God', not from biblical or theological accounts of the meaning of marriage but from the command of God in Genesis 1 to 'Increase and multiply' (Pope Pius XI 1930: no. 8), adding, 'Thus amongst the blessings of marriage, the child holds the first place' (1930: no. 11). The highly qualified acceptance of the Anglican Communion to allow contraception to married couples 'where there is a clearly felt moral obligation to limit or avoid parenthood' (Lambeth Conference 1930: Resolution 15) was roundly condemned as a 'foul stain' on the chastity of marriage (Pope Pius XI 1930: no. 56: see Thatcher 1999: 181).

The 'defence' of marriage became and remains the priority of the churches in matters of sexual morality. Betrothal, a more relaxed (and biblical) approach to the beginning of marriage, lost legal recognition in England and Wales in 1753 (Thatcher 2002; Lawler and Salzman 2015). The entry into marriage became policed by the presence of a priest or state official, and bureaucratized. Separate ceremonies of spousals and nuptials were to be combined into a single occasion— the wedding. Harsh intolerance of bastardy (a dark, sad side of Christianity) was intended to deter the arrival of children outside wedlock (Witte 2009). 'Sex before marriage' assumed a new gravity in the scale of sin (and a new understanding of when marriage begins). Whether or not God had forbidden adultery, earthly fathers worried about paternity. It suited them that, in Hegel's terms, 'the feminine life' was centred upon the home. Strict laws policed the exit from marriage, and, while Protestantism was more tolerant of divorce, the Church of England officially approved of divorce and further marriage, in certain circumstances, only in the present century (2002) (for the arguments see Working party 2000).

Marriage was also defended as a superior form of patriarchy. Timothy Willem Jones writes of Anglican missionaries encountering polygamy in the British Empire. Polygamy was

> a signifier of the inferiority of foreign religious and cultural systems to British Christianity. The barbaric treatment that men of other races and religions meted out to 'their' women under polygamy was contrasted with the respect in which Anglicanism held women in monogamy. Marriage became a key distinguishing feature between 'good' and 'bad' patriarchies. (Jones 2013: 32)

There was a consistency and unanimity within the churches throughout the period about the social, moral, legal, and theological importance of marriage. This very consistency provides at least a partial explanation for the churches' imperviousness to the growing emphasis on two sexes, followed by a growing acceptance of them. Much of the new ideology seemed to assist in the task of upholding marriage and stable families, and so did not attract opposition. Condemnation was aimed at promiscuity and adultery. Modern rhetoric about the weaker female nature of women reinforced the firm and legalistic interpretation of biblical passages about women's subordination. That rhetoric was in any case partially a product of earlier Christian teaching. The exclusion of women from the professions served to attach the locus of women's activity to the home. Patriarchal authority would not be challenged if, after two sexes, natural inequalities between them could be found. Once conception in women was understood to be controlled by ovulation and not by orgasm, then the primacy of women's reproductive purpose was thought to be confirmed, and women's sexual pleasure, long regarded with deep suspicion (to say the least), could be shown to be unnecessary. In short, if women were no longer inferior *versions of men*, then they could be shown still to be inferior by other, scientifically supported, and philosophically defended, means.

3.3.1. Three Frameworks

Earlier in the chapter it was suggested that the churches still provide a space and a discourse in which it is possible to experience the old single-gender continuum. The currents of thought explored in this chapter strengthen that claim. In most churches (including some Anglican churches), the admission of women to the priesthood and to the episcopate is barred. While this wilful exclusion is painful for and damaging to the churches that practise it and to the women who cannot fulfil their calling, it is also evidence for a deeper malaise: women's bodies render them unfit for representing the male Christ (Thatcher 2011: 125–7). On the old one-sex theory, exclusion made sense. The more perfect man was better able than the less perfect man (i.e. a woman) to symbolize and to represent the supremely perfect God, language about whom was in any case couched in a heavy masculine way. Those troublesome biblical verses insisting on the subordination of women are already the outworkings of a view of womankind that has no place in the new humanity which is being made by God through Christ.

We have now considered three frameworks or positions within theological anthropology within which women might fit. If we were not following tradition, the problem might easily have been formulated in a different way: how might men fit into an anthropology which valorized women and natality (Jantzen 1998)? Even the cumbersome term 'theological anthropology' is a replacement for the still common 'doctrine of man', another obvious one-sex expression. The three positions are: i) there is one sex, a single continuum moving from more to less perfect; ii) there are two unequal sexes; and iii) there are two equal sexes. Under position i women are inferior and are barred from sacramental ministry. They don't match the required specification. On position ii they don't match either. They have a female nature which proves to be a disabling liability, and does not allow them to exercise leadership, religious or secular. But what of position iii?

Under position iii (roughly the theological equivalent of Mill's, just considered) women are equal with, or to, men, and equally valuable in the sight of God. None of the differences between men and women are in principle socially or religiously disabling. Position iii brings down no barrier against ordination. And much of the advocacy of women's ordination operates in just this way. Certain convenient biblical texts, especially Genesis 1:27 and Galatians 3:28, are read to support the creation of two equal sexes. In position iii God is thought to have no problem with the suitability of women for priesthood and ministry. That is why God calls both women and men to that sacred work. Given the 'universal opinion' (Mill's phrase) that there are two sexes, advocacy of women's ministry is going to have to speak within the language games that are open to it.

But there is still another way, yet to be considered, that locates gender within the remaking of humanity in the likeness of Christ. Christians are not required to say how many sexes there are, especially since they hope for a time when differences of sex no longer attract discriminatory assumptions. Christians recognize the social existence of two sexes. They will not be found subversively wandering into the wrong toilet or rest room that has been provided for the 'opposite sex'. But even at the level of human biology, the assumption of two sexes cannot account for the minorities of people, increasingly visible, who are called 'intersex', or 'transgender', or 'third sex' (Cornwall 2010, 2014, 2015). The two-sex theory normalizes the modern account of heterosexuality which in turn marginalizes homosexual and bisexual desire. And we have seen in the present chapter how the assumption of two sexes needlessly polarizes human relationships in countless unnecessary ways.

The outcomes of the two-sex understanding of people are ambiguous, as this chapter has shown. Opposites generate the sense of otherness; otherness generates suspicion and power play, with predictable results. Major improvements for women in access to education, the professions, and employment, and towards equal pay with men, have been secured, always in the teeth of conservative male opposition. Legal barriers constraining women's freedom have been removed. Prejudices barring women from education (smaller brains, inability to concentrate) and from sport (no stamina, weaker bodies) are largely forgotten. But some prejudices have become worse. Women can play competitive sport provided it is organized along strictly segregated lines. The expectation that women should make themselves look attractive to secure and please men has been driven by the global fashion, clothing, cosmetics, and advertising industries that now demand women should look 'attractive' to men, wherever they are, at work, at home, on the town, or on the beach. There are 'gross exaggerations of difference by social practices of dress' (Connell 1987: 81). John Berger's *Ways of Seeing* puts the point well:

> *Men act* and *women appear*. Men look at women. Women watch themselves being looked at. This determines not only most relations between men and women but also the relation of women to themselves. The surveyor of woman in herself is male: the surveyed female. Thus she

turns herself into an object—and most particularly an object of vision: a sight.   (Berger 1972: 47, original emphases)

Male violence against women (see sections 8.2.2, 8.3) is unabated, inexcusable but so commonplace it often fails to shock. Internet pornography is a constant reminder of men's demand for power over women. Women still need protection from some men, not by other men, but by other women whom they can trust. What streets are safe at night? Men too are thrown into false consciousness by the two-sex theory. Masculinity becomes associated with fighting and wars, femininity with nurturing and compassion, each sex internalizing stereotypes which inhibit the recognition and growth of these opposite qualities in the other. In these and countless other ways accentuation of sexual difference does not further the flourishing of humanity.

With this chapter, work on the two-sex theory and its colonization of the modern mind has come to its end, in the hope that the second aim of the book can now count as being met. In the next chapter, the recent assimilation of two sexes within theology and the churches' sexual teaching will be discussed and assessed.

4

The 'Modern Mix'

One and Two Sexes Combined

Chapter 4 begins the third aim of the book: to expose the reliance of much church and theological teaching about sex and gender either on biblical proof texts or upon the language and nomenclature of late modernity, rather than upon considerations of theology and Christology. It begins by heeding the warning of historians against reading assumptions from the present into the past, and discovering them there (section 4.1). Next it turns to official Roman Catholic and Anglican teaching about sexuality and gender, and finds in each case a confused mix of one-sex and two-sex understandings of human being (sections 4.2, 4.3). Next it notes briefly how two well-known theologians claim to find the two sexes in scripture and tradition, with dire consequences (section 4.4) for their theology. Finally it notes how an insistence on heterosexuality and the condemnation of homosexuality are two sides of the same coin (section 4.5).

4.1. TWO SEXES PROJECTED BACK

Historians have borrowed (from the philosophy of time) the awkward term 'presentism' to describe a tendency to introduce present-day assumptions and ideas into analyses and interpretations of the past (Hunt 2002). This tendency is, literally, anachronistic, for it reads present ideas backwards (*ana-*) into an earlier time (*chronos*). But presentism is a particular problem for theologies of sexuality and gender.

Kim Phillips and Barry Reay have convincingly shown that much of the history of 'sexuality' is just such an exercise in presentism: the title of their book, *Sex before Sexuality: A Premodern History*, points to the dangerous distortion of the past that necessarily accompanies attempts to locate modern assumptions about sexuality (and its cognate terms homo-, hetero-, and bi-) in ancient texts. While they do not use the neologism 'presentism', they warn that modern discourses of sexuality are certain to impose on ancient peoples distinctions and attitudes of which they could not have been aware. They argue 'that historians of premodern sex will be constantly blocked in their understanding if they use terms and concepts applicable to sexuality since the late nineteenth century' (Phillips and Reay 2011: 8–9). 'Our appraisal', they say, 'based on years of reading and analysis within the field, is that premodern sexual cultures were significantly different from modern or indeed postmodern ones and we misrepresent them if we emphasize historical continuities and enduring patterns or sexual identity. Surface likenesses, we believe, should not be read as samenesses' (Phillips and Reay 2011: 10; see also 16).

The purpose of having sex used to be twofold: procreation and payment of the marital debt. The church did not insist on heterosexuality; it insisted on procreative sexual intercourse as the only legitimate sexual activity for Christians. Clearly procreation requires a fertile man and a fertile woman, but many other sexual activities requiring a man and a woman were proscribed. 'Medieval people did not draw the line between gay and straight, but between reproductive and non-reproductive sex. Same-sex activity was not reproductive, but much opposite-sex activity was not reproductive either, and was not excused by the fact that it was "heterosexual"' (Karras 2005: 8). Such was the importance of procreation to the church's teaching that 'fictive reproduction' was assigned to celibate male and female elites, 'Father' for bishops and priests, 'Mother' for abbesses, 'Papa' for the Pope himself (Karras 2015: 282). If children were not to be the fruit of their endeavours, then the birth and growth of spiritual children was an equal or better purpose in the sight of God.

The adoption of the language of heterosexuality brought a challenge to the churches' procreative understanding of sex in the second half of the nineteenth century. It signalled the replacement

of the procreative principle within sexual ethics by a new pleasure
principle:

> In the United States, in the 1890s, the 'sexual instinct' was generally
> identified as a *procreative* desire of men and women. But that repro-
> ductive ideal was beginning to be challenged, quietly but insistently, in
> practice and theory, by a new *different-sex pleasure* ethic. According to
> that radically new standard, the 'sexual instinct' referred to men's and
> women's erotic desire for each other, *irrespective of its procreative
> potential.* (Katz 2007: 19, original emphases)

The churches were confronted with a dilemma. On the one hand, the
new understanding of sex began to introduce a pleasure ethic they
were not yet able to accept. On the other hand, heterosexuality
conveniently contrasted with another opposite, 'homosexuality', and
the new language made the condemnation of some non-procreative
sexual acts (those between same-sex partners) easier. As the emphasis
on the importance of sexual pleasure for men and women grew in the
twentieth century, the churches were able to accommodate and
incorporate it (albeit within marriage). That heterosexuality was
about the pleasure principle was quietly forgotten: that heterosexuality was about marginalizing homosexuality was gratefully seized on
and extended. The normalization of this modern nomenclature
across the wide spectrum of theological and ecclesial opinion in the
last fifty years, without regard to its origins, indicates a disabling
amnesia at the basis of many modern pronouncements about homosexuality and heterosexuality.

4.2. THE 'DEADLY MIX'

In the last forty years, the Roman Catholic and Anglican churches
have combined one-sex and two-sex theories in what Jane Shaw has
called (in the Anglican case) 'a fairly deadly mix' (Shaw 1998: 21). On
the one hand, I will suggest the unwillingness of the Roman Catholic
Church (and Orthodox churches) to consider the ordination of
women is based on considerations derived from the ancient one-sex
mindset which regards women as inferior versions of the default
male. This is difficult, if not impossible, to reconcile with the simultaneous teaching that women and men are equal in dignity and

worth. On the other hand, I will suggest that the reformers' case (with its assumptions about equality, difference, orientation, complementarity) is strikingly modern and derives from the theory that there are, and (so it is claimed) always have been, two sexes. Their case is encased in presentism. Consequently ecclesial thinking already displays a mixture of theories, rather like a mix of two incompatible soundtracks in a sound recording which distorts the music as it is reproduced. Anglican thought is caught in the jaws of, on the one hand, Catholic masculinism or modern Biblicism, and on the other hand modern revisionism, with differing outcomes across the Anglican Communion. In what follows I will be looking for evidence of the mix in some key Roman Catholic and Anglican documents, and (to change the metaphor) attempting to disentangle the different threads of thought before embarking on an alternative theology of gender in part II.

4.2.1. The Catholic Case: One Sex and Ordination

The arguments against the ordination of women are well known, so I will concentrate on only those elements of it which evidence one-sex thinking. *Inter insigniores* (Sacred Congregation for the Doctrine of the Faith [CDF] 1976) begins in a conciliatory tone. It is admitted 'that in the writings of the Fathers, one will find the undeniable influence of prejudices unfavourable to woman', which were 'inspired by the spirit of the times'. 'The Church's tradition in the matter has thus been so firm in the course of the centuries that the Magisterium has not felt the need to intervene in order to formulate a principle which was not attacked, or to defend a law which was not challenged.' The attitude of Jesus to women 'was quite different from that of his milieu'. 'Contrary to the Jewish mentality, which did not accord great value to the testimony of women', women 'were the first to have the privilege of seeing the risen Lord'. But their privilege did not extend to the calling of any of them (including, pointedly, the mother of Jesus) to be apostles (CDF 1976: no. 3).

Perhaps Jesus wanted to 'entrust to women . . . a ministry assimilating them to the Twelve', but 'historical circumstances did not permit him to do so'? No. 'No one . . . however has ever proved—and it is clearly impossible to prove—that this attitude is inspired only by social and cultural reasons.' In 1994 Pope John Paul II confirmed that this document 'shows clearly that Christ's way of acting did not

proceed from sociological or cultural motives peculiar to his time'
(Pope John Paul II 1994: 2). St Paul was well able to distinguish
between 'disciplinary practices of minor importance, such as the
obligation imposed upon women to wear a veil on their head
(1 Cor. 11:2–16)', and 'the forbidding of women to speak in the
assemblies' which 'is of a different nature' (CDF 1976: no. 4). The
prohibition of women speaking in church is 'bound up with
the divine plan of creation (1 Cor. 11:7; 1 Tim. 2:12): it would be
difficult to see in it the expression of a cultural fact'. A woman
presiding at the altar alters the 'sacramental signs'. The priest acts
'*in persona Christi*, taking the role of Christ, to the point of being his
very image, when he pronounces the words of consecration'. The
bridegroom/bride symbolism of the old and new covenants, and of
the relation between Christ and the church, would be fatally disrupted
by the presence of women priests. 'The incarnation of the Word took
place according to the male sex: this is indeed a question of fact, and
this fact, while not implying an alleged natural superiority of man
over woman, cannot be disassociated from the economy of salvation'
(CDF 1976: no. 5). The priest is 'a sign', which 'must be perceptible
and which the faithful must be able to recognize with ease'. Following
Aquinas's teaching that 'Sacramental signs represent what they sig-
nify by natural resemblance', Pope John Paul II concludes:

> when Christ's role in the Eucharist is to be expressed sacramentally,
> there would not be this 'natural resemblance' which must exist between
> Christ and his minister if the role of Christ were not taken by a man: in
> such a case it would be difficult to see in the minister the image of
> Christ. For Christ himself was and remains a man.   (CDF 1976: no. 5)

Some Replies

One might ask why the tradition of ordaining only men was 'so firm
in the course of the centuries'. An answer, following the trajectory of
this book, is that women in the course of the centuries were regarded
as inferior versions of men, and so were regarded as universally unsuited
for ordination. The Vatican notes that the 'Jewish mentality ... did
not accord great value to the testimony of women'. Why was that?
Some of the Fathers were prejudiced against women. Why was
that? Can the prejudice be explained by 'the spirit of the times'?
There is a better answer—the one just given. Jesus is rightly said to

have challenged the diminished status of the women of his day, but how did that diminished status come about? Again there is a different answer to be given to this question. The prevailing view within Judaism and the surrounding culture was very far from the modern notion of two equal sexes. Women were inferior. They could not be priests in the Hebrew Bible and their disqualification there was soon extended within the emergent church.

There are other justifications for an all-male priesthood about which the Vatican is less forthcoming. Nancy Jay notes the prevalence of the phrase 'Throughout your generations for ever' (Jay 1992: 96) in Leviticus. It became the title of her well-known book. Levitical priesthood, she writes, set itself up for ever, and 'clung to patrilineal descent as the only way to legitimate' itself and Israel's sacrificial traditions. She describes how Christian clergy modelled themselves on the Levitical example, and became 'a sacrificing priesthood mediating between God and man (*sic*)', organizing themselves in 'unilineal "eternal" descent' (Jay 1992: 114). The sacrificial role of the male priest in a hierarchical structure helped to overcome the problems of continuity and succession in a rapidly expanding church. 'The Eucharist became *the* Christian sacrifice . . . the bishops who celebrated it became unilineal successors to the apostles; and clerical office became sacrificing priesthood, not charismatic ministry' (Jay 1992: 116). 'Ritual purity, as distinct from moral purity, became crucial for priests, and the reproductive powers of women were specifically polluting' (Jay 1992: 117). Jay thinks priests sought to integrate themselves into an eternal social order, an order defined, as in the Hebrew Bible, by sacrifice. Citing Job 14:1, 4 ('Man that is born of woman is of few days, and full of trouble . . . Who can bring a clean thing out of an unclean?' (version unspecified)), she thinks 'Sacrifice can expiate, get rid of, the consequences of having been born of woman' (Jay 1992: 40). The alleged polluting effects of women on men, well attested in the Hebrew Bible, confirm the gross inferiority of women consistent with the one-sex continuum. It is significant that the pollution argument for an exclusive priesthood is *not* used in twentieth-century official documents confining the priesthood to men. It is morally shameful and theologically unusable, yet it still festers away powerfully in the patriarchal imagination.

'Christ's way of acting did not proceed from sociological or cultural motives peculiar to his time.' Two issues arise. Proof is required that

Christ, in excluding women from the Twelve, *was* swayed by local or temporal considerations. It seems odd that proof should be required when an attempt is made to discern the mind of Christ. What could count as proof? More obviously, why is proof that Christ was not so swayed not required? More importantly, it is clear that Jesus (and, following him, the early churches) approved of (or did not challenge, for example) slavery, and disapproved of usury, while the modern church disapproves of slavery and approves of usury (see Salzman and Lawler 2013). The teaching and example of Jesus does not need to be protected from its situatedness in history. No one, inside or outside the Vatican, knows why the Twelve whom Jesus chose were all male. One plausible explanation is the one-sex model. In the time of Jesus, as the Vatican acknowledges, the prejudices facing women were insurmountable, and so Jesus sometimes worked within the frameworks of patriarchy, preferring to transform them from within; at other times he confronted oppression, especially religious oppression, directly.

The exclusion of women from ministry in the early church is much more contested than the document allows (Alexander 2013). It is hard to know why the requirement to wear a veil no longer has a 'normative value' whereas the silencing of women belongs to another order ('the divine plan of creation'). What women are allowed to wear and what they are allowed to do in the early church belong together. They follow directly from a patriarchal view of women, and their active, disturbing presence in the assembly. Scholars have long known there is a discrepancy in 1 Corinthians between two passages: in one (11:5) women may pray and prophesy as long as they wear veils; in the other (14:33–5) they cannot pray or prophesy at all: 'As in all the churches of the saints, women should be silent in the churches. For they are not permitted to speak, but should be subordinate . . . ' The Vatican deals with the contradiction by pressing the dubious distinction between prophecy and 'official' teaching. One is open to women; the other isn't. A more likely explanation is that the harsher passage is an interpolation reflecting a later view of a Pauline school of thought. Nascent Christian faith challenges the inferior view of women, but third-generation Christians rein in the progress that was made, fearing its radicalism. According to the Vatican here, the subordination of women is 'part of the divine plan of creation'. Elsewhere there is full equality and dignity. Here is more primary evidence of the modern mix.

We have already noted that Paul's understanding of the divine plan of creation in 1 Corinthians is far from the conventional understanding that men and women are two sexes who share equally in the image of God (see section 1.4.1). 'Man' (gendered) 'is the image and reflection of God; but woman is the reflection of man' (1 Cor. 11:7). Only man, never woman, can represent Christ at the Eucharist, for the priest acts '*in persona Christi*, taking the role of Christ, to the point of being his very image'. With regard to priesthood, then, Christian anthropology doesn't begin with Genesis but in its proper place, with Christ. Let's ask next about the priest taking the role of Christ, being *in persona Christi*. *Persona*, of course, is a Trinitarian term. God is three Persons. But the *persona* of Christ is *divine*, not human! Undergraduates are generally startled to learn that in the creedal Christology of the church Jesus has no human personality. The Personhood of Christ is divine. Christ has two natures: one divine, one human. (The idea that Christ contained or was made known in two Persons, one divine and one human, was rejected as the Nestorian heresy.) Since Christ is a Person of God, Christ's Person is beyond distinctions of sex and gender. Vatican theology at this point becomes both ideology and even heresy. Since the Person of Christ is divine and not human, it is idolatrous to confine the representation of that Person to the male sex. Since the divine Person of the Son is not male, there is no requirement that adequate representation of the Christ is open to males only (see Norris 1984: 71–5).

The concepts of representation and signification play a major part in the ideological assertion of masculinity in these documents. On an alternative but unforced reading of Nicene and Chalcedonian Christology, it follows that men *and women* do and must represent Christ. Not only *can* women represent the divine Person of the Son; given that Christian priests have historically all been men, it is urgently *necessary* for the imbalance to be rectified, and for Christians to recover and rejoice in the divine Personhood of the one Christ. Why must the faithful be able to 'recognize with ease' the maleness of their priests, especially since they sometimes dress ambiguously as women? (If easy recognition was the main issue here, perhaps priests might consider exposing their manhood a little more obviously when celebrating the Eucharist to provide unambiguous evidence of their natural resemblance to Christ? See Thatcher 2011: 126.)

Nevertheless, 'the incarnation of the Word took place according to the male sex', and 'this is indeed a question of fact'. There is a direct appeal to Christ's human nature as *anèr*, not *anthròpos*; to his humanity as *vir*, not as *homo*. Yet it is well known that the Greek *anèr* and the Latin *vir* are translated as 'man', i.e. a male human being, whereas *anthròpos* and *homo* are best translated as 'humankind'. 'Man' here means 'men and women'. 'Man' is the one-sex continuum. In the old inclusive language of the old one-sex continuum women are nevertheless included, albeit as inferior versions of the male. The creeds are silent about Christ's maleness. Of course they assume it. But the creeds do not license any talk of the Incarnation taking place 'according to the male sex'. The human nature which Christ assumed is inclusive of all humankind.

4.2.2. Two Equal Sexes, Absolutely Distinct

The *Catechism of the Catholic Church* (1994) (and several other official documents) appeals to Genesis 1:27 in order to affirm that God has created two equal sexes. This is how paragraph 2331 cites and arranges three very familiar verses from Genesis:

> 'God created man in his own image . . . male and female he created them' [Gen. 1:27]; he blessed them and said, 'Be fruitful and multiply' [Gen. 1:28]; 'When God created man, he made him in the likeness of God. Male and female he created them, and he blessed them and named them Man when they were created' [Gen. 5:2].

It follows from these texts that 'God gives man and woman an equal personal dignity' (*Catechism* no. 2334, citing Pope John Paul II 1981: no. 22). 'Each of the two sexes is an image of the power and tenderness of God, with equal dignity though in a different way' (*Catechism* 1994: no. 2335). Some modern translations of these verses replace 'man' with a term that looks less sexist ('humankind'—NRSV, 'mankind'—NIV), but the *Catechism* and all other Vatican documents use 'man' for men and women together. This language is said to be 'inclusive', and, as I suggested earlier (section 3.1.1), the insistence on its use is strong, direct evidence of the persistence of the one-sex theory.

But there is a deeper, more important, point to be made. Readers are invited to discover, from a surface reading of these Genesis texts, that God has made two sexes, and that they are equal. In advance of further treatment of these texts (see section 6.2), it should be firmly stated that the texts do not obviously provide what they are widely thought to provide. They are *at least* as compatible with the single continuum from men to women. Plausibly, what God creates is 'man' or 'Man', a singular creature. 'Man' is made in the image of God. In a subsequent step, and in order for 'man' to be able to reproduce, 'he' is created 'male and female'. These are generic terms. Only in Genesis 2 does a particular man and woman appear. There is nothing said in Genesis 1 or Genesis 2 about their equality. Jewish and Christian traditions from the beginning to the eighteenth century have taught otherwise.

The passage from the *Catechism* mixes ancient with modern thought, one sex with two, without regard to the very different locations of each. Subsequent paragraphs reverberate with the sound of late modern nomenclature. 'Sexuality' is at once catapulted into optimal theological significance because it 'affects all aspects of the human person in the unity of his body and soul' (*Catechism* 1994: no. 2332). Nothing, then, is more important than our sexuality. How can we thrive without the self-knowledge our sexuality provides? The male pronoun ('*his* body and soul') confirms that the person, like 'man', is essentially masculine. Sexuality, continues the *Catechism*, 'especially concerns affectivity, the capacity to love and to procreate, and in a more general way the aptitude for forming bonds of communion with others'. The *Catechism* gives a generous place to the contribution of sexuality to personhood, to spirituality, and to participation in the divine life. The problem is that sexuality heads a discourse which does not integrate easily, if at all, with premodern discussions of the topics within its domain. 'Sexual identity' belongs to the modern discourse, in which it is generally taken to mean recognizing oneself as one discovers one's attraction to other selves. People identify as straight, queer, and so on, as their 'orientation' to particular others announces itself over time. But sexual identity is given a very different meaning in the *Catechism*. You are either a man or a woman. There are two sexes and you identify as a member of one of them. 'Everyone, man and woman, should acknowledge and accept his sexual identity' (*Catechism* 1994: no. 2333). There is no room for ambiguity. The male/female binary is absolutized in these almost casual yet damaging dicta. Intersex, third-sex, and transgender people are officially made to vanish.

The *Catechism* derives not just two sexes but also their equality from these verses. Citing *Familiaris consortio* (John Paul II 1981: no. 22), it teaches that 'In creating men "male" and "female", God gives

man and woman an equal personal dignity.' Men, then, are male and
female. There are female men. The first half of this statement is what
the one-sex theory expects. Citing *Mulieris dignitatem* (Pope John
Paul II 1988: no. 6), the *Catechism* continues, '"Man is a person, man
and woman equally so, since both were created in the image and
likeness of the personal God"' (*Catechism* 1994: no. 2334b). The
problem is the hermeneutical sleight of hand in bypassing most of
Jewish and Christian history, which holds emphatically to a different
take on these verses, and firming up sexual difference so that it
confirms the modern theory of opposite sexes, the basis of the Vatican
binary and exclusive understanding of sexual identity. But if Genesis
1:27 confirms God made two equal sexes, then by the same hermeneutical principles Genesis 1:1–1:31 confirms God made the world in
six days, and Genesis 1:29–30 confirms that humankind is required to
be vegetarian ('Amen' to that). There is a finality about the male/
female binary ('Each of the two sexes . . . '). Two adjectives ('male' and
'female'): two sexes. A literalist, surface reading of a single verse is
supposed to release the balm of soothing words upon the gender
trouble that seethes away in every church. But the two adjectives
'male' and 'female' do not license the two sexes that modernity
takes for granted. Humanity is made in the image of God, and
humanity is 'male and female'.

Duncan Dormor calls this the 'Order of Creation Argument',
finding it in magisterial and Protestant thought alike. It consists of
three premises:

1. God has created humanity in two distinct forms, male and
   female.

2. This gendered or sexed identity is an essential characteristic of
   what it means to be considered a proper human being.

3. Gender is in a real sense also 'destiny'; that is, we are all designed
   to be attracted to the 'opposite' sex, and thus for procreation.
   (Dormor 2013: 123)

The Order of Creation Argument conveniently supports a series of
conclusions which nullify homosexual, intersex, and transgender people.
It is a poor theological argument with even worse practical, pastoral, and
missiological consequences for the victims of its abusive logic.

The Apostolic Letter *Mulieris dignitatem* deals directly with
gender (but without mentioning the term). It provides a 'study of

the anthropological and theological bases that are needed in order to solve the problems connected with the meaning and dignity of being a woman and being a man' (Pope John Paul II 1988: no. 1). The very next sentence severely qualifies how the study is to be carried out: 'It is a question of understanding the reason for and the consequences of the Creator's decision that the human being should always and only exist as a woman or a man.' There are two sexes, no exceptions, and an absolute distinction between them. We are to believe they are primordial givens, entirely beyond question, and before the creation of the world. The required study cannot include whether there are, or have always been, two sexes, or whether some people may not fit the description. It defines out any deviating ambiguities or queer propensities, notwithstanding the pain it delivers to such persons. No, the study is to be confined to what follows from God having made us this way, from 'the order of creation'.

Christian Anthropology

Great weight is placed on Genesis 1:27, which contains and 'consti-tutes the immutable *basis of all Christian anthropology*' (Pope John Paul II 1988: no. 6, original emphasis). 'Man' is 'the image and likeness' of God. 'This concise passage', the Pope teaches,

> contains the fundamental anthropological truths: man is the highpoint of the whole order of creation in the visible world; the human race, which takes its origin from the calling into existence of man and woman, crowns the whole work of creation; *both man and woman are human beings to an equal degree*, both are created *in God's image*. (original emphases)

Men and women are equally human. 'Woman' is not less human than 'man'. They derive their special human being from the image and likeness of God. This is the basis of the 'personal character of the human being'.

Since almost all Christians reading John Paul II here would probably agree with him, it may appear destructive and hypercritical to find fault with this teaching. Personhood, equality, identity, the image and likeness of God: what Christian, eager to advance the faith, would want to cast doubt upon this compelling narrative? Well, there are three reasons. The first is whether tradition has found these meanings in Genesis 1. The second is whether the two separate adjectives 'male' and 'female' provide a basis for the assumption of two separate sexes. But the third (to become a theme in chapter 6) concerns identifying the place where 'the immutable basis of all Christian anthropology lies'. The New Testament also contains references to the image of God, and it is clear from these that the image of God is not 'Adam' but *Christ.* 'He is the image of the invisible God, the firstborn of all creation.' He 'is the beginning, the firstborn from the dead, so that he might come to have first place in everything' (Col. 1:15, 18; see also 2 Cor. 4:4). Here are crucial references to the image of God that do not feature in *Mulieris dignitatem.* Whereas a biblical anthropology might be thought to have an appropriate beginning in Genesis with regard to a chronology of the 'history of salvation', a biblical anthropology which assigns to Jesus Christ 'first place in everything' might be thought to need to begin elsewhere.

Further evidence of the forced character of the papal reflection upon Genesis 1:27 lies in the treatment of Genesis 2. It has been long known that there are two different creation accounts in Genesis 1–3, and the consensus remains that Genesis 1:1–2:4a belongs to a 'priestly source' called P (dated around 500 BCE), and the second account, Genesis 2:4b–2:25 to a source called J (dated around 850 BCE, so called because it uses the name Jahweh for God). The J account helped to shape the one-sex tradition as it manifested itself in Judaism and Christianity. We have already noted how passages in the New Testament assume the priority of the man over the woman, and the J account is a principal reason why. The man is made first. The woman is made from his bone and flesh. And he recognizes her bones and flesh as his bones and flesh. The woman's bodily identity comes from the man. Her flesh is his flesh in a different form. The pope allows that the name 'woman' 'indicates her essential identity with regard to man—'is-'issah— something which unfortunately modern languages in general are unable to express: "She shall be called woman (*'issah*) because she was taken out of man (*'is*)": *Gen* 2:23' (John Paul II 1988: no. 6). Yes, the 'essential identity' of men and women is what a one-sex theory assumes, but it is never allowed to challenge the two sexes of Genesis 1:27. The two differing accounts of creation are harmonized. The Genesis 2 account is to be interpreted 'in light of the truth about the image and likeness of God' in Genesis 1. Genesis 1:27, interpreted as two equal sexes, is imposed (not without exegetical difficulty) on the whole narrative.

Gender

The *Letter to the Bishops of the Catholic Church on the Collaboration of Men and Women in the Church and in the World* (Ratzinger and Amato 2004), approved by John Paul II, confirms Genesis 1 provides the 'framework', a general account of the origin of the world and of humanity 'as articulated in the male–female relationship'; Genesis 2 'confirms in a definitive way the importance of sexual difference' (Ratzinger and Amato 2004: nos 5–6). The letter marks a yet more intransigent affirmation of sexual difference. Ratzinger writes up the discomfort of the church with regard to 'new approaches to women's issues' (Ratzinger and Amato 2004: no. 2), and gender lies at the root of it. The authors define a particular perspective (associated with the work of Judith Butler, who is not named directly) in which 'physical difference, termed *sex*, is minimized, while the purely cultural element, termed *gender*, is emphasized to the maximum and held to be primary' (original emphasis).

This singular perspective obscures 'the difference or duality of the sexes' and is said to lead to a catalogue of disasters. It inspires ideologies which 'call into question the family' and 'make homosexuality and heterosexuality virtually equivalent, in a new model of polymorphous sexuality'.

> According to this perspective, human nature in itself does not possess characteristics in an absolute manner: all persons can and ought to constitute themselves as they like, since they are free from every predetermination linked to their essential constitution.
>
> This perspective has many consequences. Above all it strengthens the idea that the liberation of women entails criticism of Sacred Scripture, which would be seen as handing on a patriarchal conception of God nourished by an essentially male-dominated culture. Second, this tendency would consider as lacking in importance and relevance the fact that the Son of God assumed human nature in its male form.   (Ratzinger and Amato 2004: no. 3)

The document oversimplifies and misrepresents the problem posed to the church by gender theory. Gender imbalance is broader than its confinement to 'women's issues', as if men have no responsibility for them. It is no secret that there are strands of scripture which are patriarchal, and strands which suggest its eventual elimination. Acknowledgement of the former is frankly unavoidable. The contribution of gender theory to theology is potentially a rich one (Beattie 2015: 32–3). It is contrary to the Catholic tradition's hospitality to reason to represent all of it in this way, and to associate it with extremism and hostility to the Faith.

This section has shown in some detail the awkward interplay of one-sex and two-sex theories of humanity in Catholic teaching. The one-sex theory is required to confine ordination to men. The two-sex theory is required to accord to women the unconditional dignity and respect that is due to them as the baptized children of God (albeit with the restrictions that belong to female nature). This is the 'fairly deadly mix' which Shaw detected in Anglican thought (see section 4.3). The great worry is the apparent threat to this firmed-up essentialism. Any possible suggestion of fluidity within human nature or desire is shunned by the appeal to the 'absolute manner' of sexual duality. But there is an unfortunate conflation between 'sexual difference' (men are not women) and 'sexual duality', dichotomously understood. Given that it makes sense to assign to human beings a nature ('human nature'), what might it mean to possess its characteristics 'in an absolute manner'? The Vatican answers the question by positing two human natures: male nature and female nature, which are absolutely different. It is vexed by any weakening of the belief that God in Christ 'assumed human nature in its male form'. But we have just noted that the Christology of the ancient creeds made nothing of Christ's male nature or form. It was enough to confess that he became 'man' (*anthròpos, homo*). Once there are male and female natures, it follows that the male Christ has no female nature. How then can he save what he does not assume? The principle that 'The unassumed is the unhealed', first found in Gregory Nazianzen's *Epistle* 101, is 'justly famed in doctrinal history' (Wiles 1976: 108). While there are different interpretations of the principle today (Wiles 1976), it is fatal to any theological rationale for separate male and female natures. If Christ has no female nature, then femaleness is unhealed. If Christ has a human nature, the problem ceases to arise. Christ in the tradition, of course, has a divine and a human nature without further division or qualification, and by further dividing human nature the Vatican may be doing violence to the very Christology it professes.

4.3. THE ANGLICAN CASE: FLIRTATION
WITH ONE SEX

Anglicans are divided into forty-four member churches worldwide, and they differ over the ordination of women, and much else. At least one is currently led by a woman bishop: in others the question of women's ordination cannot even be discussed. In 2015 the Church of England appointed women to the episcopate, and appointed a '"headship" bishop' who ensures representation in the House of Bishops of those Anglican Protestants who think women are unfit to lead or teach. Here in purple facticity is another 'deadly mix' of incompatibles requiring explanation.

There is an official Anglican report that displays a momentary awareness of the difficulties of bringing modern terminology to bear on ancient texts. In a foreword to *Some Issues in Human Sexuality*, Bishop Richard Harries introduces

> [a] note about terminology: the terms 'heterosexual', 'homosexual', 'bisexual', 'gay', 'lesbian' and 'transsexual' are all inventions of the nineteenth and twentieth centuries and their use tends to reflect the widely held modern beliefs that we each have a specific sexual orientation and that this can be distinguished from our actual sexual activity. These beliefs cannot be assumed to underlie earlier discussions of human sexuality and it is, therefore, strictly speaking, anachronistic to use the modern terminology when referring to these earlier discussions. (House of Bishops' Group 2003: x)

Perhaps the 'note' is a late insertion, after the likely realization of the working party that—yes—there actually is a disconcerting discontinuity between, on the one hand, the biblical and premodern worlds, and on the other hand the thought worlds of contemporary Christians where the modern nomenclature is assumed. The report, like most others of the genre, is strikingly 'presentist' (see section 4.1). Yes, it *is* anachronistic to use the modern terminology when referring to earlier discussions.

The fault, I think, lies not in the use of the modern bundle of linguistic inventions which characterize present discussion of human bodies and their desires. Churches need to make themselves understood. It would be impossible to return to the obscure Latinisms, coy and obfuscatory locutions like 'unnatural sex', 'unnatural' or 'marital acts', and the vicious invective of 'sodomy', 'sodomizers', and so on.

The fault lies in the unwillingness to follow through the honest admission that 'These beliefs cannot be assumed to underlie earlier discussions of human sexuality.' They don't. By the early twenty-first century, modern assumptions about two sexes have colonized the church as much as they have colonized the world.

The report shows an awareness of the danger of presentism even if it collapses into it. But there is another section of this lengthy report where the awareness of a different understanding of sexuality and gender *is* brought into focus. Adopting the detached descriptive mode, the report announces that

> [a] number of scholars have suggested in recent years that it was at the Enlightenment that modern notions of sexual difference—of women and men as *distinctly* different from each other—emerged, and that this shift was accompanied by the new idea that our sexuality is a part of our identity, that we *are* homosexual or heterosexual, rather than simply engaging in same-sex or opposite-sex activity, for example. (House of Bishops' Group 2003: 5.3.2, p. 174, original emphases)

There follows a short summary of the one-sex theory. Aristotle and Galen are mentioned. It is noted that in this theory 'Woman was the imperfect version of man' (House of Bishops' Group 2003: 5.3.4, p. 174). Matching genitals, differences of humours, and the 'more fluid understanding of gender' (House of Bishops' Group 2003: 5.3.5, p. 175) are also noted. Thomas Laqueur and Londa Schiebinger are quoted; 'the development of the two-sex model' (House of Bishops' Group 2003: 5.3.9, p. 176) is accurately described. It is admitted that the arrival of two opposite sexes led to the categories of homosexuality and heterosexuality. Laqueur is said, accurately, to point to

> the ways in which cultural understandings of women and men have in fact had an impact on how men and women were physically described and in influencing how the notion of sexual difference—two sexes—came to be predominant in the modern era. That is, both gender and sex are influenced by culture. In a way, he is making the simple point that culture does affect science. (House of Bishops' Group 2003: 5.3.30, pp. 180–1)

The one-sex theory is thought to present two challenges to 'Christian thinking about human sexuality'; the first about the extent to which 'Christian thinking in his area has been based on culturally specific understandings of sex and gender that may no longer be universally accepted today' (House of Bishops' Group 2003: 5.3.34, p. 181); and:

Secondly, and more radically, a number of scholars have argued that, once we recognize that the idea of a clear differentiation between sexes is a cultural construction rather than something that is simply given, this opens up the possibility of thinking about such differences in a new way. It has been suggested, for example, that we should think of a spectrum of sexual identity rather than a clear binary division between male and female, and that homosexuality, bisexuality and transsexualism should be accepted as part of this spectrum.   (House of Bishops' Group 2003: 5.3.34, p. 182)

These paragraphs are remarkable for displaying a knowledge of the developments in classical and historical scholarship described earlier. It appears that the one-sex theory is not forgotten after all, and that full cognizance of it has occurred. Why then does the one-sex theory not receive more weight? Part of the answer to that question is given by the bishops themselves. Without naming any of the historians who have rightly criticized aspects of the theory, they ask whether it is

really the case that it was only in the eighteenth century that people came to see men and women as distinctively and biologically different from each other? Does not the abundant evidence we have that people in the Middle Ages saw men and women as physically, emotionally and even spiritually different in a whole host of ways suggest that Laqueur's 'one-sex' model was, in fact, simply a different way of expressing physical difference on the basis of the prevailing understanding of human anatomy?   (House of Bishops' Group 2003: 5.3.36, p. 182)

They think, on the basis of a lengthy discussion of the biblical texts purporting to be about homosexuality, 'that as far back as classical antiquity people were aware that there were certain individuals who had 'an innate attraction to members of their own sex' (House of Bishops' Group 2003: 5.3.37, p. 182). Only the name 'homosexuality' has changed in relation to it.

The report relies on complementarity theory in order to clinch the claim that, from Genesis onwards, throughout biblical times to the present, complementarity—what was called (in section 3.2.2 above) 'two sexes, different but equal'—was assumed by the churches. 'It is possible to argue', they say (and that means that they *do* so argue):

That the book of Genesis does in fact teach the complementarity (the 'equality in difference') of men and women and that, on the basis of its teaching, a belief in complementarity has always been a part of ortho-dox Christian theology, even though this belief has frequently been

distorted by a hierarchical view of the male–female relationship.   (House
of Bishops' Group 2003: 5.3.38, p. 182)

The bishops say that while 'it may be both interesting and important'
to educate ourselves about understandings of gender that may have
prevailed in other times and places, historical construction always has
to give way to something more basic—the identity conferred on
Christians by Christ himself: 'we need to remind ourselves that the
Christian claim is that our identities as human beings are fundamentally determined, not by human social construction, but by the
creative and redemptive activity of God' (House of Bishops' Group
2003: 5.3.39, p. 183). The light that the old theory might have shed on
biblical sources is quickly extinguished. Doubts about its veracity (see
section 2.3) are unexplained, coupled with a sense of its intrinsic
improbability ('Is it really the case?'), and the generous use of per-
suader phrases ('abundant evidence', 'a whole host of ways') soon
indicate that the theory, while 'interesting and important', will not be
allowed to detract from the complementarian theory of the sexes that
the scriptures and right reflection on them are supposed to teach.

4.3.1. Some Replies

The bishops' response to the one-sex theory is, to say the least,
disappointing. They are worried about the *accuracy* of the one-sex
theory; about any threat to the principle of *complementarity*; about
any priority of sexual identity over theological *identity*; and about the
dangers of doctrinal and moral *development*. Let us consider each of
these worries. First, the accuracy of the theory has already been
discussed (section 2.3): it cannot be dismissed so easily. Gerard
Loughlin has commented on this section of the report that the
bishops 'fail to learn from their own learning'. 'No ancient individuals
thought that they or others were homosexual, that they could be
characterized as having an "innate attraction to members of their
own sex", let alone a "sexual orientation"' (Loughlin 2015: 613).

   Second, the claim that the principle of complementarity is present
in Genesis and has 'always been a part of orthodox Christian theology' is, well, ambitious to say the least. Complementarity has
become increasingly influential in Anglican thought (House of
Bishops 1991: 37–8, no. 4.17). The report of 2003 even elevates it to
the status of a 'core belief', deriving it not from the 'male and female'

of Genesis 1:27 but from God's creation of a 'helper' for the man in Genesis 2 (House of Bishops' Group 2003: 10, no. 1.2.9; and 90–1, nos 3.4.50–3.4.56). In some evangelical thought complementarity is affirmed just because it does *not* deliver any sense of equality between women and men, and is set against liberal 'egalitarianism', which does (see Storkey 2007: 165–6; Nordling 2010). It is a late religious equivalent of the secular theory of two unequal sexes exemplified by Rousseau (see section 3.2.2). Other evangelicals have wisely moved beyond complementarity, preferring to find their model for human relationships in the Persons of the Trinity (Storkey 2007: 169–72). From an appearance in the papal encyclical *Familiaris consortio* (Pope John Paul II 1981: no. 19) it has gained influence in Roman Catholic thought. I have offered a list of criticisms of the principle elsewhere (Thatcher 2011: 42: 185–8), not least of the incongruity that traditions which have consistently advocated the priority of celibacy over marriage and sponsored same-sex communities for monks and nuns, for most of their history, should suddenly lurch towards the dogma that men are incomplete without women, and conversely. We will come to an explanation for the rise of complementarity in a moment.

Third, the bishops do not like the suggestion that 'we should think of a spectrum of sexual identity'. Their problem is that classical and premodern people *did* think in just such a way. Some males obviously desired other males, but the description of this desire as 'innate attraction to members of their own sex' merely writes a modern theory over an ancient script. Theologians need to admit that the spectrum belongs to our history and that it can be acknowledged without embarrassment. Differences between male and female are in any case not obliterated by the idea of a gender spectrum, any more than differences between light and dark are obliterated by dusk and dawn. The avoided question is why the 'clear binary division' needs to be preserved even at the cost of extraordinary exegesis.

No one is being invited to locate homosexuality (see section 4.4) within the gender spectrum. There may be an unfortunate conflation between the *gender* spectrum of ancient thought and the *orientation* spectrum of modern thought brought into modern sexology by Kinsey (the Kinsey Heterosexual–Homosexual Rating Scale: see Kinsey et al. 1948, Kinsey et al. 1953). The ancient spectrum was an indicator of the *fluidity of sex and gender*: the modern spectrum is an indicator of the *fluidity of sexual desire* within two apparently opposite sexes. Neither should there be a worry about conflating Christian identity with *sexual* identity. Being a member of the body of Christ is obviously a different category from being a member of a sexual category (see Stuart 2003).

Fourth, the bishops worry about the legitimacy of moral change. They know that part of their constituency will be unsettled by the suggestion that there are 'culturally specific understandings of sex and gender' which may no longer be universally accepted. But the churches have recognized (to their credit) that many of their former settled assumptions have required revision in the light of the realization that they were culturally and historically specific and no longer adequate (see section 4.2.1). The persecution of Jews and witches, the geocentric universe, the demonic aetiology of sickness, the hell-bound destination of the unbaptized, and many other culturally specific assumptions and practices have all been modified, replaced, or abandoned in the light of new knowledge, and perhaps a deeper discernment of the mind of Christ about such matters. Somehow the biblical narratives of creation and fall, because they are said to teach complementarity, hold the strong prospect of unrevisability. That is a very bold claim. There is something about gender which appears to trigger additional reasons for caution.

I think the bishops are not doing what they think they are doing. They think they are being, or being constrained to be, cautiously conservative, in defending the two-sex theory (and its marginalization of homosexuality). I suggest they are actually modernists, who are so captivated by modern heterosexuality that they are determined to find two complementary sexes in the Bible even when that task requires stretching plausibility beyond the usual limits. A properly conservative mentality would not dismiss the one-sex theory, but recognize it as part of the tradition, and explore how it might actually *ease* the problem of homosexuality as modernity defines it and the churches wrestle with it.

4.4. TWO SEXES IN THE CHURCHES' THEOLOGIANS

The 'modern mix' of two-sex and one-sex theories described in this chapter is not confined to official teaching. It runs, rampant and unquestioned, among leading theologians, whose strong influence on it is unquestionable. I will mention briefly two famous and highly influential theologians of the twentieth century, the Protestant Karl Barth (1886–1968) and the Catholic Hans Urs von Balthasar (1905–88). (It is 'not without significance that both of them suffered and enjoyed close relationships with women, which scandalized their churches' (Ward 1998: 56).)

4.4.1. Balthasar

Balthasar's sexual dualities inspired John Paul II, and the latter's many writings about sex are heavily influenced by them. The astute title of Corinne Crammer's essay on Balthasar, 'One Sex or Two? Balthasar's Theology of the Sexes' (Crammer 2004), indicates that she too finds the 'modern mix' in contemporary Catholic thought. She describes how Balthasar takes for granted that there are two sexes, opposite, incommensurably different, yet made for one another. 'Man only exists in the opposition of the sexes, in the dependence of both forms of humanity, the one on the other' (Balthasar 1988: 125; in Crammer 2004: 93). Biology, for Balthasar, confirms:

> The male body is male throughout, right down to each cell of which it consists, and the female body is utterly female; and this is also true of their whole empirical experience and ego-consciousness. At the same time both share an identical human nature, but at no point does it protrude, neutrally, beyond the sexual difference, as if to provide neutral ground for mutual understanding. (Balthasar 1993: 364; in Crammer 2004: 93)

Sexual difference is a basic ontological distinction encompassing everything. Essentialism is assumed, never queried: there are men and women with fixed universal characteristics and roles.

> Wo-man (*Weib* or *Frau*), was created from the side of Adam, so that even the original *Mensch* appears to be male, since Balthasar rejects the concept of an androgynous human who preceded sexually differentiated humans. But only with the appearance of Woman (Eve) can it be established that Adam, the *Mensch*, is male (*Mann*). Just as there can be no *first* without the appearance of a *second*, so also there can be no Man without the appearance of Woman. (Moss and Gardner 1998: 383; in Crammer 2004: 95, original emphases)

While 'man' and 'woman' are essentially equal, like the divine Persons of the Trinity, 'woman' comes from the side of 'man'. The 'man' is 'first' in relation to the 'woman'. Hugely influenced by Genesis 2, Balthasar's 'man' lacks something, and that something is 'woman', who already exists in 'man' because her flesh and substance derives from his. So the theology of sexual difference bears an impossible contradiction: men and woman are equal, except that they are not, because men have 'priority' and 'headship' (based on 1 Corinthians 11). The woman is the 'helper' (Gen. 2:18) of the man: she is the 'home man needs, the vessel of fulfilment specially designed for him' (Crammer 2004: 97). Femininity is defined by receptivity, personified by the mother of Jesus; masculinity is defined by leadership. God the Father is 'Origin': everything begins with 'Him'. But origination is a masculine principle. That is why Christ was incarnate in a man, so he can represent the masculine Father. Only men can represent Christ.

I have hardly begun to expound Balthasar's understanding of sexual difference, but I hope it shows his impossible commitment to a one-sex and two-sex understanding of humanity. Genesis 1 is thought to teach two equal sexes, male and female, with any other interpretation ruled out, whereas Genesis 2 teaches the permanent secondariness and subordination of 'woman' to 'man'. The preservation of the ancient theory and the imposition of the modern theory upon it together create doctrinal chaos. In a nice judgement, the equality of the sexes is said not to have the logical form A/B, but A/not-A, where the woman is required to be all that the man is not, and to function as the definition of the man's limits (Moss and Gardner 1998: 384). It is a bogus, pseudo-equality. Current human reproductive biology will not sanction the idea that men and women are 'utterly' biologically different: rather, they are increasingly thought to be very similar. That man has a primary fruitfulness belongs to a monogenetic theory (see sections 1.2, 2.2). That God is thought to be masculine in 'His' revealed characteristics amounts to idolatry at the very heart of Catholic dogmatics. What happens to women in Balthasar's thought, despite his best intentions, is immoral, impoverishing the lives of the women who believe it. Why? Because 'woman' is 'defined only in terms of her fulfilling the needs of (what is lacking in) another (Man) and therefore being without a centre or personhood' (Crammer 2004: 105).

Tina Beattie (Beattie 2006) has subjected Balthasar's theology of sexual difference to a devastating analysis, going far into its ramifications. She lists what she calls the 'burlesque sexual parodies' (Beattie 2006: 140) of Balthasar and the 'New Catholic Feminism' based on his work. She draws attention to some of the consequences of the basic mistake of amplifying sexual difference so that it becomes the organizing principle of Balthasar's theology, skewing his ontology, anthropology, ecclesiology, and ethics. If God is masculine, the world is feminine. Sexual difference for Balthasar is

> not about two forms of human personhood—male and female—understood as co-equal but different in their capacity to image God. It is about the positioning of the human male as 'quasi-feminine' in relation to the transcendent masculinity of God, which represents the paternal origination of the world. The woman comes into being, not as a separate person, but as the man's complement and completion. (Beattie 2006: 113)

The 'creaturely femininity' of, yes, '*man*', signifies to man 'that he is not-God and therefore not masculine'. Rather, 'The female body is incidental to this whole performance: she is a wordless body that he plunders for signifiers to express his own lack of divinity and masculinity' (Beattie 2006: 146). Instead of eliminating the negative characteristics ascribed to 'woman' in the one-sex continuum, Balthasar has accentuated them. He has exaggerated the

> tendency that has been present in the Catholic tradition from the beginning—for the man to attribute to himself qualities of divinity, origination and initiative that he associates with masculinity, and to project onto the woman those rejected characteristics of his own humanity, immanence, receptivity and responsivity that he associates with femininity. (Beattie 2006: 138)

This, Beattie acidly observes, 'has now become the hub around which Catholic doctrine revolves in its human and divine dimensions' (Beattie 2006: 138), and it confirms the 'modern mix'. Crammer comes to a similar conclusion, confirming the argument of the present book, that

> despite his attempt to construct a two-sex theological anthropology (in the terminology of Laqueur), ultimately Balthasar reproduces the one-sex model in which the normative human being is implicitly male and Woman's definition is based around Man, particularly around what Man is seen to need Woman to be. The result of this methodology is that Woman in Balthasar's theology lacks substance, subjectivity, and a voice of her own. (Crammer 2004: 102)

4.4.2. Barth

Karl Barth is the best-known 'theologian of revelation' of the twentieth century. As such he rejects natural theology of any kind, calling theologians to base their art only on what God has disclosed. But Graham Ward (1998) has shown that when it comes to sexual difference, Barth relies on the very source he eschews elsewhere. As Ward explains, there are for Barth at least three layers of difference which divine revelation gives us: the difference between God and creation; between the Persons of God in the divine Trinity; and between male and female. God is in relationship to God's people and the form of this is a covenant. In Christ Jesus there is a new covenant which finds expression in the relationship between Christ and the church. And the marital covenant between a man and a woman exemplifies the covenants between God and the people of God, and Christ and the church. All this is known by revelation. 'Man', as made in the image of God, is neither male nor female, but both (*Mensch*). God created man, Barth tells us, 'in the unequal duality of male and female'. 'Man is no longer single but a couple' (Barth 1958: 308; in Ward 1998: 58). Ward explains: 'Barth describes man alone as not knowing what he lacked specifically, although knowing he was unsatisfied.' Woman, he states, 'with her special existence . . . fulfils something' which he cannot; 'woman as the one who is near and indispensable to man, as a part of himself which is lost' (Ward 1998: 59, citing Barth 1958: 296, 301). The parallels between Balthasar and Barth are obvious. Later in the *Church Dogmatics* when Barth further describes the vocations of men and women, he then 'defines their ethical and social vocation in terms of their biology alone. It is as if he returns to a natural theology his whole theological system is set up to refute' (Ward 1998: 65). What went wrong? Ward answers that question with Irigaray's term 'hom(m)osexuality'. 'Hom(m)osexuality' is 'a sexuality inscribed from the perspective of men (*les hommes*); in other words, a phallocentrism' (Ward 1998: 66). 'The consequence of this hommosexuality is that no genuine sexual difference can be established, because the other sex is always interpreted from the perspective of the one, monolithic sex, the male. The female is only a variant of the male; his other half, that which fulfils and supports him.'

Shaw has undertaken a similar analysis to that of Ward, and comes to a similar conclusion. Barth, she notes (like Balthasar), 'insists on *both* the distinctively different and complementary "essences" (and therefore roles) of women and men *and* the observance of the Pauline texts on male headship' (Shaw 2007: 225, original emphases). The different 'natures' of women and men are to be 'guarded', like their 'special vocations'. 'This notion of sexual difference', Shaw continues, 'is regarded as absolutely rigid.' Women must submit to men as the church submits to Christ. Again as Balthasar, Barth attempts, disastrously, 'to hold together the seemingly incompatible notions of *both* the mutuality *and* the hierarchy of the sexes' (Shaw 2007: 226). Shaw's criticism of Barth illustrates perfectly the dangerous nuisance of 'presentism' in theology, described earlier in section 4.1. Barth 'ignores' the contexts of Genesis 2 and the New Testament Household Codes. Possibly overstating her case she remarks, 'The irony here is that Barth has his history wrong—or just plain absent—precisely because it was only with the advent of modernity that scientists began to think that women and men were *not*, in their "nature", absolutely alike' (Shaw 2007: 226, original emphasis). Of Barth and his many conservative followers she says, 'Ideas about sexual difference and complementarity that our ancestors would have barely recognized 300 years, let alone 3,000 years, ago are regularly mapped back onto the Hebrew Scriptures, especially the creation stories in Genesis 2.' 'All of this', she continues,

> is posited as if there were a seamless line from the world of Genesis to the early twenty-first century; no account of marriage and household relations in ancient Israel is given; no account of prevailing understandings of women and men . . . is provided; modern notions of marriage and sexual difference are mapped back onto a text from a completely different culture, without explanation.   (Shaw 2007: 227)

In chapter 6 I will soon be accusing Protestant and Catholic theologians alike of devoting too much attention to the early Genesis chapters, *at the expense of due attention to the person and work of Jesus Christ*. If I am right, it will be a hard accusation for conservative theology to hear. It is an accusation that Eugene Rogers, Jr has cannily made of Barth. Commenting on Barth's asseveration that 'Man is no longer single but a couple', he finds 'unintended abstraction' in the unequal and universal roles Barth assigns to the man and the woman of the Genesis narratives (Rogers 1999: 180–91). More important still, Barth is said to have turned 'male and female into ontological categories that threaten to make the humanity of Jesus deficient'. While he has applied the notion of an 'I–Thou' relationship to the couple of Genesis 2 and 3, Rogers thinks he

> would have done better to follow his own advice and see the possibility of I–Thou not in the duality of the sexes but as the condition for the variety of relationships that Jesus Christ enacted and interpreted, relationships that are explicitly surrounded by a community and filled with the Spirit, and therefore resist dyadic reduction. (Rogers 1999: 186–7)

It is Jesus whom Christians must turn to for an ontological under-standing of relationships, and 'Jesus is not a couple but single'.

4.5. HOMOSEXUALITY ARRIVES

The link between debates about gender and the ordination of women and between debates about homosexuality is becoming clearer. Randolph Trumbach, in several works, shows that 'Europeans before 1700 presumed that all males desired both women and adolescent boys. But in the first generation after 1700, some Europeans began to think that most men desired only women and that only a deviant minority of men desired other males who might be either adults or adolescents' (Trumbach 2012: 832–3). Boldly, he speaks of a 'new exclusive desire for women' at this time (Trumbach 2012: 840, and see Trumbach 1998). Robert Shoemaker argues that the 'one-sex body', still accepted in seventeenth-century England, made the populace more tolerant of sexual relations between men:

> The fact that men and women were thought to inhabit the same bodies, except for the degree of heat and dryness present, meant that each could be more or less like the opposite depending on the amount of heat and moisture they possessed. The line between being a man and woman, and between male and female sexual behaviour, could thus be easily crossed. (Shoemaker 1998: 79–80)

But there was another reason too. Because men in the one-sex body regarded themselves as superior, more perfect, their *preference* for male company was understood even if its sexual expression was not condoned. The frequent misogyny in the tradition is also explained by the lower valuation of women in the one-sex body, while, within the spectrum, people we call 'bisexual' or 'third sex' or 'intersex' would have caused little surprise.

By the twentieth century the churches became more open to the use of the new sexual terminology while *retaining* their opposition to all sexual practices outside of marriage. Timothy Willem Jones speaks of the incompatible juxtaposition of 'moral and medical models of sexuality' in mid-twentieth-century Anglican thought (Jones 2013: 174), and 'the institutional incorporation of sexological understandings of sexuality by the church' (Jones 2013: 179). He explains, 'The adoption of sexological language, however, did not replace the previous moral paradigm. Anglican discussions recognized new sexual identities: the homosexual, the pervert, the bisexual, the invert; but maintained a moral condemnation of all sexual acts external to heterosexual marriage' (Jones 2013: 179). The new modern narratives of sexuality rendered 'homosexuality' deviant, and the churches bought into them. As Elizabeth Stuart remarks, 'The affirmation of the goodness of human (hetero) sexuality and its crucial place in human nature, providing the locus of the *imago dei*, was a radical and innovative assertion.' It signalled 'the moment when Protestant and then Catholic theology embraced the thoroughly modern notions both that people have a "sexuality" and that their "sexuality" in some sense tells the truth about who they are and what they are for, more profoundly than any other aspect of their humanity' (Stuart 2015: 21). And that 'moment' is deeply ideological. Many Protestants and Catholics alike now assert the complementarity of the sexes, their equality *and* their hierarchical order. They institutionalize the new heterosexuality, and they use it to proscribe and marginalize homosexuality.

Jay Emerson Johnson thinks the absolute confidence in these ideologies among the churches of the Anglican Communion has actually supplanted the troubles about homosexuality. 'Twenty-first-century realignments' in that Communion may be shaped 'not so much by "homosexuality" per se but by the construal of human love and intimacy as divinely gendered' (Johnson 2011: 428). Opponents of women's ordination and opponents of 'homosexuality' are often the same people, using the same language 'frame' (Parsons 2014). Shaw, also aiming her remarks at the Anglican Communion, bemoaned in 2007 'a group of texts' which, sadly much enlarged in subsequent years, 'all aimed at promoting a conservative line about homosexuality . . . in which Genesis 2 is taken as the blue-print for sexual difference and therefore heterosexuality' (Shaw 2007: 226). The almost desperate attempt to find compulsory heterosexuality in the biblical narratives yields the reason for this improbable but widespread search. As biblical proof texts which are claimed by conservatives to proscribe homosexuality become less and less plausible, the language of modernity is endorsed to enforce 'opposite' sex norms, in which of course the centrality of marriage is more important than ever. The process is well known to sociologists: 'The corollary of the privilege of heterosexuality is the stigmatization of non-heterosexual identities, manifested in many sexological studies and in the cultural and legal regulation of homosexuality' (Rahman and Jackson 2010: 114).

Part I of the book, 'Retrievals', has now come to its end. The trajectory of the one-sex model has been traced from before the time of Jesus to its baleful influence on much contemporary Catholic and Protestant thought. Different versions of two-sex models have also been discussed, and in this chapter attempts to mix one-sex and two-sex models have been considered, and pronounced to have failed. In Part II a different attempt to describe and celebrate the new life offered in Christ and the Christian faith in the area of gender will be made.

Part II

Transformations

5

Jesus and Gender

Chapter 5 begins the second part of the book, 'Transformations'. I have attempted in the first part, 'Retrievals', to show how the deluge of recent theological writing about sexuality has swept along in its path modern assumptions and ideologies about two sexes, and then read them back into scripture and tradition. Part II temporarily suspends these assumptions and attempts a 'clearing' or 'clearing away' of them. It takes up the challenge of speaking thankfully and clearly about our desires and our relationships with each other, in the light of God's self-revelation in Jesus, but without the distorting influences of rigid dimorphic theories either ancient or modern.

Chapters 5 to 8 undertake the book's fourth aim—'to show how the task of theology, in the area of gender, is to envision the redemption of human relationships'. Chapters 5 and 6 invite theology and Christology, signalled in the third aim of the book, into this clearing. Chapter 5 examines the Jesus of the Gospels and his relationships with women for signs of transformation. Chapter 6 is about the metaphysical understanding of gender which arises from the church's faith in the transforming powers of Jesus Christ, and which (I shall suggest) provides a compelling vision for redeeming or transforming gender in the present day. Chapter 7 argues for sexual *similarity*, and against entrenched assumptions of difference. Christ is upheld as the 'essence of humankind' and the vocabulary of gender (identity, difference, equality, relation, and so on) is grounded in the divine Trinity. Chapter 8 summarizes doctrinal imperatives in the area of gender, especially as these bear upon the right ordering of the church and its mission to the world.

There are three sections to the present chapter. 5.1 asks what is meant by transforming gender and sets the question both in the time of Jesus and in our own time. 5.2 draws some conclusions from the depiction of Jesus by the Gospel writers of his relationships with women. 5.3 uses the example of Jesus himself as an alternative to 'hegemonic masculinity'. The idea of an alternative masculinity is located in ancient Christianity, reinterpreted, and commended.

5.1. LOOKING FOR TRANSFORMATION

All Christians believe the Christian faith is a means of redemption. Jesus founded the Kingdom (or better, the Reign) of God, which was and is to be contrasted with all secular, demonic, and even religious expressions of domination. Baptism is an entry into a new life. 'Our "drowning" in the water of baptism, where we believe we die to sin and are raised to new life, unites us to Christ's dying and rising . . . Water is also a sign of new life, as we are born again by water and the Spirit' (Common Worship 2000b). When 'anyone is in Christ, there is a creation: everything old has passed away; see, everything has become new!' (2 Cor. 5:17). Christians believe they are incorporated into one of the forms of the very body of Christ. As sin is washed away in baptism, so a blessed and different life emerges. Christians, living between the resurrection of Christ and 'the time of universal restoration' (Acts 3:22), await the fulfilment of God's reign, and seek to anticipate this fulfilment in daily living. They pray, 'Your kingdom come. Your will be done, on earth as it is in heaven' (Matt. 6:10). In terms of *claim* all this is indubitable: in terms of *achievement*, less so. There are events in Christian history (such as Crusades), texts (such as Luther's *On the Jews and Their Lies*), and practices (such as the torture and murder of women alleged to be witches, or centuries of persecution of Jews), none of which can be countenanced without deep remorse and repentance. Despite this severe weight of counter-evidence to the claim that there is achievable personal and social transformation in the Christian faith, the hope of transformation remains alive, and can be aided by 'what is consistent with sound doctrine' (Titus 2:1). What follows is just such an exercise in sound doctrine.

5.1.1. An Enlarged Understanding of Humanity

There is redemption. That is the Good News. But, more precisely, from what, and into what? And how are relations of gender redeemed? Let us start with an answer given by the leading feminist theologian of the twentieth century, Rosemary Radford Ruether. Redemption in 'modern feminism' is, she says,

> about reclaiming an original goodness that is still available as our true selves, although obscured by false ideologies and social structures that have justified domination of some and subordination of others.
>
> Redemption puts us back in touch with a full biophilic relationality of humans with their bodies and one another and rebuilds social relations that can incarnate love and justice. (Ruether 1998: 8)

This characterization of redemption utilizes the idea of original goodness instead of original sin; offers redemption as personal authenticity ('our true selves'); leaves space for human sinfulness as ideological oppression; and finds 'at-one-ment' in restored relations of selves with themselves (no mind/body split), with one another, and within communities that practise justice and love. While these ideas are all usable in any theological account of transformation, one cannot but be struck by the lack of any reference to God in the redemptive experience. Redemption is the work of God, not just a 'reclaiming' of a non-oppressive social existence. Redemption is a state of affairs brought about by Christ, not by us: 'In him we have redemption through his blood, the forgiveness of our trespasses, according to the riches of his grace that he lavished on us' (Eph. 1:9). Sure, these notions need much unpacking to audiences less familiar, or bewilderingly unfamiliar, with basic Christian doctrines, but it cannot be overlooked that redemption is something that Christ achieves; that it is a gift; and is so because we are incapable of redeeming ourselves by ourselves. There is no mention of any possible connection here between the Incarnation of God in Christ and the incarnating of the principles of love and justice. There is no mention here of the Holy Spirit gently and invisibly creating restored relations among people and communities, nor any reference to the church or churches as an embodiment of these principles. There must be more to redemption than this.

I take issue neither with the apparent reductionism of some Western feminist theology nor with any of the global feminist theologies that have enriched theology in the last twenty years (see Fulkerson and Briggs 2012). Ruether writes as she does because she thinks that the masculinism and androcentrism of the Christian doctrine of God, of 'His' Son, and of the exclusive male priesthood, ministry, and language has rendered them inoperable impediments in the work of incarnating love and justice for women. I agree with this. They are part of the oppression. My difference with Ruether lies in the hope, indeed the necessity, that the core doctrines of faith can be recast in ways that oppress no one and embrace everyone. Ruether thinks the work of feminist theology 'involves detailed critique of how the false ideologies that sacralised patriarchy have been constructed in different historical branches of theology' (1998: 8). I try to show in the present volume that the one-sex theory and its successors lies at the very root of the problem that feminist theology seeks to address. This is a particular 'false ideology' that conceals itself in standard theologies of sexuality. Feminist theology could profit from attention to it.

Ruether, in her next paragraph, stumbles upon the one-sex theory but without naming it directly. She describes the difficulty feminist theologians have encountered in their attempt to 'reconcile a one-nature and a two-nature anthropology of gender' (1998: 9). For 'nature' instead read 'sex'. She explains that a 'one-nature anthropology . . . assumes one generic human "nature" possessed by all humans equally'. The positive advantage of this anthropology, like the theory of natural rights or Descartes's theory of mind as the essential person (see section 3.2.1), is said to be that it vindicates 'women's essential equality with men'. But it comes with an unaffordable price—it is androcentric, for 'Essential human nature is identified with qualities, such as reason and moral will, linked with males.' But the 'two-nature anthropology' (again, for 'nature' read 'sex') is 'based on male and female difference as essential'. Two-nature anthropology allows 'an equal value and even superiority of the "feminine" qualities of altruistic love and service'. Mary Wollstonecraft is a good example of this genre (see section 3.2.2). Ruether thinks the unaffordable price of two-nature anthropology is the enforcement of 'women's passive receptivity to male agency'. It results in 'modern secular complementarity' (see sections 3.2.2, 3.3).

The feminist task is 'to transcend this conflict between an androcentric one-nature anthropology and a complementary two-nature anthropology' and to 'define an enlarged understanding of the human that unites all human qualities in a transformed whole, and to define journeys of growth into wholeness for women and men by which each can reclaim those lost parts of themselves that have been assigned to the other sex' (Ruether 1998: 9–10). I want this too. In faith, there is transformation—personal and social. But doctrines, still named by abstract reifications—salvation, redemption, reconciliation, and sanctification—can still direct the journeys of growth into wholeness, and the core doctrines of Trinity and Incarnation set the origin, direction, and destination of the journey. Yet these very doctrines must also participate in the transformation that God offers to the created world. Insofar as they have become carriers of religiously enforced prejudice and discrimination, they too await redemption. The Spirit can come to the aid of the church as it encounters distortions of the faith and barriers to entering it, which are partly of its own making. With the Spirit's aid these can become opportunities for fresh discoveries.

5.2. JESUS AND WOMEN

It is right to look for, and to expect to find, evidence of the transformation begun with Jesus in the biblical record. That transformation greatly exceeds our modern interest in gender. 'Go and tell John what you have seen and heard: the blind receive their sight, the lame walk, the lepers are cleansed, the deaf hear, the dead are raised, the poor have good news brought to them' (Luke 7:22). Gender doesn't appear in the list. I won't even be looking for the equality of the sexes in the Gospels since that modern notion was unavailable and even unthinkable in the time of Jesus: 'women as such were not of particular concern to Jesus. He says nothing theologically about women as women or men as men' (Thurston 2004: 76). What might be hoped for is to find a new respect, reverence for, and re-evaluation of women as they take their full place in the Reign of God. The full significance of this might aid the churches as they begin to face up to hierarchies of gender in the world, the world's faiths, and of course the churches themselves.

5.2.1. Gender and the Gospels

There are several problems surrounding the search for transformations in the area of gender in the Gospels, but these must not be allowed to exercise a veto on the invitation to read them receptively, expectantly, and as if for the first time. Let us quickly note three such problems. The first is methodology. In the next few pages we will be looking at exchanges between Jesus and women. The very isolation of 'women' as a subject of inquiry already imposes an agenda upon the Gospels, together with the suggestion of a hermeneutical innocence which wrongly supposes that the Gospels are factual records, the truths of which can be gleaned two millennia later just by reading them. An appropriate method is what Elisabeth Schüssler Fiorenza has called a 'feminist critical hermeneutics' (1983: 3–40), which leads to a 'feminist critical method' (1983: 41–67), and then to a 'feminist model of historical reconstruction' (1983: 68–96).

But following this method prepares readers for at least two further problems, those of androcentrism and misrepresentation. Jesus wrote nothing, and had no control over the Gospel writers, so he could not influence what they wrote about him or about God's reign. The Gospels were very probably all written by men, and the various redactions of the texts already show the 'patriarchalizing' influences within and upon early churches. On the other hand the strong presence of women in the Gospels indicates the strong and inerasable memories of the women friends and followers of Jesus circulating among the second and third generations of Christians. A third problem is the danger of denigrating the Judaism of Jesus's day in order to arrive at exaggerated contrasts between Judaism and nascent Christianity. Amy-Jill Levine warns Christian exegetes against constructing women 'as the yeast which ferments the stale domestic beer of Judaism' and then becomes 'the good, imported brew of Christianity' (Levine 1994: 12, and see Schüssler Fiorenza 1983: 105–59). 'Sociological antisemitism' (Levine 1994: 12) must be avoided.

This may be able to be done by recalling that Jesus and his followers were themselves Jews; that the Judaism, or better 'Judaisms', of the period were diverse theologically (scribes, Pharisees, Essenes, sages, priests, Sadducees), geographically (urban, rural), and liturgically (synagogue, Second Temple); that the Jesus movement was not the only reform movement within Judaism and that the Reign of God proclaimed by Jesus was not a new religion but a reformed Judaism. The Reign of God begins as a Jewish movement among the diverse Judaisms of Palestine. In the end the Gospel writers sought to commend belief in God through faith in Jesus Christ. They do not pretend to adopt a position of neutrality. That is how the contemporary church should regard the Gospels now, using all the aids of modern scholarship when these assist in the kerygmatic task. We look for transformation because we already expect to find it there.

But there are Jewish feminist criticisms of Judaism in Jesus's day which are likely to be as fierce as any coming from Christians. Judith Plaskow, for example, complains about 'the unyielding maleness of the dominant Jewish picture of God' (Plaskow 1991: 123). She says the masculine language used of the divine 'maintain[s] a religious system in which men are normative Jews and women are perceived as Other' (Plaskow 1991: 125). 'Male-dominated social structures' are authorized by 'making women's oppression appear right and fitting' (Plaskow 1991: 126). God becomes the 'Dominating Other'. God's maleness makes God an oppressive power whose requirement of obedience inhibits human growth and responsibility (Plaskow 1991: 131): 'As traditionally depicted, God incorporates the "higher" qualities in a host of cleavages that correspond to various forms of human domination: He is male rather than female, regal rather than simple and poor, Jewish rather than pagan, spirit rather than flesh' (Plaskow 1991: 133). At least one strand of Judaism appears not merely masculinist but misogynist. There are rabbinic sayings such as 'Let the teachings of the Torah be burned, but let them not be handed over to women' (*y. Sota* 3:4: see Osborne 1989: 260). There is a troublesome, ancient, thanksgiving prayer, 'Blessed art thou . . . who hast not made me a woman' (*b. Menah* 43b), which was recited in the time of Jesus and is still recited in contemporary worship. Positive and negative assessments of women can be found, but the very phrase just used confirms the patriarchal framework within which the accommodation of women becomes a matter of dispute. On the one hand, Esther and Judith clearly are heroines who deliver the nation. In earlier times some women were prophetesses (Miriam, Huldah, Deborah—also a judge). All are revered in Jewish scripture. The bodies of women are honoured in the Song of Songs. Wisdom is personified as a woman. Joel awaits the time when God 'will pour out my spirit on all flesh; your sons and your daughters shall prophesy, your old men shall dream dreams, and your young men shall see visions. Even on the male and female slaves, in those days, I will pour out my spirit' (Joel 2:28–9). That time arrived, according to Peter, on the day of Pentecost (Acts 2:16–21).

On the other hand, the later Wisdom tradition appears misogynist by any standard (see Sawyer 1996: 130–45). Jesus Ben Sira, writing in the second century BCE, is less positive. His estimate of wives and daughters is coloured by the dominant masculinist interpretation of Genesis 2 and 3: 'From a woman sin had its beginning, and because of

her we all die' (Sir. 25:24). The 'good wife' is praised for the benefits
she brings to her husband, but 'A bad wife is a chafing yoke; taking
hold of her is like grasping a scorpion' (Sir. 26:7). His view of a
'headstrong daughter'? 'As a thirsty traveller opens his mouth and
drinks from any water near him, so she will sit in front of every tent
peg and open her quiver to the arrow' (Sir. 26:10, 12). While misogyny is a modern judgement, here it cannot be avoided.

Only men bore the mark of God's covenant with Israel upon their
bodies. Only men were able to be priests. Generally, only men read, or
were taught, the Torah. Only men were allowed through the Nicanor
Gate of the Temple, past the Court of Women, into holier precincts.
Only men could bear witness in court. Ruether observes how the
distinction between pure and impure, enshrined in Levitical law,
marginalized at least five classes of people. Women are marginalized
'by their very nature as women, and as causes of ritual pollution on a
regular basis through their sexual functions of childbirth and menstruation' (Ruether 1998: 17). Second, 'the vast majority of poor and
uneducated' are marginalized because of ignorance or inability to
observe the regulations. Third, these regulations also 'marginalized
the sick, the lame, the blind, the deformed, lepers, and persons with
various kinds of skin ailments and bodily fluxes'. Their ailments were
deemed to be 'caused by sin, either their own or that of their parents'.
Fourth, people 'who made their living by means regarded as polluting', such as tax collectors, prostitutes, servants, and slaves, were
regarded as permanently impure. Finally, the purity laws distinguished Jews from Gentiles. All five classes of people figure promin-
ently in the Gospels where, by a series of sharp and deliberate
contrasts, Jesus welcomes them without reserve.

5.2.2. Women in the Gospels

The woman with the flow of blood (Mark 5:24–34; Matt. 9: 19–23;
Luke 8:40–8) can be placed in several of these classes. She is permanently impure, and so is everything and everyone she touches (Lev.
15:25–7). She has spent all her money on doctors' fees. She breaks her
confinement to her home, and in touching Jesus she renders him
unclean as well. Jesus's response to her is unprecedented. By speaking
to her in a public place, he acknowledges her existence (Thurston
2004: 71), calls her 'Daughter' (Mark 5:34)—a member of the new
family constituted by the Reign of God—and tells her it is her faith

(and not his supernatural power) which has healed her. Mark depicts Jesus as one who ignores debilitating taboos and refuses to be bound by them. The woman has no male advocate (she is unnamed and unrepresented), like the unnamed woman, 'of Syrophoenician origin', later in the Gospel (Mark 7:24–30). This woman is 'of the wrong sex, the wrong national/ethnic status (Greek), and the wrong racial/religious background' (Thurston 2004: 72). She is a single parent with a daughter believed to be controlled by a demon. She comes to Jesus, begging him to exorcize the demon. Mark's record of the conversation between the woman and Jesus reveals an amazing candour. Jesus wanted to be left alone (Mark 7:24), and initially refuses the request, calling Gentiles by the unflattering colloquialism 'dogs' (Mark 7:27). Her reply, 'Sir, even the dogs under the table eat the children's crumbs' (Mark 7:28), is credited by Mark with changing Jesus's mind and healing the woman's daughter (Mark 7:29). Further reflection on the story prompts the suggestion that Jesus was open-minded towards the woman to the extent that *she* also ministers to *him*, making clear to him that his mission cannot be confined by racial, religious, or sexist boundaries (see Ringe 1985: 65–72).

The teaching of Jesus regarding divorce is evidence of his empathic understanding of the plight of divorced women, his opposition to the masculine 'hardness of heart' (Mark 10:5; Matt. 19:8), and his determination to ameliorate it. The synoptic Gospels all incorporate a rigorous strand in the teaching of Jesus about divorce and remarriage. 'Whoever divorces his wife and marries another commits adultery against her; and if she divorces her husband and marries another, she commits adultery' (Mark 10:11–12). I have long thought that

> the sayings of Jesus which protect marriage and make divorce more difficult were never intended to prevent the remarriage of people who were separated, nor to compel women to remain in marriages where their physical and mental health is threatened, by sealing off escape routes. Jesus *does* protect marriages from being broken up, and one of the ways he does so is both to seek to protect women from trivial divorces and to protect the married status of divorced women who did not wish their marriages to end.   (Thatcher 1999: 257, original emphasis)

Another difficult saying, also about adultery, may be chiding men for thinking of women as sex objects. Jesus says, 'But I say to you that everyone who looks at a woman with lust has already committed adultery with her in his heart' (Matt. 5:28). It is likely that Jesus here confronts men's blame on women for desiring them. Instead of placing restrictions of place, dress, visibility, and conduct on women, men are told to take responsibility for their thoughts and actions, and control not women's appearance and behaviour, but themselves. The saying may be best understood as 'a severe condemnation of thinking of women and relating to them only or even primarily in sexual terms' (Borsch 1990: 36).

Recent feminist analysis of the Gospel of Luke has undermined the conventional picture of Luke as the friend of women. Jane Schaberg, for example, argues that Luke portrays women 'as models of subordinate service, excluded from the power center of the movement and from significant responsibilities. Claiming the authority of Jesus, this portrayal is an attempt to legitimate male dominance in the Christianity of the author's time. It was successful' (Schaberg 1998: 363). Luke, she says, provides 'female readers with female characters as role models: prayerful, quiet, grateful women, supportive of male leadership, forgoing prophetic ministry' (Schaberg 1998: 363). But Luke also provides vital information about the women around Jesus. Unique to Luke's Gospel is the information that while Jesus was preaching the Reign of God,

> The twelve were with him, as well as some women who had been cured of evil spirits and infirmities: Mary, called Magdalene, from whom seven demons had gone out, and Joanna, the wife of Herod's steward Chuza, and Susanna, and many others, who provided for them out of their resources.   (Luke 8:1–3)

The women do not belong to the Twelve. But they travel with Jesus. They bankroll Jesus's mission, at least in Galilee. Some of them have names. Joanna was a high-born woman. They 'illustrate the breaking down of social distinctions that characterized the ministry of Jesus' (Thurston 2004: 105–6). The women 'ministered unto him of their substance' (Luke 8:3 KJV). The root verb, *diakoneò*, can be translated as 'deacon', as well as 'minister', 'helper', 'server'. Since there were deacons in the earliest Christian communities, it is likely the text preserves an ancient practice. Even 'with him' is 'a technical term for discipleship elsewhere in Luke' (Thurston 2004: 106), leading Thurston to conclude that the text 'is a powerful description of the ministry of women in the community of Jesus. It grants them a status close to that of the Twelve and may describe them in semitechnical terms.' Yes, women are cast in the role of helpers and servers in Luke's Gospel, but so is Jesus himself. 'The Christology of Luke's gospel, which depicts a serving Lord Jesus, in fact gives increased dignity to the roles of service undertaken by the women' (Thurston 2004: 107).

All four Gospels record the anointing of Jesus by a woman (Mark 14:3–9; Matt. 26:6–13; Luke 7:36–50; John 12:1–8). In the synoptics she is unnamed and does not speak. Jesus speaks *about* her, and only in Luke does he speak *to* her (Luke 7:48, 50), where what he says is intended for the audience to hear as well. Feminist criticism makes much of this tableau for the male audience, directing ire in particular at Luke for converting her from one who is to be remembered wherever the gospel is preached (Mark 14:9; Matt. 26:13) into a model of feminine piety, a penitent sinner, weeping on account of her sins, and begging forgiveness. But the presence of the story, or versions of it, in all four Gospels testifies to the impact that the historical scene must have made on the memory of the earliest Christians. There is plenty going on in the story signifying the arrival of God's reign. Jesus and other guests are in the company of another social outcast (Simon the leper—Mark 14:3; Matt. 26:6). They are in his house, having a main meal with him. The openness of Jesus's practice of 'table-fellowship' (Mackey 1987: 104–9) shocked the Pharisees. They want to know, 'Why does he eat with tax collectors and sinners?' (Mark 2:16) This contrast between the open practice of Jesus and the closed practice of the Pharisees with regard to eating together may be responsible for Luke's change of venue for the incident to the house of Simon the Pharisee. It was a practice so scandalous that the opposition to it 'finally destroyed the man who in any case had no table of his own' (Mackey 1987: 106). The woman is also credited with a theological understanding of the significance of Jesus's impending death. This had not occurred to any members of the male audience, who evaluate the woman's symbolic action purely in cost-effective terms. The penitence of the woman is simultaneously the humiliation of the man and his manner of religious observance.

Luke's story of Mary and Martha (Luke 10:38–42) can be understood as an adjudication between two models of women's service, one listening, the other serving. But there are other elements of the story which are too often neglected. Martha is an independent woman. She owns her own home. She invites Jesus in for a meal. It would probably be unprecedented for a single Jewish woman to invite a rabbi into her home. The story preserves the memory of the presence of such women in the historical ministry of Jesus, and Jesus's glad acceptance of them and their hospitality. 'Martha was distracted by her many tasks' (Luke 10:40). The KJV's rendering of the key phrase is 'cumbered about much serving', and 'serving' (the noun *diakonia* is again used) may recall Martha's holding the office of deacon. The well-known detail that her sister Mary 'sat at the Lord's feet and listened to what he was saying' (Luke 10:39) need not be seen as another Lucan model of feminine passivity. Another remarkable element of the story is that Mary takes the role, not of passive listener, but of active disciple. There was an argument whether women should be allowed to learn the Torah at all. 'The very posture of Mary "sitting at the Lord's feet" was reserved for disciples' (Paul sitting at Gamaliel's feet is the obvious example) (Osborne 1989: 281; and see Illig 2007: 35). By depicting Mary in this way, Luke may be confirming her as a disciple. John's Gospel records Martha's confession, 'Yes, Lord, I believe that you are the Messiah, the Son of God, the one coming into the world' (John 11:27). Here is a profession of faith at least as dramatic as that of Peter in the synoptics (Borsch 1990: 38).

All the Gospels record the presence of named women at the tomb, with Mark (16:1) and Luke (24:1) explaining that their purpose there was to prepare the body of Jesus for burial. They are told to convey the news of Jesus's resurrection to the apostles. In Mark the women are the ones who were witnesses to his death and burial, the ones who 'used to follow him and provided for him when he was in Galilee' (Mark 15:41). The verb *diakoneò* is again used (KJV = 'ministered'), again leading to the suggestion that the women may be 'followers' and 'deacons' belonging to the expanded circle of disciples, while being more faithful witnesses than their male counterparts (Osborne 1989: 269). In Mark there is an escalating process of learned discipleship among the women, as they 'move from being the passive recipients of miracles, to being active examples of faithful response, to being given an apostolic commission . . . The women were not only capable of following, serving, and suffering, but in Mark's narrative did so more faithfully than the male disciples' (Thurston 2004: 77). Luke adds that the women are given the kerygma of the gospel at the tomb (Luke 24:7), and this is included in what they are to tell 'to the eleven and to all the rest' (Luke 24:9). Only Luke observes that the women's testimony was not believed: 'But these words seemed to them an idle tale, and they did not believe them' (Luke 24:11). The faithfulness of the women is contrasted with the incredulity of the disciples. The

testimony of women in court was generally disregarded or dis-
counted, as the apostles knew. That may have been an additional
reason for their scepticism. That Luke chose to emphasize the testimony of the women, and the incredulity of the apostles, underscores
their centrality, fidelity, and inclusion around Jesus.

5.2.3. Three Conversations

John's Gospel contains three extended conversations between Jesus
and different women. The first of these, like the Syro-Phoenician
woman in Mark, is of the wrong gender, the wrong race, the wrong
religious background. We can be confident John intended to disrupt
essential conventions governing Jews and Samaritans, and men and
women. In his narrative the woman is, unsurprisingly, startled by
Jesus's request for a drink: 'How is it that you, a Jew, ask a drink of
me, a woman of Samaria?' (John 4:9). It is often overlooked that the
conversation would have been in Aramaic, and that it is probably
governed by the text of 2 Kings 17:24–41 (see Thurston 2004: 84–5),
where 'The king of Assyria brought people' from five separate dis-
tricts 'and placed them in the cities of Samaria in place of the people
of Israel; they took possession of Samaria, and settled in its cities'
(2 Kgs 17:24). The writer explains, 'So they worshipped the Lord, but
they also served their own gods, after the manner of the nations from
among whom they had been carried away. To this day they continue
to practise their former customs' (2 Kgs 17:33–4). So the Samaritans
were thought to be apostate, idolatrous Jews, and Samaritan women
according to the Mishnah were viewed as 'perpetually unclean, men-
struants from the cradle' (see Thurston 2004: 83). The Aramaic word
for 'husband' supports a reading of the five husbands as the five gods
of the Samaritan occupation. Such a reading makes good sense in a
long tradition of the use of marital imagery to describe the covenant
between God and God's people.

John's Gospel records that the disciples 'were astonished that he
was speaking with a woman' (John 4:27). That detail takes the
modern reader into the androcentric world of the male disciples,
together with its expectations and exclusions, and Jesus's partial
challenging of these. Even Samaritans can drink the 'living water'
Jesus offers the woman at the well. The woman is theologically
sophisticated (John 4:12, 19–20, 25). John contrasts her ready belief
with the incomprehension of Nicodemus earlier (John 3). She is an

effective evangelist, since 'Many Samaritans from that city believed in him because of the woman's testimony' (John 5:39, 42). Her 'word' (*logos*) convinces them and bears fruit (4:37). Equally astonishing in relation to the gender conventions of the time is the attitude of Jesus to the woman accused of adultery, a narrative preserved in later manuscripts of the fourth Gospel (most commonly at 7:53–8:11). The narrative wonderfully exposes the unthinking hypocrisy and cruelty of the representatives of the religious establishment and contrasts it with God's forgiveness and mercy. Scribes and Pharisees are made to appear godly and righteous, even as they are exposed as merciless and legalistic. The absence of the male partner in the crime draws attention to the obvious injustice that was being perpetrated. Appeal is made to the relevant proof texts (Lev. 20:10; Deut. 22:22). Any sense of clemency on Jesus's part would have brought a charge of heresy. The dissipation of her accusers as Jesus invites 'anyone among you who is without sin' to be 'the first to throw a stone at her' (John 8:7) is among the most dramatic in all biblical literature. Three verses later, Jesus says, 'I judge no one' (John 8:15). Perhaps this saying, and his persistent practice of forgiveness, is responsible for the juxtaposition of the narrative at this placing in the Gospel.

In John's Gospel the woman who anoints Jesus is Mary, the sister of Lazarus whom Jesus has raised from the dead. 'Jesus loved Martha and her sister and Lazarus' (John 11:5). The Beloved Disciple in John is not the only 'beloved disciple'. Jesus has no unease in their presence, and no inhibition about Mary's extraordinary gesture of wiping his feet with her hair. 'Martha served' (John 12:2), again suggesting the possibility of a memory of her as a deacon. A burning issue in this part of the Gospel is the death of believers before the end of the age. John deals with the issue by having Martha and Mary face the death of their brother while Jesus is still with them. Jesus challenges Martha whether she believes he is 'the resurrection and the life', and she replies, 'Yes, Lord, I believe that you are the Messiah, the Son of God, the one coming into the world' (John 11:27). So Martha makes a full confession of faith in Jesus before his resurrection, easily equivalent, again, to the confession of Peter in the synoptics (Mark 8:29; Matt. 16:15–19; Luke 9:18–20). Mary's anointing of Jesus (as in Matthew and Mark) is an anticipation of his death (John 12:7). Both women are devoted disciples. The 'fragrance of the perfume' (John 12:3) which anoints the body of Jesus, who is about to die, is contrasted with the 'stench' (John 11:39) of the body of Lazarus who has been dead for four days. That Mary anoints Jesus's feet (instead of his head) anticipates the following scene where Jesus washes the feet of his disciples. That Mary dries the feet of Jesus with her hair, and Jesus dries his disciples' feet with a towel, serves to emphasize the proleptic character of the incident. When the incident is over Jesus tells the disciples to follow his example (John 13:14). But Mary is doing that already. And she has not merely washed the feet of Jesus and dried them. She has anointed him.

Mary of Magdala is the only woman at the tomb, according to John. She is grief-stricken, and takes her determination to follow Jesus to his grave, while the disciples remain at home. She runs to tell Simon Peter and the 'other disciple' that the body of Jesus is missing. They run to the tomb, inspect the abandoned burial clothing, and return home again, 'for as yet they did not understand the scripture, that he must rise from the dead' (John 20:9). Mary is the first person to whom the risen Christ discloses himself. She thinks he is a gardener, until the moment of intimacy when 'Jesus said to her, "Mary!"' (John 20:16). Mary is the first to be brought to the recognition of Jesus, as the One who kept his word in rising from the dead. Jesus is the One who 'calls his own sheep by name and leads them out' (John 10:3). Mary of Magdala is the first disciple after the resurrection to be called by name.

In contrast, the address of Jesus to his mother, 'Woman' (John 20:15, *Gunai*), may sound detached. However, if Schüssler Fiorenza is right, the generic form is used because Mary represents all women followers of Jesus and, through her, all his followers, whose sorrow is turned into joy (Schüssler Fiorenza 1983: 333). Mary, not John (and certainly not Peter), stands for the believing community and believes before the male disciples. The force of Jesus's question to her, 'Whom seekest thou?' (John 20:15 KJV), is lost by the NRSV's prosaic and grammatically awkward 'Whom are you looking for?' The verb *zètein* has a rich meaning for the Johannine community, which probably knew its technical meaning of '"to study" and "to engage in the activities of a disciple"' (Schüssler Fiorenza 1983: 333). Mary calls Jesus 'Rabbouni' or 'Teacher' (John 20:16), confirming her place as Jesus's foremost disciple. Mary does not get the embrace to which she may have been accustomed ('Touch me not', John 20:17 KJV). The risen body of Christ is not accessible in the old familiar ways. Instead she is sent to the brothers of Jesus with the news of his impending ascension. That is why she was known as 'the apostle to the apostles'. She says emphatically, 'I have seen the Lord' (John 20:18). Hers is the first appearance of the risen Jesus.

5.2.4. A Rewarding Search?

We may seem to have wandered far from the one-sex theory explored in Part I. However, confirmation of the one-sex continuum described by Laqueur can be found in the material surveyed in this chapter. The inferiority of womankind, sealed by the foundational myth of Genesis 2 and 3, is enshrined in Jewish law, language, and practice. It is not anti-Semitic to say this, because it is also being said of much of the Christian tradition. At this juncture it is appropriate to recall that Laqueur's purpose in writing *Making Sex* was

> to show how a biology of hierarchy in which there is only one sex, a biology of incommensurability between two sexes, and the claim that there is no publicly relevant sexual difference at all, or no sex, have constrained the interpretation of bodies and the strategies of sexual politics for some two thousand years. (section 1.1.2; Laqueur 1990: 23)

Laqueur is eager to deny the possibility that any empirical or factual account of human being, in any period, can justify an ideology of the superiority of some over others, whether or not the ideology is religious (see section 1.1.2). I have tried to break out of the 'constraints' on 'the interpretation of bodies', not by adopting secular interpretations (and their constraints!) but by rethinking the gift of salvation given in Christ which, when allowed to do its work, will itself bring about the new community where no human difference will lead to prejudice and disadvantage. That is why it is particularly important to be able to observe a real change in human relations as a result of the coming of Jesus, vindicated by the church's interpretation of his being (Christology) and its implications for humanity.

I think the search for gender transformation in the Gospels is rewarded. The Jewish and Graeco-Roman worlds all thought, with many variations, that women were inferior versions of human creatures, and their inferiority was manifested to different degrees and in different ways. It is not necessary to depict the Judaisms of Jesus's time as 'stale beer' in order to enliven them with feminist yeast. Jesus does not dismantle the one-sex continuum. He calls twelve male apostles as his inner circle, and the Gospels are mostly about men. Instead the Reign of God brings a respect for, an engagement with, and an involvement of women, that can rightly be claimed to be novel. The Kingdom of God is a realm where the usual power relations are reversed (see section 5.3), especially those of men over women. In God's reign sexual difference in the male–female continuum matters less. Women are true disciples, whose faith, devotion, and perseverance sometimes exceed (and expose) that of the apostles. Women have a ministry in the earliest churches. Their word and witness is trusted. In John's Gospel, where the ethics of God's reign are summarized as the practice of love and service, women are even pre-eminent. 'As it becomes increasingly evident that at the heart of Jesus' ministry was a passionate desire to gather and reform the people of Israel in as inclusive a manner as possible for the coming of God's reign, one recognizes how fully women were to be part of this renewed community' (Borsch 1990: 30). I agree with Thurston's judgement that

> Jesus' characteristic behaviour of including, affirming, accepting women as equals is part of his larger inclusion of and preference for the marginalized. This is supported by his calling women to be disciples with men, and this was undoubtedly part of his offense in the eyes of the religious establishment. (Thurston 2004: 94)

The New Testament churches, in the absence of any central organization, developed differently, and this is evident in particular in the role accorded to women within them. The Gospels of Mark and John contain the strongest memories from communities where women may have been leaders. For different reasons, the Petrine and Deutero-Pauline communities represent a conscious muting and diminution of Jesus's radical practice, largely on the ground of avoiding a clash with Roman authority and the inevitable persecution. The sure Pauline corpus of seven letters acts as a bridge between the Gospels and the later New Testament letters, although there are obvious complexities in Paul's thought regarding the ministry and place of women. There are large themes in New Testament theology which tend towards the further elimination of patriarchy. The family of God consists of his mother and sisters and brothers, not as kin but as members of the new community of God's reign. The continuing presence of Christ in the world described through the metaphor of the vine and branches; or the depiction of the church as the body of Christ with its many members and organs; or the new creation brought about by Christ Himself: all require the dismantling of patriarchy for their full potentiality to take effect and their transformation of gender to become obvious.

5.3. JESUS AND GENDER

5.3.1. Jesus and Alternative Masculinities

After the foot-washing scene in John's Gospel, Jesus tells the disciples:

> So if I, your Lord and Teacher, have washed your feet, you also ought to wash one another's feet. For I have set you an example, that you also should do as I have done to you. Very truly, I tell you, servants are not greater than their master, nor are messengers greater than the one who sent them. If you know these things, you are blessed if you do them. (John 13:13–17)

The priority of the foot-washing scene in John can be in no doubt, for it replaces the institution of the Eucharist recorded in the other three canonical Gospels. The same discourse also contains the saying, 'I give you a new commandment, that you love one another. Just as I have loved you, you also should love one another. By this everyone will know that you are my disciples, if you have love for one another' (John 13:34–5). The requirement to love and serve one another, exemplified in Christ's own act of humility in the foot-washing ceremony, is central to the Gospel of John: indeed, the abasement of Christ is given as an example to follow all over the New Testament. Power is reversed in the new order. The synoptics all record the dispute among the disciples about who is to be the greatest (Mark 9:33–7; Matt. 18:1–5; Luke 9:46–8). They are told, 'Whoever wants to be first must be last of all and servant of all' (Mark 9:35). The same Gospels re-emphasize the importance of service as the sons of Zebedee seek top positions in the coming kingdom (Mark 10:35–45; Matt. 20:28; see Luke 22:24–30). The refusal is very direct:

> You know that the rulers of the Gentiles lord it over them, and their great ones are tyrants over them. It will not be so among you; but whoever wishes to be great among you must be your servant, and whoever wishes to be first among you must be your slave; just as the Son of Man came not to be served but to serve, and to give his life a ransom for many. (Matt. 20:25–8)

This emphasis on service in the teaching and example of Jesus particularly interests New Testament scholars who approach the New Testament in gender-critical ways (for the references see Conway 2008; 2015: 224). We have already noted patterns of masculinity in the Graeco-Roman world (see section 1.3), against which the Gospel writers may have wished to portray Jesus. Colleen Conway sees in these recent writings 'an inherent ambiguity in the gendered portrayal of Jesus'. They show:

> On the one hand, the gospel writers have an interest in highlighting the ways that Jesus measures up to the standards of hegemonic (and imperial) masculinity ... The gospel writers find ways to make clear that Jesus' power and authority surpasses that of the emperor. On the other hand, all of the gospels relate the story of Jesus' passion which, in the context of the first century is a story of humiliation and emasculation. It is not surprising, then, that gender analyses have produced interpretations of Jesus as a figure who assimilates Roman imperial masculine ideology as well as one who represents alternative, marginal expressions of masculinities. (Conway 2015: 230)

But while Conway is cautious in finding only an 'inherent ambiguity' in the gendered portrayals of Jesus in the Gospels, she is rightly impatient with the dominance of the method of historical criticism in Gospel study insofar as it results in a hermeneutical paralysis when readers want to make claims of contemporary relevance from scriptural texts. 'There is no theological reason that interpretations of the biblical text need be constrained by the "hegemony of historical criticism"' (Conway 2015: 229, citing also Martin 2006: 88). But there is no need for interpreters to leap into subjectivity either. The power and authority of Jesus is a different kind of authority from that of the emperor, so it is inevitable that different understandings of power and authority will be woven together in the New Testament. The Reign of God is not a theocratic state rivalling the imperial one, but its implications for the citizens of the imperial power are immense (and soon resulted in a reining in of its radical character). In the Reign of God greatness is to be recognized by becoming a slave. Power is radically reversed. Jesus is 'Lord' (Vulgate *dominus*) and the function of a *dominus* is to dominate. But there is always a paradox in the 'Lordship' of Christ, for it is in the exercise of 'non-dominance', or 'non-mastery' (Milbank 1990: 6), or 'un-mastery' (Coakley 2013: 43), that the divine love exercises the power which it has and is.

This dialectic of humiliation and exaltation lies behind the ancient Christological hymn embedded in Philippians 2:5–11. Being 'in the form of God' Christ 'emptied himself, taking the form of a slave, being born in human likeness. And being found in human form, he humbled himself and became obedient to the point of death—even death on a cross'. These abasement statements become the premises of an argument that concludes with a triumphant 'therefore':

> Therefore God also highly exalted him and gave him the name that is above every name, so that at the name of Jesus every knee should bend, in heaven and on earth and under the earth, and every tongue should confess that Jesus Christ is Lord, to the glory of God the Father.

These are not contradictions or ambiguities, as much as reflection by very early believers on the learned experience of discipleship which indicated that the triumph of divine love can never be brought about by coercion, but only by treading the way of abasement which was the way of Christ himself. But this renunciation of power in due acknowledgement of the power of love is hugely important for the negotiation of relations between men and women.

5.3.2. Manly Men

Mathew Kuefler (Kuefler 2001) has shown how ascetic Christian men in the third to fifth centuries CE managed to practise an alternative masculinity based on celibacy, sexual restraint, and even, in a few cases, castration. So successful was this new masculinity that, within the Christian church, it largely replaced the 'hegemonic masculinity' found in the empire and itself became 'hegemonic', that is, a dominant male practice that all Christian men were obliged to recognize as superior, even if they took the inferior path of marriage. The superiority of this version of masculinity is preserved in the Roman Catholic and other churches even now with regard to ministry. This is a story of how a new model of 'manliness', based on 'sexual renunciation' (Kuefler 2001: 170), became dominant. The 'new men' turned away from political, military, and ecclesial struggles and towards the more private struggle against sexual and other temptations. Men who held office in the imperial church faced the problem of combining executive authority in the church while maintaining the profile of servants to the people of God. The growing expectation of celibacy did not fit well into the paradox of clerical power on the one hand, and the renunciation of power on the other. Christian ascetic males were not exercising 'non-mastery'. They were turning the full force of mastery upon themselves in forging an alternative, and eventually a dominant, masculinity in the church.

Christians today are likely to find these ancient masculine struggles puzzling and ill-grounded. They give the model of women as deficient men theological legitimation and elucidation. Women are temptresses; they are responsible for the arrival of sin into the world; they are often impure; and for these and other reasons their company is to be avoided where possible. They represent the converse of male perfections, and become the source of evil thoughts that arouse the male body and imperil the male soul. The respect for women learned from the Gospels seems to have been largely unlearned in the 'patristic' period. There is nonetheless a case for taking these heroic masculine struggles seriously, and even emulating them. In late capitalist societies, where the bodies of women are regularly objectified and commodified, and in emerging societies and ethnic groups where the bodies of women are hidden from public view, the male control of women remains the problem (though exercised in very different ways). Renunciation in such circumstances might be adopted, rather than ridiculed, but directed not against the temptations arising from the alluring bodies of women, but against the temptation to *control* them by excluding them, confining them, and requiring pleasing behaviour or pleasing appearance from them (whether veiled or exposed). In short the temptation to perform hegemonic masculinity by dominating, controlling, excluding, objectifying, and manipulating women in different ways must be renounced. The Christian virtues are available to men who would forsake the deeply rooted structures of sexism, and allow their masculinity to be reshaped, not by the control of women but by rejoicing in sexual difference and performing the Kingdom values of mutuality, respect, and neighbour love.

There are hegemonic masculinities routinely performed all around us, which are no go areas, inconsistent with holiness. Appropriate renunciation would be not of sexual contact per se, but of all sexual contact that exploits or uses another, including within marriage, together with the mindsets that perpetuate the falsehood of women's inferiority to men. There is also a need for renunciation of all religious ideologies which, having posited women's inferiority, then legitimize forms of exclusion and control, or invent specious forms of 'spiritual' equality to mask continuing prejudice. Is there not a strong case today for redefining manliness as boldly as the early Christians appear to have done, albeit with a different outcome? Manliness which is predatory, or macho, or promiscuous, and which creates among women the expectation of receptivity, availability, and conformity to a masculine hegemonic culture, cannot be reconciled with any version of Christian faith. It is inconsistent with the simple practice of neighbour love. It must be renounced. When the falsehood of women's inferiority is renounced, churches will be able to become the communities of sexual and relational justice they are intended to be.

The turn to gender studies in theology leads to criticisms of yet more androcentrism (references in Conway 2015: 223–4). The spotlight shines again on men, their masculinity, and their mores, and the extent of their possible condescension to the other sex. If men are urged to emulate the humility and example of Christ in cultivating an alternative masculinity, how is the humility of this male Christ to be appropriated by women? What men and women are given in Christ is entry into a new humanity where sexual difference should enliven and liberate, where all human creatures enjoy the fullness of life which God intends for them. When human creatures respond together to the power of God, the transformation can begin. The next three chapters shine the spotlight not on men, but on how women and men can enjoy the life God has for them.

6

'... No Longer Male and Female...'

Chapter 6 moves from the transformation of relationships around Jesus as recorded in the Gospels to the continuing transformation of relationships by the presence of Jesus in the new communities that recognize him as the Christ. The chapter reviews the three positions about sex arrived at in chapter 4 in order to specify what a robust doctrinal faith can contribute to resolving the confusion left by this threefold legacy (section 6.1). With papal and evangelical attempts to find two separate sexes in Genesis 1 and 2 in mind, the chapter asks several questions about the use of Genesis 1:26–7, concluding that it is to Christ, the very image of God, that the church must look for the peace of its corporate mind as it continues to wrestle with gender (section 6.2). Life in Christ as it transforms gender is glimpsed, together with alternative visions of an afterlife where gender trouble will cease (section 6.3). Maleness is accorded no priority either in the Christian doctrine of God or of Christ (section 6.4). The celebration of difference, divine and human, is postponed to chapter 7.

6.1. ONE HUMANITY

At the end of chapter 3 we arrived at three possible answers to the question 'How many sexes are there?' The first answer was the ancient view that there is a single human continuum, male-and-female, incorporating sexual difference on an elemental and teleological scale whereby men are hotter, more rational, more perfect than women (position 1). In the seventeenth and eighteenth centuries this view began to be replaced by two versions of a rival view. There are two distinct sexes. In one view, the sexes are unequal (position 2);

in the other they are equal (position 3). I argued in chapter 4 that Christian teaching often but unhelpfully combines position 1 with position 3. Position 2, however, while generally disavowed, remains strong. Equality in position 2 is confined to a moral or spiritual quality, or converted into an attribute of divine love—God loves men and women equally—or is given an anodyne human characteristic like dignity. This manoeuvre enables material, social, and religious inequalities to remain intact, and patriarchy undisturbed, while at the same time pretending to follow the modern equality agenda. How do we move beyond these views, while learning from them at the same time?

Position 1 helps us to understand where modern ideas about sex and gender have come from and how much has changed. But the same could be said for the history of medicine or the history of science, littered as they both are with benevolent malpractices and abandoned hypotheses. If position 1 is to be retained at all in theology, it must contribute to an understanding of human being that advances the gospel for all women and men. Its advantage lies, I tentatively think, in its vision of men and women as a sort of unity. What God makes is a single 'earth creature' (*ha'adam*, Gen. 1:26). This creature, in order to 'Be fruitful and multiply', is sexed—is male and female. There is solidarity rather than syzygy or opposition between them. That is the core of acceptable complementarity theory. There is no opposition but a purposive unity in difference. Moreover, the universal 'man', the neologism 'humankind', and the substantive 'human nature' are all *inclusive* (in the carefully described sense of section 3.1.1). There is no space in theology for 'male nature' and 'female nature' as modern Vatican thought requires. There is human nature (as Mill also argued; see section 3.2.3). What is intolerable about the one-sex continuum is, of course, the gradation of perfections, the gender slide, the hierarchical ordering of relationships, all of which are rightly dismissed in our time as baseless prejudices. A 'continuum' is 'a continuous sequence in which adjacent elements are not perceptibly different from each other, but the extremes are quite distinct' (Oxford Dictionaries Pro n/d). There is much value in continuing to think of human being as a single continuum, provided its axis is horizontal, not vertical or requiring a descent from male perfections to female impurities.

Position 2 has no place in contemporary theology.

Position 3 has several advantages. It is the modern default position believed by almost everyone in the West. When churches utilize it they can assume a certain degree of comprehension. In the hands of liberals, reformers, and early feminists, appeal to two equal sexes has achieved much for women. Reformers within churches have appealed to it with some success. It may be the best of the three views we have so far considered. It could even be considered as an appropriate *development* of Christian tradition in the modern period. So why not settle for it?

There are several reasons. First, theology can do better. There are many neglected resources and riches in the traditions of Christian faith which are capable of appropriation by a grateful contemporary church. Doubts can be raised about the sexual binary not just because it is a product of modern secular thinking. Christians are the friends of reason. The issue is whether the language game of sexuality can tell the entire truth about relations between people, or whether a honed theology can provide a vital and missing dimension. Second, the oppositional character of the two sexes has affected the lives of both men and women, adversely and adversarially (see section 3.3). The subsidiary place of women in the one-sex continuum may have been replaced by a 'battle of the sexes' which exaggerates sexual difference and normalizes conflict.

Third, why should biological difference matter so much? Within the separate categories of 'men' and 'women' there are differences as great as those between men and women considered as two sexes. Why emphasize biological difference between women and men, and ignore the kaleidoscope of differences *within* each 'sex' and the many similarities *between* the 'sexes' (see chapter 7.1)? Gender intersects, as we have noted (section 1.3), with several other material and social categories, not least race, religion, ethnicity, and class. Why fixate on raw biological difference to the detriment of further examinations of human difference which may be life-denying and unjust? Biology has never been able to support the social and cultural constructions of embodiment that it has been supposed to justify, and the new biology of the eighteenth century is no different. That said, there are clearly bodily differences between men and women as well as many similarities. Theologically these are given, among other reasons, to enable us to share with God in the work of creation and reproduction, as the author of Genesis 1 assumes.

Fourth, the arrival of opposite, incommensurable sexes produced a state called 'heterosexuality', which creates the expectation that *everyone* should find themselves in a male or female body, always desiring a female or male person of the 'opposite' sex. One is either a man or a woman, as modernity defines each. While a clear majority of people are like this, that is, they would say they 'identify' as 'heterosexual', it is an alarming and damaging assumption to think that all people are, or ought to be, like this. Anne Fausto-Sterling recently argued that, when intersex conditions are taken into account, there are not two but *five* sexes (Fausto-Sterling 2000: 78). Heterosexuality, innocuous for many of us, is for several minorities an alarming social straitjacket, which flies in the face of how some people find themselves, and causes much pain and suffering. The older one-sex theory perhaps accommodated experienced sexual difference better, since it entertained no expectation of rigidly defined opposites within the gender spectrum. Fifth, the normalization of heterosexuality brought about another binary, not the male/female binary but the homosexual/heterosexual binary, at once relegating male and female homosexual people to the social and moral margins of deviancy. Finally, the two-sex theory polarized not just the two sexes, but the characteristics thought to attend each of them. If it is manly to be aggressive, and womanly to be nurturant, then gentle men and single women with careers are thought to be unnatural and exceeding their proper roles. Licence is then given to yet another misleading language game whereby men are encouraged to seek their neglected feminine side, and women are encouraged to seek their hidden masculine strengths.

I take from position 1 that there is a basic solidarity in simply being human. The single continuum is a whole. Eugene Rogers, Jr has helpfully suggested to me that a circle is a better figure than a continuum, for in a circle 'there would be no privileged ends, and perhaps even mild-mannered men and self-assertive women would have not a privileged but a typical place' (private correspondence). A circle indicates unbroken continuity: perhaps in the Christological account in this and the next chapter, the Christ might be seen as the centre around whom all humanity revolves. In the thought of the church there is a single human nature, one not two, and this is what the divine Son of God assumed. This human nature is prior to any subsequent division between male and female. Position 1 without the slide into imperfection is a serviceable understanding of male and female human being. It allows for sexual difference, among many others. It accommodates everyone who does not straightforwardly identify with either of the sexual binaries. And it knows nothing of the opposition of sexes. But there never has been a single continuum in which women and men were valued equally on a horizontal axis. That is why it does not deserve reinstatement without considerable revision. Position 3 has gone some way to achieve the horizontal axis, except that it has split the axis, and also spawned several harmful unintended consequences such as those just listed. If theological anthropology cannot help us here, one wonders why it exists at all.

In what follows in this and the next chapter I look for a Christian theological approach to gender which *does* affirm a single continuum but which also incorporates human difference, not just sexual difference, without valorizing either end of the continuum above the other. The name of the continuum has to precede sexual difference. Several abstract terms might suffice for the purpose: human being or beings; human reality; humanity; human creatures; persons; people; and so on. The terms remain abstract, of course, prior to deployment, and they need to be filled with content. Any attempt to speak this way can of course be criticized for being 'essentialist', 'universalist', even 'masculinist', in its embrace of abstraction. But I think theology must speak this way, since it speaks of Christ as the new creation, the second Adam, the One in whom 'all will be made alive' (1 Cor. 15:22). Christian faith takes these matters as joyful realities not overblown abstractions. But in making Jesus Christ the focus for our understanding of human being (see section 6.3) it will be necessary first to return to the influence of the creation accounts upon our topic.

6.2. 'MALE AND FEMALE': PROBING GENESIS 1:26–8

We have seen that these verses constitute the basic text, not merely of Rome's theological anthropology, but a proof text for the existence of two equal sexes, and we have already found good reason to challenge this view (see section 4.2.2). The Hebrew Bible displays no further recognition of this verse: indeed, the 'narratives about creation and Fall have hardly any effect on the other writings of the Old Testament, in terms of specific reference to these texts' (Zamfir 2007: 505). The passage has fascinated Christian theologians probably in every generation, and perhaps today more than ever. The literature is vast, and from the late thirteenth century a particular genre arose—the *Querelle des femmes* ('Quarrel about Women')—in which strikingly egalitarian interpretations of Genesis 1:27 were advanced (O'Neill 2011: 446). Four particular questions are relevant to the argument of the present volume.

6.2.1. Four Questions about God's Image

The four questions are:

1. How is 'humankind' to be understood in Gen. 1:26 ('Let us make humankind') and 1:27 ('So God created humankind')?
2. Do the two verses describe two separable 'events' or one singular 'event'?
3. What might be meant by the 'image' and 'likeness' of God in 1:26 ('Let us make humankind in our image, according to our likeness') and 1:27 ('So God created humankind in his image, in the image of God he created them')?
4. What significance might be given to 'male and female he created them' at the end of 1:27?

All four questions are unfortunately complicated by an interpretative conundrum. It is well known that Genesis 1:1–2:4a and 2:4b–3:24 are two different accounts of the creation, conventionally P and J. Whether one attempts to read the two accounts as a single narrative and to attempt (*per impossibile*) to reconcile them, or whether the differences are allowed to stand unresolved, influences the answers to each question.

The first two questions can be taken together. Most Christians in the West might raise their eyebrows at the suggestion that there are two distinct events described in Genesis 1:26–7. They are likely to think, after Augustine, that 'Genesis 1.27 is understood as a one-stage event: right from the start God created man and woman, and this grants to woman a validated *Ur*-status as physically different' (Coakley 2013: 289; see Ludlow 2007: 166–81). Gregory of Nyssa, however, famously argued 'that Genesis 1.27 should be taken in two parts, as the Hebrew text itself suggests: first a non-physical, non-sexed, angelic creation; and only then, with the Fall becoming imminent, sexual differentiation' (Coakley 2013: 281). The Fall confirms sexual difference. Humankind, the earth creature, is originally *un*differentiated. For Augustine, male and female were originally differentiated, while at the Fall, original difference is distorted by divine punishment.

Several ancient theologians accepted the myth of the 'primal androgyne' (see Meeks 1974, Knust 2011: 51–3). Margaret Farley explains: 'Adam was both male and female until the creation of Eve, which in some traditions was interpreted to mean (like Aristophanes's myth) that Adam was split into two (Eve taken from Adam's side), so that only then did human gender come into the picture' (Farley 2006: 143). 'By the first century CE', writes Colleen Conway, 'the two Genesis creation stories were frequently interpreted through the lens of this myth, where Genesis 1:27 detailed the creation of an original androgynous progenitor of the human race, and Genesis 2:22 expressed the tragic bifurcation of that being into two distinct sexes' (Conway 2015: 228; see Shaw 1998: 16, 20). If there are two events in Genesis 1:26–7, then the first is 'Let us make . . . ' (1:26), and the second is 'So God created . . . ' (1:27). The first of these, following the abstract nature of Greek thought, need not be concrete or historical. Humanity could be angelic, or an essence in the divine mind. It could be the collective human race. The second event could be an actual creation by God at 1:27, or, reading the text continuously, it could be what Genesis describes in 2:18–25. These alternatives point up a key issue: is human unity, 'humankind', the fundamental ontological 'fact' prior to sexual difference, or is sexual difference equally fundamental?

The third question suggests a very wide range of answers (see Grenz 2001). The contemporary Orthodox theologian Verna Harrison describes the *imago dei* as 'multidimensional' and unable to be 'limited to one defined characteristic'. She explains, 'Since in Late Antiquity it was taken for granted that an image arises through contact with its model and God is immediately present in his activities, the *imago Dei* means first of all that the inmost core of the human being is ontologically connected to God' (Harrison 2002: 347). It follows, she thinks, that 'we are created to enter into communion with God and participate in the divine life'. She goes on to say that 'the divine image describes certain innate human faculties associated with *nous* or *logos*, such as rationality, freedom, and the capacity to perceive spiritual realities', and in addition, 'the ability to participate in divine attributes such as life and immortality and, most importantly, the virtues such as goodness, wisdom, justice, compassion, and, of course, love'. None of these characteristics is derived from Genesis at all, though she goes on to mention 'dominion over the earth' and 'human creativity' (Harrison 2002: 348), which are found there. All this is well said, even if much of it is not to be found in the Genesis texts. But she also says, 'The fathers, following St Paul, think of the divine image primarily in Christological terms.' Exactly. It is Christ, and not Genesis 1, to whom ancient theologians give preference when looking for the embodiment of the divine image. But the very comprehensiveness of the possibilities of interpretation of the *imago dei* in Genesis should make us wary of fixing particular meanings of it, particularly when they are replanted in the less hospitable soil of modern sexuality debates.

Our fourth question is also open to several possible answers. The familiar phrase 'no longer male and female' (Gal. 3:28 NRSV) very probably mirrors the 'male and female' of Genesis 1:27. Mary Rose D'Angelo finds at least four meanings of the phrase in the early Common Era (D'Angelo 2002). As Farley summarizes, 'male and female' may be 'a figure of speech (used frequently in antiquity) which names a whole reality by naming its opposite poles'. Second, it may refer to a 'relation of disadvantage'. Third, it can mean '"sex and marriage", so that "no male and female" in Galatians means no more sex and marriage'. Fourth, it may refer 'to the original Adam, the image of God, as androgynous' (Farley 2006: 142–3). But the figure of speech 'which names a whole reality by naming its opposite poles' is the *very same thing* as the one-sex continuum which moves from male to female (and Farley invokes Laqueur's one-sex model in order to explain D'Angelo's meaning (Farley 2006: 144–5). The one-sex model is clearly, for women, also a 'relation of disadvantage'. This interpretation, together with the androgynous one, is much at odds with the casual and increasingly popular assumption that there are two sexes and that God revealed this truth to us in the first chapter of the Bible long before modern scientists thought they had discovered it by themselves.

These options, avers Farley, 'offer a radical challenge to later theological traditions in which gender distinction becomes central to an understanding of the human (as it does in Barth, von Balthasar, and John Paul II, for example)' (Farley 2006: 144; see section 4.4

above). I will try to answer the four questions listed above without assuming either the texts or their modern readers have two sexes as their shared a priori. This is not because I am a biblical scholar (I am not) with right answers, just a reader of Genesis operating with a non-standard view of 'the sexes'. So (question 1), God's intention is to make an 'earth creature', *Adam*, humanity, humankind. All women and men are included in the intention. Humankind is to 'Be fruitful and multiply' (Gen. 1:28). That is why earth creatures are male and female. Being sexed is necessary for human reproduction (although it could have been otherwise: Messer 2015: 75), but sexual difference need not be prioritized or valorized (given '*Ur*-status') by these verses. I make no room for puzzling distinctions between God's intention to make humankind ('Let us make . . . ') and God's making ('So God created . . . ') of humankind, so question 2 ceases to matter (unless one is a Platonist or an advocate of homogenizing readings of Genesis 1–3).

The very broad range of understandings of the image and likeness of God (question 3) precludes specificity. Harrison might have added further candidates to her list, including relationality, an 'I–Thou' relationship, or likeness to the Persons of the Trinity. I conclude, with Norman Kraus (Kraus 2012), that theologians should not find exclusive heterosexuality or modern complementarity in these verses (question 4). Whereas Genesis 1 does not provide automatic valid-ation of modern two-sex theories, Genesis 2 massively supports the one-sex continuum. God makes the man first, and on this basis the man has priority over the woman, as the New Testament several times attests. While the etymology of 'helper' need not imply infer-iority (Gen. 2:18), the role does. The narrative emphasizes that the woman comes from the flesh of the man; that he recognizes her derivation: 'This at last is bone of my bones and flesh of my flesh' (Gen. 2:23). No opposite sexes here. Even the derivation of 'woman' expresses one sex: 'this one shall be called Woman, for out of Man this one was taken' (Gen. 2:23). Marriage notwithstanding, the man and the woman are not opposite sexes, but 'one flesh' (Gen. 2:24).

Theologians who find sexual equality in Genesis 1:27 are likely to end up affirming position 3 (two equal sexes) while practising pos-ition 2 (two unequal sexes). Those complementarians who find equality here are placing their trust in contested details of ancient creation myths instead of elucidating the New Testament and patris-tic conviction that *Christ* is the image of God and anchoring gender statements in Christology. Jo Wells, to take a single example, glibly reiterates (in a popular study guide) the common view that 'from the outset of Scripture we find Genesis 1 proclaiming the foundational equality and complementarity of the sexes' (Wells 2013: 7). Not only does this ignore Genesis 2, most of the subsequent Jewish and Christian traditions, and the familiar reasons why Christians until recently have refused to ordain women, it pointedly diminishes the work of Christ in bringing about the realm in which there is 'no longer male and female'. Wells is not wrong in wanting sexual equality. A better way of finding it is to look, not to disputed readings and questionable literal interpretations of Genesis, but to the person and work of Christ through whom the equality of all human beings becomes a real possibility.

6.3. CHRIST AND THE NEW HUMANITY

Let us first assert, with Paul and the author of Colossians, that Christ is to be understood as the image of God. In the case of 'those who are perishing', Paul writes, 'the god of this world has blinded the minds of the unbelievers, to keep them from seeing the light of the gospel of the glory of Christ, *who is the image of God*' (2 Cor. 4:4, emphasis added). Christ 'is the image of the invisible God, the firstborn of all creation' (Col. 1:15). Giving priority to Christ over Adam in any appropriation of the *imago dei* should not be a controversial move. Meditation on the Person of Christ soon arrived at the conviction that Christ was not only the reflection of God as the divine image: Christ was so identifiable with that reflection that He was to be confessed as God's very self. A similar confession is found in several places in the New Testament (e.g. Heb. 1:2–3; John 1:1–5; 1 Cor. 8:6). The question then arises how this New Testament assertion squares with the uncompromising papal insistence that Genesis 1:27 'constitutes the immutable basis of all Christian anthropology' (see section 4.2.2).

6.3.1. The Image of the Invisible God

The answer is that the earlier text provides the central concept—the *imago dei*—for subsequent Christological development; it is in that sense the 'basis' of further reflection on the being of the Christ. But

Genesis 1 is not the determining factor in God's self-revelation by means of the divine image. More was to come—the fullness, the complete embodiment of the divine image in the Word made flesh. 'To call Christ the image of God is to say that in Him the being and nature of God have been perfectly manifested—that in Him the invisible has become visible' (Bruce 1984: 101). Whereas the New Testament authors *found* the idea of the image of God in Genesis, they apply the idea not to Adam, but to Christ. Because Christ has come everything has changed. Chronologically Adam is first; ontologically Christ is first. The story of salvation is that the image of God, manifested in the first earth creature and marred through human wilfulness, is re-presented to the world in a radically new form. The re-presentation is not a restoration of the *status quo ante* but a new, material, given manifestation of the image of God in the coming of Christ. The theological problem of gender is how the relations between men and women are transformed by sharing in Christ, the new image of God.

Having established the priority of the image of God as Christ over the image of God as 'male and female', let us ask how the image of God as Christ is itself reflected in and by Christian communities. The answer that the Colossian author gives is by participation in four related and overlapping entities: a new kingdom (Col. 1:13); a new creation (Col. 1:15–17); a new body (Col. 1:18); and a new humanity (Col. 3. 9–15). I will call this the 'fourfold reality'. Chapter 5 has already detailed the arrival of the kingdom in the ministry and Person of Jesus. New creation is linked with creation in Genesis by the argument of Colossians 1. Verse 15 continues by designating the Christ as 'the firstborn of all creation', explaining 'for in him all things in heaven and on earth were created, things visible and invisible, whether thrones or dominions or rulers or powers—all things have been created through him and for him. He himself is before all things, and in him all things hold together' (Col. 1:15–17). Christ is linked to the creation narratives only for them to be relativized in relation to Himself. In the beginning God created, but 'before' even the beginning was the eternal God whom Jesus also was and is. The chronological and ontological priority of Christ over Adam is asserted, with a corollary that all lesser (that is, created) entities derive their being from the One who sustains them in their being. The fourth Gospel makes similar claims (e.g. John 1:1–14).

There is a second reference to the image of God in Colossians. While making the familiar Pauline contrast between the old lives of Christians and their new life in Christ, the author tells them they 'have stripped off the old self with its practices and have clothed yourselves with the new self, which is being renewed in knowledge *according to the image of its creator*' (Col. 3:9–10, emphasis added). 'There is a correspondence between these old and new ways and what Paul calls "the old and new humanity" (*ho palaios anthropos* [3:9] and *ho neos [anthropos]* [3:10])' (Johnson 1992: 11). The first reference to the image of God describes who Christ is (Col. 1:15); the second is about how Christ's followers reflect the image of God in their transformed lives and conduct. Translators have struggled with the common abstract noun *anthròpos*. The KJV speaks of 'the old man' and 'the new man', using the old inclusive and generic sense of that troublesome, polyvalent term. But the NRSV has 'the old self' and 'the new self'; the Colossian Christians 'have clothed yourselves with the new self, which is being renewed in knowledge according to the image of its creator' (Col. 3:10). This seems unfortunate, for nothing less than a 'new humanity' is presaged in these lines, whereas 'the new self' individualizes and privatizes what Christ has done, ignoring its universal scope. 'The terms "the old humanity", "the new humanity", derive their force not simply from some individual change of character, but from a corporate recreation of humanity' (Moule 1962: 119). Old and new selves resonate well with the experience of conversion, but they eclipse the prior sense of the broad inclusive humanity into which conversion and baptism incorporate the new believer.

The new body into which new Christians are incorporated is, in Colossians, the church, with Christ as its head. 'He is the head of the body, the church; he is the beginning, the firstborn from the dead, so that he might come to have first place in everything' (Col. 1:18). Again the prior, protological status of Christ over against Adam is stressed. 'Body' or *sòma*, is another highly polyvalent term. The narrower term 'body of Christ' is said to have at least five meanings in Paul's letters—the physical body that suffered on the cross; the mystical body into which Christians are incorporated; the sacramental body of bread and wine; the ecclesial body or church; and the ethical body, which is the ecclesial body as it performs Christlike activities (Dinter 1994). We might add beyond the Pauline list, the resurrected and ascended body of Christ. If we add the strong presence of Christ, or his solidarity with, for example, children, the 'outcasts' at the Day of Judgement, and so on, which the Gospels emphasize, we are confronted with a joyful, colourful, kaleidoscopic series of images of the body of Christ. The mind of the Colossian writer has such a pervasive view of the body of Christ that he exclaims, 'He himself is before all things, and in him all things hold together' (Col. 1:18). There is a generous metaphorical indeterminacy about the body of Christ that literalism cannot begin to capture.

So the question arises regarding this fourfold reality: why should it be thought to be masculine, or to give priority to the masculine in any sense? Why should it incorporate the subjugations of the old order, since it exists to replace that order? What room is there in it for the power differences which have always been associated with sexual difference in a 'fallen' world? Of the five meanings of 'body of Christ' in Dinter's list, only one of these, the crucified body of Christ, is noticeably male. The risen body of Christ is a transformed body (see section 6.4.2); the mystical body, while partially instantiated in worship and prayer, exists beyond even space and time; the sacramental body, being bread and wine, is genderless (and, for some, miraculous); the ecclesial body cannot be male because it comprises men and women; and the ethical body is known by its practice, not by its gender. If it helps to call this concatenation of body language 'queer' (Cheng 2015), so be it. The body of Christ, we may safely conclude, is polymorphic. It has blurred edges and permeable boundaries. Its members are members of other bodies too. The body of Christ is both ineffably mystical and factically material, as it oscillates between the agony and ecstasy of flesh, and the timeless purity of eternity. Always given, always broken, it is also our triumphant destiny, that on which, in this life, we feed in our hearts 'by faith with thanksgiving' (Common Worship 2000d).

6.3.2. The Spectre of Feminine Obsolescence

The fourfold reality proclaims a different way of human relating than the hierarchical one. The influence of the one-sex model has perpetuated the subjugation of women within the single humanity, and Benjamin Dunning's *Specters of Paul: Sexual Difference in Early Christian Thought* shows how this happened in early Christianity. The 'perduring problem at the heart of Pauline theological anthropology' is, according to Dunning, 'the difficulty of situating sexed human subjects (male and female) within an anthropological frame-work bookended by two enigmatic figures—Adam, the first human, on the one hand, and Christ, the "second Adam", on the other' (Dunning 2011: 4). That Christ is the 'Second Adam' is a central idea of Paul's doctrinal scheme (Rom. 5; 1 Cor. 15). Where are women to be found within either figure, considered as a prototype? The 'spectre' of Dunning's book, haunting future interpreters of Paul, is how women might be included within this masculine schema.

The problem is compounded for modern readers by the 'hermen-eutical conundrum' (Dunning 2011: 6) of attempting to reconcile the apparent dismantling of male and female difference in Galatians 3:28 with Paul's teaching about the subordination of women in 1 Corinth-ians 11. A similar formula to Galatians 3:28 is used in 1 Corinthians but the reference to male and female is conspicuously avoided (1 Cor. 12:12). But Galatians 3:28 may *not* be a blueprint for modern equality at all. Rather, the text may speak of

> the subsuming of the weaker female into the stronger male, the mascu-linization of the female body, the supplying of male 'presence' (heat, for instance) for the former of female 'absence' (cold, understood as a lack of fire). In this system, which is the overwhelmingly predominant kind of 'androgyny' in the ancient world, it would be a mistake to portray androgyny as implying any equality at all between male and female. Ancient 'androgyny' . . . *embodies* the unequal hierarchy of male over female; it does not dispense with it or overcome it.   (Martin 2006: 84, original emphasis, and see Conway 2015: 228–9)

The hopes pinned on this verse by progressive Christians may be another example of presentism (see section 4.1), finding two sexes in the New Testament and claiming the work of Christ equalizes them. The likelier understanding of the 'male and female' clause in Gal-atians is a 'unity in masculinity' (Dunning 2011: 6) whereby, as Chrysostom taught (Martin 2006: 86), 'Galatians 3:28 teaches the obsolescence of the female, not its elevation. The message is unity in masculinity, not equality between the sexes.' Variations of Gal-atians 3:28 'circulated in multiple contexts in the earliest movement', including 2 Clement, the Gospel of the Egyptians, and the Gospel of Thomas (Martin 2006: 32). We are back with the one-sex model as the ancient framework for thinking about gender. '"No male and female" promises the abolition of dimorphic sexuality, not sexual equality' (Martin 2006: 87).

Specters of Paul analyses the accommodation of women into the Adam–Christ typology of Paul in various Valentinian texts, in Clement of Alexandria, in a Nag Hammadi text, and in Irenaeus and Tertullian. Dunning's judgement is that none of them succeeds: the 'spectre' of Paul's dilemma about gender haunted them all and haunts Christians still: 'these multiple early Christian thought-experiments together constitute a large-scale discursive failure'. But these same 'rich and variegated failures of discourse' tell us something about 'a necessary instability in the very categories that constitute theological anthropology' (Dunning 2011: 154). The very irresolution of the problem, thinks Dunning, has a positive conclusion. That conclusion does not contribute to a final resolution given only in the eschaton. Rather, it motivates towards a living with the problem that recognizes the subtleties of sexual difference, and acknowledges, through learned ignorance, that we can and must live peaceably with our differences, however complex and variegated they are.

6.3.3. A Better Vision

It is possible to accept Dunning's detailed analyses without coming to his rather disappointing conclusion. Yes, from our modern perspective there is a 'large discursive failure' to deal satisfactorily with gender in early Christian thought, and indeed subsequently. That failure is still with us in contemporary Christian thought, as churches prevaricate over the ordination of women or demonstrate the weakness of the exclusive case by closing down discussion of it. But the failure is traceable to the sexual framework within which those debates were conducted. As long as there is a gender slide, a continuum moving from perfect to imperfect, there will always be an impasse in elevating the female end, for that would entail an end to femaleness (which is what happens). There is no sexual equality in the New Testament (see chapter 5) and well-meaning attempts to find it there are probably as fanciful as they are optimistic. But that conclusion does not entail pessimism either. An appropriate theological assessment of the gender slide is required.

Euro-American cultures are generally comfortable with a two-sex theory despite its distortions and weakening heterosexual assumptions. But Christians cannot acquiesce in modern sexual binaries, not least because they have something better to offer. The conceptual transformation needed is already given in that triptych of Galatians 3:28—'no longer Jew or Greek', 'no longer slave or free', 'no longer male and female'. The conviction that salvation had come to the Gentiles took several decades to register. It was the cause of the early church's most troublesome dispute. The occasion of writing the letter to the Galatians was the expectation, introduced by Paul's opponents, that (male) converts to the faith should be circumcised. Paul mounts a fierce argument against them. Gentile Christians are justified by faith, not by the works of the law, including, prototypically, circumcision. The law 'was added because of transgressions' (Gal. 3:19). Like Abraham, who believed God, prior to the giving of the law, 'which came four hundred and thirty years later' (Gal. 3:17), Christians are made righteous by their faith in Christ and by nothing else. The 'offspring' of Abraham is 'one person, who is Christ' (Gal. 3:16). Because the Galatians have been 'baptized into Christ' and have 'clothed' themselves with Christ, they have no need of Jewish law, and so no need of the ethnic identity that circumcision or the observance of the law confers. This is the argument that takes Paul into his great assertion, 'for all of you are one in Christ Jesus' (Gal. 3:28b). God has now 'sent his Son, born of a woman, born under the law' (Gal. 4:4) to make the Gentiles God's adopted children (Gal. 4:5), 'and because you are children, God has sent the Spirit of his Son into our hearts, crying, "Abba! Father!"' (Gal. 4:6).

Nothing is more central to Pauline theology than the belief that God has sent the Messiah to deliver the Gentiles from the domain of sin and the works of the law. There is, then, in Pauline and Deutero-Pauline thought alike, a fourfold reality that confers on everyone, whatever their ethnic identity, potentially at least, to become the children of God (Gal. 4:5–6). These realities carry with them a remarkable sense of solidarity of God in Christ with all humankind, overcoming the sinful state of affairs which alienates people from each other and from their Creator. The great, all-encompassing vision of the Pauline school was hard won in the face of principled opposition from those many Christians who still thought of themselves primarily as Jews. The fourfold reality, however, did not obviously or immediately bestow equality on its members. It could hardly be more obvious that slavery, while softened as an institution among Christians, was not abolished. Slaves have a place in the Christian household and in the fledgling churches, and masters have a duty towards them. In Colossians, slaves must serve their masters as they serve their Lord (Col. 3:24). Only towards the end of the second millennium does slavery come to be seen by a majority as deeply evil and inhuman. The biblical principles of justice and neighbour love, and the sense that all women and men are the children of God, led, in conjunction with other social and political factors, to its dismantling.

In the case of gender, the time frame is even longer. For slavery there is clear textual support in the Bible. It is taken for granted (see Thatcher 2008a). Only a deeper understanding of divine love, revealed by the Gospel, overcame the texts which assumed and affirmed slavery. Contextual readings of the New Testament, and in particular the Household Codes, were partly responsible for the change, relativizing the influence of the ancient imperial world. What is needed now inside the churches is a similar relativizing of the ancient view of the one default male sex which incorporates lesser males as women while ensuring their inferiority. As with slavery, the same Gospel principles apply. There is no room in the new fourfold reality for the sinful prejudices that marred the old ones. The new creation is not the same thing as the liberal proposal to advocate the equality of the sexes, achieved (to some extent) in modernity, and dubiously read back into the Bible. It is nothing less than a new start for humanity where divisions of race, sex, and class are exposed as the sinful structures of an older order. The proposal is theological and Christological, based on no particular text, but on faith in Christ as the bringer of New Being, the image of God, and instigator of a new model of humanness.

The fourfold reality also offers an alternative to the masculinist eschatology in which perfection entails a perfected masculinity which women achieve or join. Perhaps we can say Christians looked towards a future when troublesome gender differences would be overcome, but their understanding of its accomplishment—in a new all-male humanity—like their understanding of much else—is necessarily historical and no longer able to speak to us. We *can* affirm the attempt to envision a new humanity where sexual difference was no longer troublesome, without affirming the form (a single, male sex beyond both) in which that vision was expressed, and femininity eliminated. Masculinity beyond male and female is, for us, a nonsense, for it remains masculine. The redeemed community in Christ, realized fully only in the afterlife, could be found realized partly in this life, where sexual difference is no longer the opportunity for hegemony, for power games, and for old dominances to appear in new guises.

6.4. BEYOND MALE AND FEMALE

The maleness of the incarnate Christ has been hyperbolized by a patriarchal church. Obviously, Christ became incarnate in a male human being, a *vir*, an *anèr*, but the nature the creeds ascribe to him is a *human* one, which, like his divine nature, is neither male nor masculine. The Kingdom of God (Col. 1:13) consists of both women and men, but when the character of the Kingdom is explored further, and the presence of the risen Christ among His followers is theologized, more complex metaphors are employed and adopted, and the fourfold reality comes into view. Whereas the contrast between the old and new is depicted dramatically in the New Testament, and especially when it is symbolized in immersive baptism, the relationship between the old and new is often blurred, compromised, and tentative. Nonetheless these metaphors do not float in the air; they attempt to make sense of a historical people, not divided by class, gender, and sex, who continue to be and to effect the presence of the Christ in a world still awaiting its final redemption. This same people is otherwise described as the church (Col. 1:18), which continues to embody the Christ in its worship and service. Its fallibility, failure, and ignorance are always matters requiring repentance and forgiveness, but its witness to the renewing ongoing presence of Christ in the world remains stolid in every generation. Discrimination in the new body on the grounds of sex is doomed, for it perpetuates the old creation which is passing away.

6.4.1. God beyond Gender

Confirmation of the final irrelevance of sexual difference in the new body is found by returning to standard and orthodox beliefs which Christians hold about God, and receiving these with fresh gratitude. Elizabeth Cady Stanton, in her *Woman's Bible* of 1895, found in Genesis 1:27 'a plain declaration of the existence of the feminine element in the Godhead, equal in power and glory with the masculine' (Stanton 1895: ch. 1). In her opinion,

The first step in the elevation of woman to her true position, as an equal factor in human progress, is the cultivation of the religious sentiment in regard to her dignity and equality, the recognition by the rising generation of an ideal Heavenly Mother, to whom their prayers should be addressed, as well as to a Father.

Long before Luce Irigaray complained about the lack of feminine representation of the divine within Christianity, and the deleterious consequences of that lack for women's sense of their own subjectivity and worth (see D'Costa 2000b: 1–11 for a summary), Stanton blamed a male God for oppressing women, and like Irigaray, she thought the male God impacted negatively on women's souls and bodies. Stanton's solution was the rediscovery of the Heavenly Mother. She (the Heavenly Mother) was not the human creation of an image of God in feminine form, but was the counterpart of the Heavenly Father in the plural avowal 'Let us make man in our image after our likeness.' Since male and female alike image God (she renders part of Genesis 1:27 'male and female image, created he them'), God must be both male and female, Father and Mother, and women are free to worship this God as their Heavenly Mother. Yes, Stanton is disdainful and dismissive of the doctrine of the Trinity, while understandably unaware of the possibilities of Trinitarian doctrine for resolving at least part of her problem.

That problem was the masculinity of God and its legitimation of patriarchy. The problem is similar to that of the male Christ, flung down by Rosemary Radford Ruether with her question 'Can a Male Savior Save Women?' (1992 [1983]: 98). Since God is not a male God, the assertion of a balance between 'His' male and female 'elements' (as Stanton calls them) cannot be the solution. It does not lie either in the invention of a Heavenly Mother in the image of women's religious needs, but in the rereading of the Christian revelation of God in Jesus. The solution lies in the discernment that God the Creator is above the creaturely distinction between male and female, while being the author of both. What is required is a non-sexist, non-patriarchal understanding of the doctrine of the Trinity, and this understanding is no invention (like the Heavenly Mother) but fundamental to what Christians mean by 'God'. It begins by probing beneath the surface grammar of 'Father' and 'Son'.

In an earlier work I noted that to speak of God as 'Father' may be to assume that 'Father' functions as a name; as one of the divine Persons;

as a relation (a child is required for anyone to be a father); or as the cosmic Parent in the sense that all human beings are God's children, the ones God created and loves (Thatcher 2011: 120–2). In several articles Harrison has helped readers to appreciate the subtlety of patristic teaching about the ungendered nature of God. For the Orthodox teachers, she writes, 'actual gender is unthinkable in the divine nature or the eternal existence of the three hypostases regardless of the grammatical gender of words used to name the divine' (Harrison 1998: 113). But is not the very thought of the Father 'begetting' the Son hopelessly gendered in its subject, its verb, and its object? Not at all. The church fathers were aware of the metaphorical and symbolic nature of the language they used, especially if they used it of God, and

> the affirmation that the Father begets the Son means that the Son comes from the Father's own person and is consubstantial with him. It does not mean that maleness or sexuality are in any way involved in the divine generation any more than time, change or partition of the Father's being.   (Harrison 1998: 13)

She notes that at the Council of Toledo in 675, 'the idea that the divine generation transcends gender was expressed explicitly' (Harrison 2011: 524). The council taught that 'For neither from nothing, nor from any other substance, but from the womb of the Father (*de Patris utero*), that is, from his substance, we must believe that the Son was begotten or born (*genitus vel natus*).' There is no difficulty in imagining the Father having a womb or describing the generation of the Son 'in language appropriate to both male and female parents'. God's fatherhood, then, turns out to be 'a unique mode of generation characterized by a wholeness that includes as well as transcending aspects of both forms of human parenthood' (Harrison 2011: 524).

6.4.2. The Sexed Body of Jesus

The maleness of Christ belongs to him as a characteristic of His incarnate humanity. It 'is not a feature of his divine ontology, nor is it the ontological link between our Lord's humanity and his divinity' (Harrison 1998: 114). Rather, 'God the Son as a person possesses maleness as one of the particular human characteristics he has assumed and enhypostasized in the incarnation. However, since there is no confusion between his two natures, this must not be understood as making his eternal nature as God somehow male' (Harrison 1998: 114). Discussion of his maleness belongs to 'the relationship between the particular human characteristics of our Lord and the universality of the common human nature he assumed' (Harrison 1998: 115). Being a man belongs to Christ's particularity, like being a Jew, living in first-century Palestine, being a carpenter, and being the son of Mary and Joseph and brother to his brothers and sisters. It is possible to speculate that, given the position of women in the ancient world, no sense could have been given to a divine *female* incarnation, but it is Jesus's real particularity of which maleness is a part that also constitutes its importance. God 'could not have become incarnate as "humanity-in-general" because human nature exists only in particular persons'. The human nature of Christ enables Him

> to share the humanity that is common to all people. This universal humanity, the common 'substance' of which the concrete totality of all human persons throughout time and throughout the world are made and which unites them all with each other, is what he unites to God through the incarnation.   (Harrison 1998: 115)

In terms of binary sex we could say that being sexed is more important than the sex one is or has, and that is as true for the incarnate Word as it is for everyone else.

The question just raised, 'Can a male Saviour save women?', has, as one answer, that the Christ is not male. The Word made flesh is the divine Word. The human nature of the incarnate Word belongs to all human nature; the maleness of Jesus belongs to that nature because that nature cannot exist merely abstractly. The personhood of the Son is divine. But Harrison has another answer to the same question: the male Saviour can save women because one of them gave birth to Him. 'The Church's answer is that he dwelt in his mother's womb and was born of her, and thereby he united with God and thus healed and sanctified what is distinctive in woman's biology, namely what belongs to the reproductive process' (Harrison 2011: 525–6). Theologians from East and West are said to agree that 'both genders are united with God in him, and both, insofar as they differ, are saved'. The salvation offered to everyone in Christ must, if it is to be effective inclusively, be grounded in what everyone is—'In order for Christ's salvation to be effective for every human person who chooses to receive it, the divine image and the potential for the divine likeness must be understood as inhering in what everyone shares, namely the ontological structure of personhood and the common nature' (Harrison 1998: 116). (There are dangers here for a theology awaiting the redemption of animals and other living things. Perhaps *sarx*, 'flesh', provides the more appropriate medium which the Word became.) Sexual differences cannot be ultimate matters on a properly Christological view of humanity. What Christ shares with us in order to save us is our human nature without further distinction. R. A. Norris concludes:

> Thus we may say quite firmly in summary that the maleness of Jesus is of no *Christological* interest in patristic tradition. Furthermore, it is possible to detect in the development of patristic ideas on the subject a logic which suggests why it never occurred to the Fathers to make any more play with Jesus' sex than they did with his race. What the Fathers learned to understand by 'incarnation' was *the likeness of the Word of God in his humanity to all those who are included within the scope of his redemption.*   (Norris 1984: 78, emphases added)

In the previous section we noted the tendency of early interpreters of Paul's Christology to think that since human perfection requires maleness, in the next life people will be all male (or will assume a form beyond maleness and femaleness, which more resembles maleness in this present life, since it is more perfect to be male than to be female). But Harrison suggests there may be clues from the post-resurrection appearances of Jesus that suggest His risen body may not be unambiguously male after all. The implications, therefore, for our eternal destiny, may be far-reaching. Beginning with the observation that the Risen Christ 'did not always appear in the precise form he had prior to his death', she notes that

> he still possessed that form but was not limited by it and could manifest himself in other ways also. These new forms suggest that human nature has added possibilities in the resurrection. Without losing the aspects of goodness and excellence it has acquired in this life, a person's particular embodiment of human nature gains a new openness to the vast potentials inherent in universal human nature.   (Harrison 1998: 124)

But the unconstrained form of the risen body of Christ is not the only hope of gender transformation in the next life. In the ongoing process of sanctification (or deification), the saints grow in holiness as their virtues 'converge with divine properties', that is, they 'share in the likeness, identity and identifying marks of Christ'. While descriptions of what is intended here are perilously difficult to articulate, she suggests

> the ontological openness and movement toward universality of particu-larized human nature mirrors and manifests the boundlessness of divine virtue and life, as the eternal progress of the saints in God (*epektasis*) becomes the created icon of divine infinity. As this occurs, nothing intrinsically good is lost but the limitations and self-enclosing boundaries inherent in gender and other characteristics that define partial and incomplete human identity are overcome through the actual-ization of wholeness, fullness of life and unity in Christ.   (Harrison 1998: 124–5)

The evangelical theologian Elaine Storkey is right to embrace what she calls the 'relational Trinity' as a more appropriate way of thinking theologically about gender. Taking her cue from the idea of the Persons of God as Persons-in-relation, she takes aim at evangelical and Catholic theologians who alike seize upon particular proof texts in order to maintain women's subordinate position vis-à-vis men. She thinks the 'recovery of human identity as relational rather than some substance with an essence or nature changes the focus of the gender debate' (Storkey 2007: 168; and see Grenz 1998: 615–30). She perhaps overlooks the potential that the term 'human nature' still possesses in deconstructing the male and female natures that continue to surface. Relationality, she suggests,

> mounts yet another challenge to the assumptions undergirding the attempt to find some definitive biblical gender characteristics. For it does not presume that the defining characteristic of the man–woman polarity is difference, reflected at the very center of our spiritual being; it does not see men and women as having distinct natures, brought together under the principle of complementarity. It does not posit some hierarchy of relationship, or call upon an authority structure within which men and women live with separate and distinct roles of rule and submission. It holds that the reifying of human nature or essence, and its distillation into the polarized concepts of 'manhood' and 'woman-hood,' are fundamentally flawed. Ontologically, our very identity lies in who we are in relationship.   (Storkey 2007: 169)

There are no reasons for thinking the doctrine of God gives priority to maleness, or that the Incarnation of God as a man valorizes it. The attempt to load a robust sexual dimorphism onto Genesis 1 occludes a proper treatment of Christ as the image of God. Beginning with

Christ opens up the fourfold reality of a new kingdom, a new creation, a new body, and a new humanity, and where sexual difference no longer becomes a means of domination and oppression. The theological treatment of Christ as the *imago dei* blends into an understanding of God as a Trinity of Persons which, while due care is directed to the analogical character of the language by which it is possible to speak of God at all, is of the utmost importance for our experience of sexual and gendered relationships. It is scarcely controversial to claim that in God, as expressed in the Athanasian Creed, there is both difference and otherness; there is mutuality, equality, and reciprocity between the Persons; and there is a unity in their communion and loving purposes (Thatcher 2011: 105). These are themes to be explored in the next chapter.

7

Against Sexual Difference

A Theology of Similarities

There has been much discussion in this book about 'sex' and about how many sexes there are. A pathway has been traced from the ancient to the late modern world where the discourse of sex has become sufficiently authoritative for its categories to be accepted by nearly everyone—majorities and minorities alike find their place within it; theologians of all persuasions think with it and endorse it; church reports even assign biblical authority to it; while social scientists, having ascribed *Ur* status to it, have allowed it to shape both their inquiries and their results. Yes, modern scientific discourse may have been misled by it as much as the church's theologians. But the sheer contingency of the two-sex theory is now increasingly understood by the natural and social scientists, by philosophers and gender theorists, and it is the task of dissenting theologians both to assimilate critically their findings, and, as theologians, to propose ways of relating between women and men that are faithful to the Gospel promise of fullness of life for everyone.

Continuing the fourth aim of the book, 'to indicate how theology and Christology, in the area of gender, envisions the redemption of human relationships', the chapter is in two parts. The troubling ontological question regarding sexual difference is asked in section 7.1. If there are two sexes, are there therefore two human essences? Two humankinds? I will be arguing for similarity, not difference, in the discussion of gendered relations. These seemingly abstract questions about essences and kinds are raised in order to support the ontological claim in section 7.2, that Jesus Christ is to be able to be acknowledged and confessed by Christians as the essence of humankind. Gender is redeemed by a full incorporation into the new humanity (the four-fold reality of the last chapter), which Christ is, and wills to share with all humankind. Similarities between the vocabulary of gender (identity, equality, and so on) and the vocabulary of Trinitarian doctrine are explored, concluding that the divine Trinity provides the foundational basis for full equality between women and men. The goal of redeemed human relations is the relationality that already and eternally exists in God.

7.1. AN END TO SEXUAL DIFFERENCE?

There are strong reasons for abandoning all talk of sexual difference, both in the church and in the academy, and speaking instead of sexual similarity (when we need to speak of 'sex' at all). Let's begin, following Michael McKeon, by suggesting that prior to the seventeenth century, roughly speaking, the meaning of the term 'sex' could be found in a particular reference to 'the two divisions of organic beings distinguished as male and female respectively'. During that century 'sex', he continues, also became a generalization, 'the class of phenomena with which these [distinctions] are concerned' (McKeon 2012: 795, citing *The Compact Edition of the Oxford English Dictionary*, 1971). As a consequence 'it became possible to write not only about "the male sex" or "the female sex" but also about "sex" as such'. The earlier meaning envisaged a distinction within the same species between male and female, but not a separation. I think the earlier meaning remains useful. The later meaning converted the distinction of the sexes into a separation. How? By foregrounding 'sex as such' to the extent that it becomes the principal source of human identity, grounded now in biology alone, no longer with reference to the wider web of social relations within which individuals were necessarily involved. Sex later became 'sexuality', and the very basis of one's identity as male or female. The new view 'disembedded' men and women from the earlier 'complex experiential network so as to isolate each as a fundamental and differential physiological identity' (McKeon 2012: 795).

McKeon's essay was originally an introduction to a symposium in 2009 entitled 'Before Sex'. All the contributors (including Laqueur) explore the shift in the social and cultural understanding of sex in the seventeenth and eighteenth centuries. As McKeon explains:

> The tacit category 'sex' became unprecedentedly explicit in Western Europe during this period because it was disembedded from the socio-cultural, economic, and religious ground that before then had made it functional and purposive in other terms. People have always understood the disparity between men and women as essential to their experience of the world. But the customary distinction between the genders *along a shared and common spectrum* was replaced over the course of this period by the tendency to view men and women as *basically different* from each other, separate ways of being whose difference is crucially marked by a preference for the other sex and crucially mediated by the existence of a category of people who, on the contrary, prefer the same sex.   (McKeon 2012: 791, emphases added)

The contrast between 'before sex' and 'after sex' mirrors the contrast we discussed (section 4.1) in Phillips and Reay's *Sex before Sexuality*. The heightened emphasis on sexual difference *is*, or is the principal characteristic of, the watershed between 'before' and 'after'. That emphasis continued and even accelerated for a further three centuries. A sex difference, says Melissa Hines (whose work, as we will shortly see, challenges sexual difference fundamentally), is a 'characteristic' that '*differs on the average for males and females of a given species.* Thus, a human characteristic is considered to show a sex difference if it differs for a group of boys or men in comparison to a group of girls or women' (Hines 2004: 3–4, original emphasis). Reported sex differences, she observes, frequently suffer from various distortions such as the over-reporting of results where differences are slight; the 'influences of stereotypes ... on the perceptions of researchers and research participants'; the contextual specificity of results, and common disagreement about what the results mean (Hines 2004: 5, 5–8; Maccoby and Jacklin 1974). Biological or reproductive difference is wrongly assumed to be the natural basis for a host of further alleged differences between the sexes, for example,

> bodily strength and speed (men are stronger and faster), physical skills (men have mechanical skills, women are good at fiddly work), sexual desire (men have more powerful urges), recreational interests (men love sport, women gossip), character (men are aggressive, women are nurturant), intellect (men are rational, women have intuition), and so on. It is widely believed that these differences are large, and that they are 'natural'.   (Connell and Pearse 2015: 36)

Language further naturalizes these differences by using the terms 'feminine' and 'masculine' to describe social behaviours (Leaper 2014, 1995; Lott 1981) and character traits. Campbell Leaper shows how devices like the Bem Sex-Role Inventory (Bem 1974), which use separate femininity and masculinity scales, 'perpetuate(s) the notion that certain behaviors are inherently either female or male'. 'Thus, for a man to show affection implies that he is somehow not masculine; conversely, for a woman to act confident implies that she is somehow not feminine' (Leaper 2014: 66).

Popular psychology has extended the alleged dichotomous nature of sexual difference into the further idea of character dichotomy. This development has continued even though a 1975 study (and many others since) concluded that on character trait after character trait there is no difference between girls and boys:

> [I]t is *not* true that girls are more social than boys, that girls are more suggestible than boys, that girls have lower self-esteem, that girls are better at rote learning and boys at higher-level cognitive processing, that boys are more analytic, that girls are more affected by heredity and boys by environment, that girls lack achievement motivation, or that girls are auditory while boys are visual. All these beliefs turn out to be myths. (Connell and Pearse 2015: 43, original emphasis).

Forty years on, after torrents of research, the 1975 conclusion holds: there are no significant differences in the character traits of girls and boys, women and men.

The question therefore arises (a *genuine* psychological question) why there appears to be an unshakeable attachment to the idea of character dichotomy. 'Most people still believe in character dichotomy. Pop psychology is utterly committed to this idea' (Connell and Pearse 2015: 43). The answer lies in the entrenchment of the idea that there are two opposite sexes. Every area of human life has been subject to scientific investigation in order to yield the secrets of masculine and feminine dichotomies, and 'evidence' for them has been found, appearing to justify the legitimacy of the research questions. Belief in two distinct sexes is a 'master narrative', a 'dominant ideology' which shores up other beliefs about personal identity, individuality, naturalness, and normativity which are themselves in constant need of re-enforcement and justification. In cultures where a two-sex ideology is recent, 'evidence' of difference is always news, eagerly sought and devoured. Yet evidence of sexual similarity is never news and never sought—'gender similarity is not a positive state; it is merely the absence of proven difference (literally, the "null hypothesis")' (Connell and Pearse 2015: 44).

The human two-sex dichotomy was given a further boost in the nineteenth century when Charles Darwin extended his theory of natural selection to apply to human *sexual* selection.

> In *The Descent of Man, and Selection in Relation to Sex* (1871), Darwin extended these conclusions to humans, and further elaborated his theory of sexual selection: male characteristics (for example, strength, intelligence, virility) are evolutionarily favoured in the competition for females, who will be selected for beauty, health and fecundity.   (Rosario 1997: 10; in Rahman and Jackson 2010: 111)

A proper theological critique of Darwin's later thought ought to occupy itself, not with his theory of evolution, but with the use of it to explain gender differences in humans by naturalizing them. The critique might then accelerate its momentum by describing sexual selection as the primary 'example of the expansion and institutional-ization of natural science during this era' (Rahman and Jackson 2010: 111). While humanity has gained much from the rise of the modern natural and social sciences, the benefits do not extend to the elimin-ation of other, more holistic forms of knowledge; or to the pretence that its methods of inquiry are objective and value-free; or to the triumph of an overarching secular world view, *etsi deus non daretur*, over the historic Christian faith, itself evolving in response to the revolutionary changes of the modern period. With regard to sexual matters, the dimorphic view became ever more fully anchored in the turbulent sea of public perceptions about sex. Science gradually came to 'replace religion as a dominant cultural framework, but simply reproduced and elaborated upon essentialist patriarchal ideas' (Rahman and Jackson 2010: 114).

We have already noted that Freud loaded heavy cultural meanings onto genital organs (see section 3.1.2). It is easy to see how terms like 'penis envy' and the pressure-cooker metaphors of sexual 'drives' and sexual 'repression' received an enthusiastic welcome in the arena of public discourse as it sought to extend itself beyond religious under-standings of sex. Anatomy not only lies at the basis of sexual differ-ence; unnoticed in this cultural elevation of psychological language is the smuggling in of 'the social concepts of masculinity and feminin-ity', and the further identification of these 'with orientation towards

the opposite sex/gender' (Rahman and Jackson 2010: 116). But anatomy, now at the level of chromosomes and genes, continues to rely on
and to import social meanings of sex in its attempt to tell its particular
story. Sarah Richardson provides a fine example of this in her account
of the history of chromosomal research. In 'Sexing the X: How the
X Became the "Female Chromosome"' she documents how

> the X chromosome has not only become female identified as an object
> of biological research, but has, more broadly, become a highly gendered
> screen upon which cultural theories of sex and gender difference have
> been projected throughout the twentieth century and up to the present
> day. The case of how the X became the female chromosome presents a
> prominent example of how unquestioned gender assumptions can
> distort and mislead, not only within the biological sciences but more
> generally in the production of knowledge.   (Richardson 2012: 927–8)

7.1.1. An End to 'Sex and Gender'?

The purpose of the distinction between sex and gender for the last
forty years has been to distinguish between those human characteristics which are rooted in biology and those which humans acquire
through social and cultural influence (Nielsen and Norton 2015).
This 'two-realms model' (Connell and Pearse 2015: 40) was intended
to limit the influence of biology to biological matters only, while
offering the hope that gender, freed from biological constraints,
would be seen to have a thoroughly contingent historical character.
It was hoped that, as individuals became aware of the diverse social
influences impinging upon them, relations of equity and justice
would be easier to forge. The pervasiveness of sexual dimorphism
began to be understood. It began to be realized that 'biological,
psychological, and social differences do not lead to our seeing two
genders. Our seeing two genders leads to the "discovery" of biological,
psychological, and social differences' (Kessler and McKenna 1978: 1).
'Queer biology'—a 'school of thought [which] argues that our understanding of the biological world is framed by *what we think we
already know*' (Amy-Chinn 2009: 50, original emphasis)—is becoming better known. From this perspective, 'absolute sexual dimorphism
remains one of the last false metanarratives governing our thinking,
and contributes to a relationship between the sexes grounded in
hierarchy and privilege'.

The two-realms model, like its counterparts essentialism/constructionism and nature/nurture, had its advantages, but there are good reasons for concluding that the model should now be abandoned completely. Hines flings down three such reasons at the beginning of her book *Brain Gender*. The first of these is sheer human ignorance. Of the distinction between sex and gender, she remarks: 'Given our limited knowledge of what is socially or biologically determined, I believe it is impossible to make this distinction' (Hines 2004: 4). The second reason is the entanglement of social and biological influences, together with more specific influences, on the actions of people: 'it is likely that many behavioural sex differences result from complex interactions among different types of influences, some generally considered biological, others social'. The third reason is the presence of a functioning brain as a necessary condition of our behaviour (amply illustrated throughout her book): 'all our behaviour is controlled by our brain and, in this sense, is biologically based'. In her view sex and gender 'cannot be separated' (Hines 2004: 4, and see Malabou 2011: 137–8).

Like the concepts 'sex' and 'gender', the concepts 'male' and 'female' also (in Hines's view) tend to float above the messy particularities of human life. 'Few, if any, individuals correspond to the modal male pattern or the modal female pattern. Variation within each sex is great, with both males and females near the top and bottom of the distributions for every characteristic' (Hines 2004: 18, and see 35), although most of us appear to be either clearly male or clearly female, we are each complex mosaics of male and female characteristics' (Hines 2004: 19). We should not think, as most of us apparently do, that our brains remain 'hardwired' so to speak, while 'we' are changed by our many experiences. Brains change too. 'Experience can alter sex differences in brain structure' (Hines 2004: 211). Yes, there are structural differences between male and female brains, but brains are 'malleable' and when neural sex differences have been found they can be 'surprisingly responsive to environmental factors' (Hines 2004: 218). Social experience can influence hormones (Hines 2004: 218). 'Expectations and beliefs, as well as hormones, can engender the brain' (Hines 2004: 227). However, expectations and beliefs, for example about the limited ability of males to care for children, and much else, based on biological difference are not currently supported. 'The empirical data on hormonal influences on the brain and behaviour suggest flexibility and variability in outcomes that argue against these conclusions' (Hines 2004: 229).

There are other problems with the two-realms model. Human life does not simply divide into two realms. Feminist thought is suspicious of the generalizations 'man' and 'woman' even prior to the operation of biological and social distinctions, because the extensity and diversity of possible social conditions governing the lives of men and women cannot be subsumed by theory, and give rise to the question 'Which women?' The intersectionality of gender with 'a range of social and material categories' (see section 1.3) complicates the distinction further. The question impels itself: is there a future for gender? McKeon states the problem well:

> Premodern 'gender' acknowledges the distinction between men and women without positing their separability, their difference. But the modern concept 'gender' is self-consciously sponsored by, and depends for its intelligibility on, the equally modern premise that men and women are separable and different; that they are hence susceptible to categorical reconciliation insofar as their difference is judged to be cultural, not natural; and that their difference is therefore restatable as a distinction between the masculine and the feminine.   (McKeon 2012: 797)

Both 'sex' and 'gender' emerge from the widespread adoption of a two-sex ideology and its subsequent aporias. I can't advocate abandoning either term (especially as one of them appears in the title of this book). I don't think using them interchangeably, as Hines does, is finally satisfactory since there remain contexts, especially in theology, where the distinction between sex and gender, body and society, is a useful one. Connell and Pearse leave the distinction behind but continue to speak of gender. They say, 'Social science provides a solution to these difficulties. The key is to move from a focus on difference to a focus on *relations*. Gender is, above all, a matter of the social relations within which individuals and groups act' (Connell and Pearse 2015: 11, original emphasis). This is a decisive shift which correlates well with my initial stipulative definition of gender as about the relations between women and men (see Introduction), still a crucial issue for churches worldwide. That gender is about relations will be an illuminating idea when we think soon about the difference the Trinity makes to our understanding of human relations (see section 7.2).

7.1.2. An End to 'Men' and 'Women'?

These challenges to sexual difference are decisive. It is time to rename the one-sex continuum the 'human continuum'. A key to understanding male/female relations is similarity. But to speak of men and women as similar is not to deny difference altogether, for similarity is only possible where there is *dis*similarity. Otherwise women and men would be identical, and it could hardly be clearer that they are not. There are 'men' and 'women', and so there is sexual difference. But there are also 'third sex' people (see Herdt 1996), and intersex and transgender people for whom the cultural normativity of sexual difference is exceedingly problematic and oppressive. If there are men and women, then it should be possible to say what each is. And if it is possible to say what each is, it seems hard to avoid saying that men and women each have an 'essence'.

Reflexive Essentialism

Essence has a long history in Western philosophy, going back at least to Plato. It can mean the reality of a thing over against its appearance; the substance or essential being of a thing over against its properties or accidents; the definition of a thing marking it out from other things; a synonym for the nature of a thing; or the judgement *what* a thing is (its essence), against another judgement *that* a thing is (its existence). The peculiar problems of theology with regard to the essence of men and women are no greater than the problems for the biological and social sciences, for secular thought is also impregnated with assumptions about the essential man and woman. 'Scientific essentialism remains a ubiquitous feature of contemporary culture and continues to give rise to "research" purporting to demonstrate "natural" differences between men and women—whether these are based on hormones, brains, genes or the supposed conduct of our evolutionary ancestors' (Rahman and Jackson 2010: 116). But Rahman and Jackson go further. They identify what might be called a state of self-consciousness, a mindset, even a way of being, that internalizes tropes of what a man or a woman is, and places these at the heart of the self (or, as Christians might say, has colonized their souls). They call this 'reflexive essentialism'.

Similar to the term 'gender', 'reflexive' also has its origins in grammar, where it denotes a kind of pronoun (e.g. 'myself', 'yourself') that refers back to the subject of the clause in which it is used. Heightened individualism is a common theme of social analysis. One's personal identity, self-defined in relation to peers, becomes a matter of much importance, the project that is the fashioning of the self. Reflexive essentialism picks out the point that the project of the self is carried out in cultures where the division between men and women, even in a time when human rights are affirmed and sex discrimination is illegal, has reasserted itself and become a pervasive force:

> We suggest therefore that contemporary culture is marked by a *reflexive essentialism*: reflexivity combined with essentialist notions of sexual identity. The reflexivity expected of the self in a consumerist, post-traditional culture requires the widespread deployment of sexuality as the definitive aspect of our social identities ... Whilst the power of media-driven consumerism is now a global phenomenon, as is the discourse of women's and gay rights and identities, these are still dependent upon essentialist understandings of identity—a reformulated, reflexively produced essentialism organized primarily around sexuality, but nonetheless a continuation of modernity's emphasis on the innate origins of the sexual. (Rahman and Jackson 2010: 149, original emphasis)

Whereas 'the new moral frameworks that permit the existence of women's rights and some gay rights indicate the shift towards new self identities ... it is far from certain that such individual "projects" of the self are occurring in the context of wider, structural gender and sexual equality' (Rahman and Jackson 2010: 209).

If this analysis of reflexive essentialism is correct, the circumstances surrounding and producing it require extensive theological critique, because a different vision of the relation between women and men is given in the Christian revelation of fullness of life. An exclusionary priesthood, sexist liturgical practice, the practice of 'headship' in millions of conservative Protestant homes and the damaging effects of this on the bodies and souls of the women and men who suffer from it—these too are forms of essentialism, the precursors of the forms of essentialism that modern cultures and sciences proclaim.

7.1.3. 'Gender Realism'

The essence, then, of man and woman—seemingly an abstract question—turns out to be of vital importance inside and outside the churches. Remaining for the moment with theory, two further ancient terms, 'realism' and 'nominalism', may facilitate an answer. A nominalist would be expected to explain why we classify individual things like men or computers by appealing to resemblances between those things. A realist would be expected to reject resemblances as inadequate, and to posit a universal, a real referent to which nouns like 'men' or 'computers' refer (see Armstrong 1978). So are there men and women beyond the resemblances occurring between members of the *class* of men and of the *class* of women? (And is not 'class' in any case a universal?)

'Gender nominalism' is associated with the influential work of Judith Butler, who 'rejects both the idea that there are particular traits or experiences that naturally belong to particular genders and the idea that individuals possess core gender identities' (see Nielsen and Norton 2015: 145). Sexual difference, she thinks, is itself constructed and 'inscribed' on bodies. Catherine Malabou angrily rejects gender nominalism, which she sees as an attack on feminism by postmodern writers, including some writers calling themselves feminist. She thinks the denial of an essence to womankind is yet another instance of violence against women that smacks of ancient prejudices:

> That 'woman' finds herself now in the age of post-feminism deprived of her 'essence' only confirms, paradoxically, a very ancient state of affairs; 'woman' has never been able to define herself other than through the violence done to her . . . The critique of 'essentialism' (i.e., there is no specifically feminine essence) by gender theory and deconstruction is but one more twist in the ontological negation of the feminine. (Malabou 2011: v)

There is a surprising congruence between Malabou's complaint and the complaint against the two-sex theory that has been accelerating throughout this book. Whereas 'post-feminism' denies that there is an essence—woman—'traditional' feminism 'analyzes relations between the two sexes in terms of power and domination without ever questioning the presupposed dualism within the imperative of equality, parity, and reciprocity' (Malabou 2011: 1). Malabou has correctly discerned, not that the analysis of relations between men and women in terms of power is mistaken, but that 'traditional' feminism' takes the two-sex theory for granted. I too have complained about this (see section 5.1). The 'presupposed dualism' of which she complains is the two-sex theory inscribed in the sciences and the churches alike. Her complaint that 'the idea of "gender" has never been taken back to its ontological source' (Malabou 2011: 1–2) is to be applauded.

For Malabou there is an essence of womankind. But what then, is it? Malabou's answer seems pessimistic to this male author: 'I propose', she writes, 'a minimal concept for woman, an ineffaceable "remains" in which "woman" refers to a subject overexposed to a specific type of violence' (Malabou 2011: 93). Pope Francis has another answer. He recently affirmed (in an address commemorating the twenty-fifth anniversary of *Mulieris dignitatem*, and commenting on the theme of paragraph 30 of that document, 'God Entrusts the Human Being to Woman'):

> It seems evident to me that my Predecessor was referring to maternity . . . the fact remains that it is woman who conceives, bears in her womb and gives birth to the children of men. And this isn't simply a biological fact, but entails a wealth of implications be it for the woman herself, for her way of being, be it for her relations, for the way of positing respect for human life and for life in general. By calling woman to maternity, God has entrusted the human being to her in an altogether special way.   (Pope Francis 2013)

While Pope Francis was not responding to the philosophical question about the essence of women, his reflection on 'woman' in terms of reproduction, maternity, and the feminine respect for life gives a clear example of essentialist thinking, continuous with previous popes. (There is a more positive way of understanding his remarks. If he had written 'many women' instead of the generalization 'woman', the implication would have been avoided that reproduction is what *all* women are for.)

Similarity and Difference

Linda Alcoff, in a detailed and nuanced treatment of sexual identity, offers a third way between the essentialism exemplified in the previous paragraph and the constructionism that gives little or no weight to sexed bodies. She invites readers to

> [c]onsider the following as a possible objective basis for the category of sexed identity:
>
> *Women and men are differentiated by virtue of their different relationship of possibility to biological reproduction, with biological reproduction*

referring to conceiving, giving birth, and breast-feeding, involving one's own body.   (Alcoff 2006: 172, original emphasis)

These few words demonstrate the subtlety of her position. She speaks not of an essence, but a 'category'. 'Male' and 'female' are 'categories'. Other writers have avoided the loaded term 'essence' by speaking of 'series' or 'groups' (see Warnke 2011: 88). The basis for Alcoff's categories is 'objective', grounded in bodies, 'out-of-theory'. This is 'gender realism'. She explains that 'possibility' means 'something more than mere logical possibility, something closer to Aristotle's idea of concrete potentiality, in order to capture the idea that females are expected to have, or have had, the ability to give birth and lactate, whereas males are not'. By choosing 'possibility' she tries to avoid the essential implication that *all* women might be expected to become involved in reproduction. Instead, all women have a relationship of possibility to reproduction that men cannot have:

> By 'possibility' here I mean I want to capture the reality that this differential relationship of possibility to biological reproduction remains in place even for women who have had hysterectomies, women who have no desire or intention to reproduce, and women who are not fertile. Those classified as women will have a different set of practices, expectations, and feelings in regard to reproduction, no matter how actual their relationship of possibility is to it. That is, even infertile, prepubescent girls or postmenopausal women, and women who have no intention to reproduce *still* have a relationship to biological reproduction that is different from what males have.   (Alcoff 2006: 172, original emphasis)

Because women *may* give birth to children it does not at all follow that they *ought* to give birth or that they *ought* to adopt maternal and domestic roles. Of course many women *want* children, and the theory accounts for this. 'Men' and 'women' are 'categories', 'classes' or 'types' within human life, but they are not essences.

Lisa Cahill describes how the vulnerability of the female pregnant body provides both a reason and a specious over-justification for the gendered power of men over women. 'Because pregnancy, birth and infant care require a protected environment, and because these activities have historically tended to reduce the ability of pregnant and child-bearing females to fend off enemies and obtain food for themselves and their young, corresponding male roles of hunter and protector have also developed' (Cahill 2011: 103). One might go further and add that pregnancy and breastfeeding may provide a bonding between mother and child which some fathers can only envy. But, she asks, why should reproductive difference extend to 'different psychological and cognitive traits in women and men, or different social roles in other areas? To what degree are women by nature designed for child-bearing and child care, and men for warfare and material productivity? . . . To what degree are these roles pliable?'

If there is an essence to woman, it is very clear man has an essence too. Essences are supposed to delineate at a basic level, to say why x, being x, cannot be y. What might man's essence be? Almost all the historical discussion—theological, scientific, philosophical—about woman's essence seems to have been undertaken by men eager to maintain their dominant position in the gender hierarchy. In a moment I will suggest there is only a human essence, and that men and women are categories or classes within it. There are deeply theological reasons for suggesting this, indeed, insisting upon it. Nonetheless it will also need to be shown that any postulated human essence is not merely a male essence in disguise.

Hines, who, as we have noted earlier, thinks any distinction between sex and gender is untenable, is highly sceptical about different psychological and cognitive traits in men and women which, if proven, might constitute an essence. But they are far from proven; indeed, she finds them to be over-reported, and to conform to gender schemas which influence both expectations and the design of experiments and their results. She observes that 'the hormones of pregnancy may play a role in human parenting or attachment behaviour', and 'the early hormone environment, particularly levels of androgens prenatally, may influence interest in infants', but 'the role of hormones, if it exists at all, is relatively minor'. An example of a psychological trait is male violence. Men commit many more violent crimes than women but, given the state of current knowledge, it is safe to say, counter-intuitively, that *hormones play little or no part in any explanation*. While the hormone testosterone is popularly linked to male aggression, the question needs instead to be put, 'Given the paucity of rigorous, empirical evidence that adult levels of testosterone or other androgens contribute to aggressive behaviour in human beings, *why is the assumption that androgen has powerful influences on aggression in males so persistent?*' (Hines 2004: 143, emphasis added). One familiar answer is that gender schemas distort perceptions. Hines explains, 'Everyone, scientist, and non-scientist alike, has cognitive schemas (or informal scientific theories) about these topics. These cognitive schemas about sex or gender are composed of groupings of characteristics associated with males versus females, and they usually function to allow people to reach conclusions based on limited data' (Hines 2004: 143–4). So anyone with the gender schema that (rightly) 'includes the idea that men have higher levels of testosterone than women and that men are more dominant, more aggressive, and more likely engage in antisocial behaviour than women' is likely 'to associate testosterone not only with males, but also with dominance and aggression'. However, the association is shown to be unwarranted. If there is a causal connection between testosterone and male violence it is likely to be the opposite of the popular assumption that one causes or helps to cause the other. Rather, 'it is more likely that aggression, or factors associated with it, influence levels of testosterone than that testosterone influences aggression in adulthood' (Hines 2004: 225).

Genesis, Essences, and Kinds

We have spoken of essences and categories. It is now appropriate to speak of the biblical notion of a 'kind'. 'Kinds' provide a surprising and illuminating link between the creation story of Genesis 1, the modern notion of two sexes, and the present discussion about possible human essences. Despite many standard assertions to the contrary, Genesis 1 provides no support for male and female essences. 'A natural kind refers to a category that exists independent of the observer and that can be defined in terms of an essence, a set of properties common to all members of the kind' (Hawkesworth 2013: 34). Leaving aside the more advanced problems of description and reference associated with natural kinds, let us accept this definition of a natural kind and turn to the twelve references to kinds in Genesis 1. These include 'fruit trees of every kind' (Gen. 1:11); 'plants yielding seed of every kind' (Gen. 1:12); 'the great sea monsters and every living creature that moves, of every kind, with which the waters swarm, and every winged bird of every kind' (Gen. 1:21); 'the wild animals of the earth of every kind, and the cattle of every kind, and everything that creeps upon the ground of every kind' (Gen. 1:25). Finally there are two references to 'humankind'—'Let us make humankind' (Gen. 1:26) and 'So God created humankind in his image' (Gen. 1:27).

There is, of course, no obvious continuous semantic meaning between the Hebrew word for 'kind', *miyn*, and the definition just cited. However, the definition fits well. Let us note that every kind listed is capable of reproducing itself. Most of these kinds reproduce sexually but no mention of this is needed or made in the narrative. Only with humankind (the creature in which the author thought sexual difference was most obvious?) is there the inclusive mention of 'male and female' (Gen. 1:27). Every creature belongs to a kind, and humans too belong to a kind—humankind. The problem with the modern opposite-sex theory is that it assumes humankind is actually two kinds—'malekind' and 'femalekind'—and this assumption cannot withstand scrutiny. Hawkesworth observes:

> Within the version of biological dimorphism cultivated over the twen-
> tieth century, male and female are construed as natural kinds, distin-
> guished by unique configurations of chromosomes (xy–xx), hormones
> (androgens–estrogens), gonads (reproductive organs such as testes and
> ovaries), internal morphology (seminal vesicles and prostate as opposed
> to vagina, uterus, and fallopian tubes), external genitalia (penis and
> scrotum, clitoris and labia), as well as secondary sex characteristics
> (body hair, facial hair, breasts). *Feminist scholars have shown, however,
> that none of the typical correlates of biological sex conform to the
> demands of a classification as natural kinds.*   (Hawkesworth 2013: 34,
> emphasis added)

The conclusion follows that 'there are no behavioral or physical characteristics that always and without exception are true only of one gender' (citing Kessler and McKenna 1978: 1). 'Chromosomes, hormones, sperm production, and egg production all fail to differentiate all men from all women or to provide a common core within each sex.' There is no clear biological dividing line between men and women:

> Indeed, both men and women have testosterone and estrogen in their
> systems and the human X chromosome, wantonly mischaracterized as
> the female chromosome, is not only common to both men and women
> but also carries a large collection of male sperm genes (Richardson
> 2012). *Even the insistence that there are two and only two sexes is
> mistaken.*   (Hawkesworth 2013: 34–5, emphasis added)

Hawkesworth's arguments concur with others in this chapter, and with the emphasis throughout this book on people who are unable to identify with the modern sex binary. Whereas modern science once insisted on two sexes, it is backtracking fast, and it is time for theology to do the same. In the case of theology, the process would be facilitated by revisiting the ancient one-sex continuum in which it has a longstanding investment. The wider consideration of Genesis 1 as a series of kinds runs counter to the endless assertions that the chapter supports the creation of two separate sexes, whether 'egalitarian' or 'complementarian', equal or unequal. The alternative narrative in Genesis 2 contains no support for two sexes either. The woman comes from the man's flesh, who then recognizes her flesh as his: 'This at last is bone of my bones and flesh of my flesh; this one shall be called Woman, for out of Man this one was taken' (Gen. 2:23). Neither account supports two modern sexes. There is a surprising convergence here. While historians are more aware of presentism in the interpretation of texts (see section 4.1), scientists are beginning to understand that the dimorphic understanding of women and men has been much overdone.

7.2. A TRINITARIAN ONTOLOGY

We have just noted Malabou's contention that 'the idea of "gender" has never been taken back to its ontological source', and that 'the presupposed dualism within the imperative of equality, parity, and reciprocity' has not been properly questioned. Hers is an analysis of gender that supports the claims in the present volume. One wonders, however, where the ontological source is coming from. Christian theology, waiting in the wings for its cue, is well able to provide an ontology that insists on equality and reciprocity in human relations— one which is rooted in the divine revelation to which it bears its fragile witness. Theology can never acquiesce in a mode of thinking that calls itself postmetaphysical, anti-ontological, or anti-foundational, and it must either speak compellingly about *theos* or eventually retire from the academy. But 'compellingly' must refer to the attractiveness of its narrative, the open invitation of its story, not a retreat to an imperial past that preaches in a loud, superior, and incontrovertible voice. While *theos* is an unacceptable premise for many, it is a foundation, indeed *the* foundation, for Christian faith. In the case of gender in particular, Christian theology is able to provide 'the imperative of equality, parity and reciprocity' which looks and feels very different from the harsh masculinism, androcentrism, subordinationism, and misogyny that is still poisoning Christian witness in many parts of the world. Thomas Laqueur pointed out (see section 1.1.2) that 'no set of facts ever entails any particular account of [sexual] difference' (Laqueur 1990: 19). That contention remains true today. This lacuna in gender studies provides an auspicious space for theology, which it may occupy with humility, wonder, and excitement. In the next few pages some points of contact between Trinitarian ontology and gender theory will be noted. The way into the Trinity will be via the Christological conclusions reached earlier.

7.2.1. Christ: the Essence of Humanity

I wrote (section 7.1.3) that is a mistake to hunt for the essence of man and woman. That was not to deny differences between men and women as defined earlier (section 7.1). It was to assert, at the climax of a long argument, that there is an essence, not of man and woman, but of humankind. Humankind is a kind, male and female. Theologically, its kind is to be made in the image of God. But, after the Fall (allowing for diverse interpretations of that 'event'), and now that the Christ has come, it is Christ who is the image of God. The divine image is now restored, revealed, and shared. The essence of humankind is Christ. Christ for Christian faith is the Head of a transhistorical, transcultural body of people that relativizes all other human distinctions without eliminating them. That is the only morally permissible doctrine of 'headship'. This body purports to be the 'tangible presence of Christ in the world—a "body" that like other bodies is a system of cooperative movement among subsystems' (Williams 1990: 6).

It is not imperialistic to make this claim. The claim arises rather out of basic beliefs about who and what Christ is: it is part of Christian 'auto-interpretation' (D'Costa 2000a: 100). The problem lies with a particular 'hetero-interpretation' of the claim—the assumption outside the faith that old-style imperial claims and strategies are intended. Love and service are the instruments of mission, while at the level of theological and inter-religious encounter, the equality of women with men should be and perhaps one day will be a strong element in gaining new followers of Christ. While hierarchy falls to the ground in the renewed humanity of which Christ is the Head, difference does not. It becomes instead a means of communion. If Christian theologians have anything useful to say about gender it is to proclaim the difference that Christ makes to the performance of it, with profound implications for the 'community of practice' ('community of performance'?) which is the church.

The whole Christ in his/her divine being is beyond distinctions of sex, and the humanity of Christ, as tradition east and west insists, is inclusive of all humans whatsoever, for He is confessed by the church as *homo* not *vir*, *anthròpos* not *anèr* (see section 4.2.1). That the incarnate Christ was also *vir* and *anèr* cannot be doubted. What must be doubted is the overemphasis on the maleness of Christ by derogatory one-sex and two-sex theories respectively. God creates 'humankind in his image'. Humankind is what gets *Ur* status in normative readings of this verse. Humankind is the essence. Being made in the image of God is what unites male and female and does not divide them. It is more an expression of similarity than one of difference. Whatever may have befallen humankind since its prelapsarian state, a newer, deeper, Christological understanding of the image of God has occurred.

Deep in the corporate understanding of Christian people is the conviction that, together, they constitute the very body of Christ. One of the forms of the presence of Christ in the world is the *corpus Christi*, which embodies women and men without ontological superiority, hierarchy, or rank. They are *ta tekna tou theou*, the 'children of God' without distinction (as the neuter *teknon* implies). They have received the Holy Spirit without distinction of sex (or nation or race, as the Pentecost narrative of Acts 2 insists), and await the day when the same Spirit is 'poured out' 'upon all flesh, and your sons and your daughters shall prophesy' (Acts 2:17). I have sought to ground relations between men and women within this redeemed Body. It is now time to see how what Christology proclaims, Trinitarian ontology confirms.

7.2.2. Individuals and Persons

There is a striking overlap between the basic items used in the vocabularies of gender and Trinity: individuals and persons; persons and relations; identity and difference; equality and diversity, and so on, all have key places in the discussions of each. These overlaps prompt and invite a series of cautious analogies between the two sets (see Thatcher 2011: 102–3). Let us start with individuals. The notion

of a free agent as an individual underwent a change beginning in the
seventeenth century, coterminous with the arrival of two sexes. An
'individual' used to require belonging to a community. Then it came
to mean being *separate* from a community. McKeon explains:

> According to traditional views, the liberty of one member of the com-
> munity is achieved in and through association with all others. Bodily
> health is a function of temperance, a state of balanced equilibrium that
> is maintained by the equilibrium of the collective body. To be an
> individual is to be subsumed within this greater body, a role within a
> greater drama that precludes the conceptualization of the individual self
> in the modern sense of the term.   (McKeon 2012: 795)

In the seventeenth century 'individual' changed in meaning from
'indivisible' to 'single, as distinct from others of the same kind'.
What lay behind the change was 'the growing conviction that liberty
requires the liberation of the passions from the control of external
institutions such as the state—the conviction that individuality entails
individualism' (McKeon 2012: 795). Charles Taylor has undertaken a
similar (and extended) analysis, calling the modern individual 'the
buffered self', contrasting him or her with the premodern 'porous
self'—'open and porous and vulnerable to a world of spirits and
powers' (Taylor 2007: 27), and of course other selves. By the
twenty-first century, the buffered self became a gendered self with a
'core gender identity' (Hines 2004: 83). The buffered self thrives in a
climate of 'reflexive essentialism' (see section 7.1.2).

Much has been written about the modern sense of self and its
various routes towards the disseverment of individuals from community. There are two points to emphasize (from many that might be
made) in the present context. First, gender is theoretically irrelevant
to the modern concept of the individual, because human individuals
are members first of human groups, not gendered ones, just as they
theoretically enjoy human rights on the same basis. But the second
point derives from the nature of God. God is *treis hypostaseis, mia
ousia*—three individuals, one being or essence. Gregory the Great
explained how these terms were to be used in relation to God (Allen
and Springsted 2007: 69, citing Gregory of Nyssa, Letter 38.3). While
Peter, Andrew, and Paul, he wrote, are three individuals, 'man' is an
essence, what Peter, Andrew, and Paul have in common. Father, Son,
and Spirit are three individuals, but they are also one in their being.
'That which is spoken of in a special and peculiar manner is indicated

by the name of the hypostasis' (i.e. individuals are particulars), whereas 'being' is a general term—what the particulars have in common. However, there is a difference between speaking of God as a unity (of Father, Son, and Spirit) and speaking of 'man' as a unity comprising what men all hold in common. Why? Because the unity of God transcends ordinary comprehension of commonality: 'Peter, Andrew, and Paul share a common nature as men—they are of the same *ousia*—but they are not so united that they are *one man*.'

Analogies are already in play in Gregory's account. The analogical element I wish to place in the centre of the discussion about gender is the *balance* between sameness and difference, unity and diversity when speaking of God. The individuals who are the one God differ. Yet their unity is greater than the unity of any human essence, and so any extreme of identity and difference, so fractious in the human case and leading to solipsism or violence, is avoided. The Athanasian Creed declares, 'And the Catholick Faith is this: That we worship one God in Trinity, and Trinity in Unity; Neither confounding the Persons: nor dividing the Substance' (Book of Common Prayer 1662). The balance between sameness and difference is unmistakable. When the human mind opens itself in worship and contemplation, it is not only licit to begin by thinking of the one God, and moving to the separate Persons. It is also necessary to begin with the different Persons and to move to the divine unity. But a balance of the two approaches must also be struck. At the very edge of human language and comprehension, both approaches must be held together; both stories must be told. The truth about God cannot be well articulated without each. So important is the balance that the creed warns, 'unless a person keeps this faith whole and entire, he will undoubtedly be lost forever'. But the balance of sameness and difference is just as important in the human essence as it is in the divine essence. In the divine case the individuality of each of the Persons is without domination or subordination, without otherness or alienation. There is no better way of imitating or embodying the divine Persons than by the equal and reciprocal treatment of human persons. Gender is an obvious test case.

7.2.3. Identity and Difference

The gospel invites people to enter into a new life, the divine life, where identity and difference are held together in the being God is. We might note in the human case, our affixing to ourselves labels, however ill-fitting, which proclaim us as heterosexual, male, black, vegetarian, republican, etc. People who are different from us serve to *confirm* our identities and perhaps make us uncomfortable in their presence. Difference can become the justification for treating people with suspicion, hostility, inferiority, or violence. Human beings long for a peaceful existence where difference entails co-operation not competition. The divine life, the *perichoresis* of the Trinity, offers this. The Athanasian Creed spells out repetitiously, almost tediously, how God's life reconciles identity and difference. The Persons are not confused or mixed up ('Neither confounding the Persons . . . '). They have a strong identity. At the same they do not divide the substance (*neque substantiam separantes*). Their individuality is not actualized at the expense of the others, and the being of God is not divided by their separate roles.

> For there is one Person of the Father, another of the Son: and another of
>   the Holy Ghost.
> But the Godhead of the Father, of the Son, and of the Holy Ghost, is all
>   one: the Glory equal, the Majesty co-eternal.
> Such as the Father is, such is the Son: and such is the Holy Ghost . . .
> So the Father is God, the Son is God: and the Holy Ghost is God.
> And yet they are not three Gods: but one God.
> So likewise the Father is Lord, the Son Lord: and the Holy Ghost Lord.
> And yet not three Lords: but one Lord. (Book of Common Prayer 1662)

The creed continues with its affirmations of identity and difference, its play between unity and diversity and its warnings about what faithful Catholics must and must not believe. There is no doubt that the creed assumes a different milieu from our own. Theologians were battling against accusations of tritheism, monism, subordinationism, and many other 'heresies', and compromises may have been achieved as much for peace in the empire as in the church. The composition of high doctrinal formulae was not influenced by considerations of gender such as those which have come to the fore in modern times. The church has nonetheless bequeathed to us a vision of God which resonates vibrantly at a time when relations between women and men are under scrutiny. Subordination remains an acute theological problem in the churches today: not of the Son and the Spirit to the Father (though even this has its modern advocates), but the subordination of women to men, in the sanctuary and in the world. Redeemed human life is life in communion, as God's life is communion. Hierarchical power plays belong to the old order which is passing away.

7.2.4. Equality

A Trinitarian ontology also contributes decisively to the understanding and realization of equality. Elizabeth Anderson helpfully distinguishes between equality as a 'distributive principle' and as 'an ideal of social relations' (Anderson 2012). In secular thought egalitarians 'aim to replace social hierarchies with relations of social equality on the ground that individuals are fundamentally moral equals' (Anderson 2012: 40). A social hierarchy is said to consist of 'durable group inequalities that are systematically sustained by laws, norms, or habits. The inequalities are durable in that they are reproduced over time by the social arrangements that embody them. They are also group based: They create *classes* of people who relate to one another as superiors to inferiors' (Anderson 2012: 42).

There are three types of social hierarchy, she continues. First, there are 'hierarchies of domination or command' in which 'those occupying inferior positions are subject to the arbitrary, unaccountable authority of social superiors and thereby made powerless' (Anderson 2012: 43). Second, there are 'hierarchies of esteem' in which 'those occupying inferior positions are stigmatized—subject to publicly authoritative stereotypes that represent them as proper objects of dishonor, contempt, disgust, fear, or hatred on the basis of their group identities and hence properly subject to ridicule, shaming, shunning, segregation, discrimination, persecution, and even violence' (Anderson 2012: 43). Finally there are 'hierarchies of standing' in which 'the interests of those occupying superior social positions are given special weight in the deliberations of others and in the normal (habitual, unconscious, often automatic) operation of social institutions. As a result, those of higher rank enjoy greater rights, privileges, opportunities, or benefits than their social inferiors' (Anderson 2012: 43).

Egalitarians have proposed various alternative regimes, from anarchism to communism. Democracies too are undermined by abuse of power, greed, misinformation, persuasion, etc. Women and sexual minorities recognize themselves in all three types of social hierarchy, and many continue to suffer from explicitly religious institutions which claim divine legitimation for the discrimination they practise. But it need not be like this. The creed goes on to specify differences between the divine Persons, only to conclude:

> So there is one Father, not three Fathers; one Son, not three Sons: one Holy Ghost, not three Holy Ghosts.
> And in this Trinity none is afore, or after other: none is greater, or less than another;
> But the whole three Persons are co-eternal together: and co-equal.
> So that in all things, as is aforesaid: the Unity in Trinity, and the Trinity in Unity is to be worshipped.
> He therefore that will be saved: must thus think of the Trinity.

Christians are entitled to muse that the equality which egalitarians seek has its roots in divine, not human, being, and requires divine grace to realize it in this life. It is found in the fourfold reality of the previous chapter. There are Nonconformist churches where decisions are democratically taken and the doctrine of the priesthood of all believers held. But the old churches, including the Anglicans, are still in thrall to the one-sex theory or to a literal reading of subordinationist biblical texts. Yet, at the very heart of the Catholic faith stands the conviction, which is not permitted to Catholics to deny, that 'in this Trinity none is afore, or after other; none is greater or less than another. But the whole three Persons are coeternal together: and coequal.' In the divine life there are no hierarchies, power plays of greater and less, more and less perfect, more or less divine. And the insistence on the unity of the Persons requires that their relations are ones of reciprocity, mutuality, and symmetry. There is scarcely a more appropriate analogy for gendered relations than the equality and reciprocity of the Trinity.

7.2.5. Communion and Love

Pope John Paul II made his own the earlier teaching that God is a *communion of Persons*, a *communio personarum* (e.g. *Familiaris consortio* (1981), *Letter to Families* (1994)). Here, the basic statement that God is Love is explained by the *communio personarum*: the Persons of Father, Son, and Spirit constitute the dynamic flow of Love that God is. Human persons too, being made in the image of God, are made for love and for communion, and they share this communion with friends and strangers, and if they are married, with their spouses and any children they have (Thatcher 2008b: 203). Communion is essential for the fulfilment of men and women. Marriage, of course, is inessential for communion, but because it assumes the intimacy of lovemaking, it provides an intense form and experience of it. The *unio* or 'one flesh union' of marriage is thought to symbolize and enact the union of the Persons within God, one in being yet distinct from each other, each an individual expression of the infinite love that God perfectly is.

Relations

There is a logical truth about the Persons of the Trinity (and about human persons too). It is this: there cannot be Persons without Relations. You cannot be a mother or father if you have no child, for having a child is a necessary condition for being a parent. God is called Father principally in relation to the Son. In this sense, without the Son, God the Father could not be Father. God the Son could only be the Son in relation to the Father. That is why the names 'Father' and 'Son' do more than name particular Persons. They name Relations. What is at stake in calling God 'Father' in this sense is the insistence that God is intimately in relation, in the first instance to Christ, but also to the world, and to ourselves: not that God, being named Father, approximates to a masculine gender.

Miroslav Volf has pointed out that, whereas human beings share sexual difference with animals, we cannot share these differences with God, for God is not a creature and is beyond distinctions of sex. Allowing for gender differences worldwide, he wants these to be shaped by the differences in the triune God. He proposes

> that we locate normativity in the formal features of identity as we encounter it in the identities and relations of divine persons. Instead of setting up ideals of femininity and masculinity, *we should root each in the sexed body and let the social construction of gender play itself out guided by the vision of the identity of and relations between divine persons.* (Volf 2003: 170, original emphasis)

Here, then, is an admission of gender difference. There are many of them. But Christians take what is important about gender difference from the difference that is to be found, not in society or church, but at the heart of divine reality. There is difference in God certainly, for the three Persons are different. But in God the three Persons are also equal. Taking our cue for handling difference from the differences that subsist in the life of God, Volf argues that 'we must both affirm equality between men and women and seek to change social practices in which the inferiority of women is embodied and through which it is perpetuated' (Volf 2003: 173).

Volf, then, is another theologian who finds resources for dealing with gender at the very heart of the Christian tradition. The life of the Trinity is a communion or community where difference does not need to be overcome by elimination, domination, repression, or oppression, for each Person is already 'in' the other, in the one Life that pours itself out in self-giving Love.

> But though self-giving has no assurance of success, it does have the promise of eternity because it reflects the character of the divine Trinity. It is on account of self-giving that divine persons exist in a perfect community in which each is itself only by being inhabited by the others. And it is through the power of self-giving that a new community of men and women will emerge, in which distinct but dynamic gender identities that are 'not without' the other will be fashioned and refashioned in peace. (Volf 2003: 177)

One might quibble about *how* the vision of the identity of, and relations between, divine Persons is to be a guide in the construction of just human relations. Others will worry about the abstractness of the formulae of the Athanasian Creed. Others will say its function is to *pro*scribe heresy, not to *pre*scribe relations of equality between human persons. Others will find the pressing of the analogy between divine and human persons startling, novel, even illegitimate. But the creed is the clearest articulation of the doctrine of God that the church has bequeathed to us, and my use of it as the foundation for relations of equality between men and women is unapologetic. It is the 'ontological source' at which (as Malabou laments) secular thought never arrives. If it occasions surprise to use the Athanasian Creed in the context of twenty-first-century conversations about gender, the surprise may be akin to reading Pope John Paul II twenty or thirty years ago. Whereas it was far from novel to speak of God as a *communio personarum*, it was novel indeed to extend the *communio* to the domain of human persons, and to press the divine Person/ human person analogy into service in order to depict God at the heart of the relationship of marriage, and indeed beyond. A similar novel connection may be made here, where not marriage but gender is given theological form, and the presence and activity of God located where human relations are loving and just, and where love and justice are expressed reciprocally and equally between women and men.

8

Redeeming Gender

This final chapter concludes the fourth aim of the book, to indicate how theology and Christology, in the area of gender, envisions the redemption of human relationships. 'Human relationships' are extended here beyond the confines of churches. The chapter first summarizes the doctrinal imperatives requiring action in the field of gender. Second, it indicates areas of unfinished business in the churches, which, with notable exceptions, fail to embrace the doctrinal riches and transformational opportunities offered to them by the Spirit. Third, some brief indication of the urgency of the problem of discrimination against women throughout the world is made, followed by a short reflection on the contribution of gender justice to mission.

8.1. TRINITARIAN ROOTS OF REDEMPTION

I have concentrated in Part II of the book on the theological reasons why 'there is no longer male and female'. Strong philosophical reasons accompany these. Whatever reservations Christians may understandably entertain about Enlightenment thought, over the question of gender there is a certain congruence between theology and philosophy which to some extent confirms the argument in these pages. For example, if people are fundamentally 'souls' attached to bodies, as the Catholic Descartes thought, then women are equal to men, spiritually, intellectually, and morally (see section 3.2.1). 'The mind has no sex.' If there are such things as natural rights, then men and women have them, irrespective of the fiction of natural inequalities invented to perpetuate male privilege. Human rights are human rights regardless of gender. If human rights exist there are no humans without them. Mill supported the 'principle of perfect equality' (see section 3.2.3) with a battery of sound arguments. It is possible to propose a sexual and gender ethic based on the principle of justice for all women and men (and distinguished Christian ethicists have achieved this; see e.g. Farley 2006, Ellison 2012). Western democracies no longer deny the vote to citizens because they are women. Democracy is the rule of the *demos*, the people, not just certain privileged males. The 'Greatest Happiness Principle', the foundation principle of utilitarianism, 'holds that actions are right in proportion as they tend to promote happiness, wrong as they tend to produce the reverse of happinesss ' (Mill 1879: ch. 2). This principle, and the calculations that flow from it, are gender-blind. Whatever reservations Christians may rightly entertain about the vocabularies of rights and happiness, they are congruent with the striving for gender equality.

I have concentrated on theology and Christology in this book, while remaining appreciative of other critical arguments which nonetheless lead (as far as they go) to similar conclusions. We have already considered the fourfold reality of new life based in Jesus Christ (see section 6.3), and a Trinitarian ontology (see section 7.2). But these are not the only considerations. The problem of gendered oppression is much worse in some cultures than it is in those influenced by the churches, and it is necessary to emphasize (albeit with much humility) the universality of Christian claims about gender and the need for liberation from other incidences of oppression. Theology asserts a common humanity prior to its division into races, religions, cultures, and nation states. Humanity itself is made in the image of God. God the Word illuminates this common humanity. 'What has come into being in him was life, and the life was the light of all people. The light shines in the darkness, and the darkness did not overcome it' (John 1:3b–4). The *general* presence of the Word in all humanity is the precursor to the *particular* presence of the Word in the flesh (John 1:14) of Christ. The Word is the light of all people, whether they are aware of the Word or not. This, of course, is another example of Christian auto-interpretation which disregards cultural and religious divisions because it lies prior to any of them, including Christianity (as John clearly states). It takes for granted that comparable assertions may be available within some of the other religions. The light of all people may be the basis for a universal ethic, even though it has (like all ideas) a particular origin, and is quite different from the 'light of reason' trumpeted by the Enlightenment. The light of all people shines upon inhuman practices, exposing them for the evils they are, while it illumines a fairer vision of how all people might share in the Life that the Word gives them.

That Word for John has a particular form, which is Christ, the Word made flesh, and the Light of the world (John 8:12). Justin Martyr famously spoke of the *logos spermatikos*. 'The idea lurking in his mind', explains J. N. D. Kelly, 'seems to be that His presence in Jesus Christ should be understood as similar in kind to this universal presence, *though much greater in degree*' (Kelly 1965: 146, emphasis added). But it is through the Spirit that the healing presence of God *extra ecclesiam* is discerned. Timothy Gorringe concludes that 'on the Christian understanding all cultures, and therefore all religions, in what is life affirming, represent a response to God's Spirit' (Gorringe 2004: 258). Gavin D'Costa's cautious analysis of Catholic teaching about the presence of the Spirit in the world's religions still permits him to say:

> Through the witness that non-Christians give through their lives and teachings, Christians have often been called into more faithful discipleship. The Spirit's presence in other religions is also the source of promise and great joy to the church, for in being open and attentive to the Holy Spirit, it grows in its own relationship to God and those from other religions. (D'Costa 2000a: 130)

The universalist strand of Paul's thought confirms that the locus of God's salvation is the whole of humanity, indeed, of all creatures: 'in Christ God was reconciling the world to himself' (2 Cor. 5:19); 'for as all die in Adam, so all will be made alive in Christ' (1 Cor. 15:22); 'Therefore just as one man's trespass led to condemnation for all, so one man's act of righteousness leads to justification and life for all' (Rom. 5:18). Jesus represents all humanity before God, just as he represents God to all humanity. The solidarity of Jesus with everyone, regardless of ethnic, religious, or any other difference, is obvious from the Gospels: 'looking at those who sat around him, he said, "Here are my mother and my brothers! Whoever does the will of God is my brother and sister and mother"' (Mark 3:34b–35). The depiction of the Last Judgement in Matthew's Gospel illustrates assessment criteria in the afterlife, the implications of which are seldom noticed. Jesus identifies himself totally with people, any people, who are suffering (for whatever reason). The 'righteous' who 'inherit the kingdom' are those who *minister to Jesus*, whose incognito presence among hungry, thirsty, alien, naked, ill, and imprisoned people counts their actions as righteous irrespective of whether they recognize him (they don't). There can be no doubt that in a Christian understanding of the Incarnation, all women and men are subjects of God's love, infinitely precious, made in God's image, the sisters and brothers of Jesus, and the children of the heavenly Father.

The import of these features of Christianity's global scope is that there is more to the Christian mission than the making of Christians. The divine gift of life is universal, like the extent of redemptive grace in Jesus Christ and the unanticipated and ungraspable roaming of the Spirit who 'blows where she wills'. The redemptive scope of God's redeeming love through Christ requires opposition to a complacent cultural relativism. Cultural relativism is 'the view that norms of justice are always relative to the society in which they are formed, reflecting values and practices that vary enormously from one society to another' and that 'there is no "truth" outside these various local standpoints' (Phillips 2010: 16). An obvious problem with cultural relativism is that it 'seriously overstates the incommensurability of the discourses that arise in contemporary societies, and wrongly represents the difference between cultures as a difference between hermetically sealed, internally self-consistent wholes' (Phillips 2010: 17). Religious relativism is the view that religions too are like hermetically sealed wholes, any or all or none of them proving to be ways to 'God'. I agree with Gorringe that 'the prioritization of difference . . . allows people to get away with murder, as we saw throughout the twentieth century' (Gorringe 2004: 215), and that much that passes for cultural and religious difference is patriarchy—brash, assertive, and cruel—under another name.

8.2. UNFINISHED BUSINESS IN THE CHURCHES

8.2.1. Ordination

Across the churches throughout the world it is still widely believed that the bodies of women, being in many ways inferior to those of men, preclude them from ordination to the priesthood. We have already observed how the Roman Catholic exclusion of women is mired in the one-sex theory (see section 4.2.1). The continued exclusion of women from ordination should now be seen as an act of spiritual violence against them. While all churches test vocations to priesthood and ministry in various ways, the blanket exclusion on grounds of sex is blatant discrimination, and, worse, a refusal to heed God's call to countless female candidates for ministry. Whatever rationalization and prevarication is offered for the exclusion, the reverberation around the world is clear: women are not worthy to represent Christ. Men must remain in charge.

No Orthodox church ordains women to the priesthood, although women can be ordained to the lesser order of deacons. Father Maximos Aghiorgoussis's response to the decision of the Episcopal Church of the USA to ordain women as priests in 1975 may still represent the majority opinion within Orthodox churches. He called it an 'uncharitable act perpetrated not only against the people within the Anglican communion who do not accept this decision, but also against the Churches of apostolic tradition and especially the Eastern Orthodox Church', and claimed it disregarded 'the symbolic and iconic value of male priesthood, both as representing Christ's malehood and the fatherly role of the Father in the Trinity, by allowing female persons to interchange with male persons a role which cannot be interchanged' (Aghiorgoussis 1976: 1).

In the tiny Church of England, however, where I belong, women are now bishops, and all candidates for ministry (at least in 2015 as I write) are required to subscribe to Five Guiding Principles. The first of these is that

> the Church of England is fully and unequivocally committed to all orders of ministry being open equally to all, without reference to gender, and holds that those whom it has duly ordained and appointed to office are true and lawful holders of the office which they occupy and thus deserve due respect and canonical obedience.   (Ministry Division 2014)

This represents great progress after years of tenacious struggle. However, principles 4 and 5 state:

> Since those within the Church of England who, on grounds of theological conviction, are unable to receive the ministry of women bishops or priests continue to be within the spectrum of teaching and tradition of the Anglican Communion, the Church of England remains committed to enabling them to flourish within its life and structures; and

> Pastoral and sacramental provision for the minority within the Church
> of England will be made without specifying a limit of time and in a way
> that maintains the highest possible degree of communion and contributes
> to mutual flourishing across the whole Church of England.

The first principle is undermined by what follows. Communion within the church is no longer a matter of grace; it is a matter of degree. Ordained women have to work with their opponents who believe that 'in order for people of God to fully flourish, the leadership of the church needs to be male' (Cotton 2015: 15). The document proclaims its principles as the 'basis' for 'mutual flourishing'. The traditionalists are required to accept that ordained women are 'true and lawful holders of the office which they occupy', even though they 'on grounds of theological conviction, are unable to receive the ministry of women bishops or priests'. That cannot be a comfortable or consistent position for them to occupy. This book has shown that the 'theological conviction' that is the basis of the traditionalists' objection is fallacious. Ordained women now have to strive to reach the highest possible degree of communion with Christians who cannot receive their ministry, and, as Hilary Cotton explains, this creates a 'high expectation . . . that women will take the first steps in being generous to those who dissent from their ordination. This feeds beautifully into women's conditioning to give up their needs and wants for the sake of their brothers and sisters' (Cotton 2015: 16).

What may be happening, she continues, is that the church 'has preserved a form of unity that is sick at its heart'.

8.2.2. Violence

Violence against women remains a huge problem within Christian families. That is why evangelical organizations like PASCH ('Peace and Safety in the Christian Home') have been set up in North America to attempt to mitigate it. The range of the problem is disturbingly outlined in a collection of eighteen essays in the book *Responding to Abuse in Christian Homes* (Nason-Clark et al. 2011). Some ministers, we learn, still counsel submission of wives to husbands as a divine command however much suffering is involved. There are calls to the evangelical churches to face up to truths about themselves (Tracy 2011) and a frank section on the patriarchal culture of evangelical Christianity (Sevcik et al. 2011: 176–89). Some ministers are reluctant to work with shelters for victims or with victim advocates on the ground that they are pro-feminist or pro-divorce (Owens 2011: 152). Evangelical women who are victims of domestic violence testify that they want personal safety to be ranked higher than 'preservation of the marriage relationship' (Sevcik et al. 2011: 185). As a survivor says, 'Victims of abuse don't want to hear Scriptures, they want someone to listen to them, to validate their experience' (Sevcik et al. 2011: 172). While references to pastoral ignorance, incompetence, prejudice, and biblical 'misinterpretation' abound, so does solid and heartening evidence of determination in overcoming these evils, and making churches and homes places of peace and safety. The headship doctrine has been linked with countless cases of violence against women in Australian churches. It has become 'the strong structural framework within which unquestioned abuse can occur' (Porter 2015).

But the reformers run into theological problems they cannot resolve. The hermeneutical problem will not go away. Everyone knows that the New Testament contains passages requiring women's silence, obedience, subjection, submission. But the Bible is also understood among evangelical constituencies as a divinely authorized guidebook (the Word of God) which tells Christians how to behave. Authors are clear that when these troublesome passages legitimize violence they are 'misinterpreted', but the masculinist leadership and ministry of these churches already profoundly affects the achievement of gender equality, and remains largely unable to identify one of the sources of the problem (that is, the leadership itself) that the book confronts. The attempt to reread the Bible in order to make it say what the reforming evangelicals want it to say must be regarded (sadly) as a failure. 'Mutual submission', supposedly sanctioned by Ephesians 5.21, is offered as a basis for egalitarian marriage, but any such egalitarianism is clearly contradicted in the next few verses and elsewhere. The dubious appeal to Galatians 3.28 as a biblical warrant for gender equality is also amply countermanded several times in the New Testament. There *is* hierarchical leadership in the Bible as well as 'servant leadership' (Owens 2011: 14). Submission is unconvincingly made into something else like 'adherence' or 'loyalty' (Kroeger 2011: 83). 'Headship' is defined, apparently in a liberal way (Owens 2011: 14), but which does not properly comprehend the offence that headship causes, or make allowances for its historic context. There is little or no attempt to think about the problem as a *theological and*

Christological one (as I have attempted in the previous two chapters), and there are signs of deep and commendable worry about having to defend the passages which Phyllis Tribble once called 'texts of terror'. While ancient gender understandings are perpetuated, the hermeneutical task of reconciling these texts with modern notions of two equal sexes remains daunting.

The subordination and oppression of women is a common feature across many cultures, and in Christian parts of Africa male supremacy is regularly perpetuated and legitimized by notions of male headship and centuries of power inequality between women and men. African Christian feminists angrily denounce 'the eloquent silence of the churches' (Chitando and Chirongoma 2013: 9) about sex and gender-based violence (SGBV). They speak for Christian women everywhere when they say:

> Churches can respond to SGBV effectively if they set their priorities right. For example, why do male church leaders seem to have limitless energy when it comes to debates on homosexuality, but they appear frozen when it comes to confronting SGBV? Why is it that many of them are eloquent when it comes to challenging colonialism, but are completely speechless when the issue of sexism comes up? (Chitando and Chirongoma 2013: 10)

In 2002 Churches Together in Britain and Ireland produced *Time for Action*, in which the churches are called upon to recognize the ways in which their institutional life has silenced the abused and protected the abusers (Galloway and Gamble 2002). Since then some progress has been made among the churches, but they are still reeling from the global revelations of the abuse of women, children, and otherwise vulnerable people within churches and church institutions. An Anglican report, *Protecting All God's Children*, was explicit about its theological approach to the crime of sexual and other abuse:

> From beginning (in the cry of a baby) to end (in the cry from the cross), the life and death of Jesus Christ illustrates the willingness of God to be vulnerable in order to share to the full our world of pain, poverty, suffering and death. In his earthly ministry, Jesus constantly showed himself to be compassionately on the side of the outcast, the marginalized and the stranger, reaching across social barriers with the inclusive love of God. This was wholly in line with the Hebrew Bible's priority concern for orphans and widows, its obligation to provide a voice for the voiceless, and its prophetic call for justice to 'roll down like waters,

and righteousness like an ever-flowing stream' (Amos 5.24)... The heart of Christian pastoral care is this: love for God and love for our neighbour, the social expression of which is justice in all human affairs. (Church of England 2006: 3)

Another Anglican document recommends

that each of the theological colleges and training schemes of the Anglican Communion ensure that curricula include at least one component designed to train all clergy and other ministers concerning:

a. the nature and dynamics of gendered and domestic violence;
b. how positive attitudes and behaviours among women, men, girls and boys can be encouraged and affirmed;
c. awareness of the indicators often present in situations involving trafficking of girls and boys, women and men for sexual purposes and exploitative labour;
d. the scriptural and theological basis underpinning the work of eliminating gender-based and domestic violence. (Anglican Consultative Council 2012)

The flurry of documents in many of the churches indicates a fast-growing awareness of the problem of violence and abuse within and outside the churches, especially where women's voices can speak and be heard. I worry though about several features of the new awareness, especially when it is expressed by male-only or male-dominated committees or benches of male-only bishops. While it is difficult not to applaud the resolution just cited, worries remain. Do the document's authors comprehend the breadth and depth of the problem? What is the point of training programmes if the prior patriarchal ethos is not first removed? Isn't a searching repentance for male agency in the violence a prior requirement? Is it really self-evident that there is a 'scriptural and theological basis' for combating gender-based violence? The problem here is that the scriptures do not obviously and unanimously combat gender inequality, and the theological basis for equality is sounder and more comprehensive than the regular appeal to two sexes which are allegedly 'equal' because they have each been made in the image of God.

There can be no doubt that a deeply rooted patriarchy is responsible for SGBV. But users of the concept, myself included, need to hear the warnings issued by Adriaan van Klinken's *Transforming Masculinities in African Christianity: Gender Controversies in Times of AIDS* (2013). He finds the concept 'monolithic' when superimposed upon cross-cultural

diversity; admonishes that it 'runs the risk of reinforcing and reproducing colonial and essentialist representations of African men as
dominant and oppressive'; and avers it is unclear how it 'relates to
the conceptualisation of multiple masculinities' (van Klinken 2013:
16). Fieldwork in a Roman Catholic parish in Lusaka, Zambia, leads
him to conclude that the thriving men's society there, at a parish level,
takes issue with promiscuity, alcoholism, irresponsibility in marriage
and family life, injustices to women, and low commitment to church
and faith. An 'alternative understanding of manhood is promoted'
(van Klinken 2013: 97). Catholic women support it too, because they
are aware of its power to change men's lives for the better. During
fieldwork in a second church in Lusaka, an 'Assembly of God' which
promoted 'biblical manhood', van Klinken found similar attitudes and
behaviour among the men. Not just sex before marriage, but even
kissing before marriage was found to breach the church's guidelines
for sexual conduct. Responsible fatherhood, marital fidelity, and
abstinence from alcohol are encouraged: homosexuality and domestic
and sexual violence are abjured. According to the local pastor, male
domination 'stinks in the nostrils of God' (van Klinken 2013: 115)!
Both churches commend male headship and the complementarity of
the sexes, and both of them acknowledge the potential for the abuse of
each. The experience of being 'born again' and the insistent demand
for personal holiness provide ample proof of the transformation of
(some) male lives. Manhood is thought to need a thorough remaking,
and the church tirelessly seeks to bring this about. Feminist and
liberation theologians are thus left with a paradox: men are taking
'responsibility for their own lives' and developing 'more positive
attitudes towards women' (van Klinken 2013: 198) in churches thoroughly informed by a gendered theology which African feminist and
liberationist theologians strongly oppose.

It ought to be possible to thank God for any sign of gender justice
while working out a postcolonial theology of gender that anticipates
and promotes it. The church does not yet have it. The fixation with
male transformation may merely perpetuate androcentrism. It may
leave women where they are: at home with the children, hoping soft
patriarchy will be soft on them. If male headship were renounced, it
would not need to be redefined as something else. The modern notion
of complementarity deeply lodged in Vatican teaching and in evangelical Protestantism is the real sign of colonial theology. A vision of
the full redemption of men, women, and society is needed, where 'soft

patriarchy' is but a step from blatant inequalities towards the grace
and freedom that is to be enjoyed by all God's children.

8.3. GENDER, VIOLENCE, AND PEACE

The issue of SGBV globally is reaching epidemic proportions. An
internet list of types of violence against women currently run by
Wikipedia (2015) includes acid-throwing, breast ironing, bride burning, date rape, domestic violence, dowry death, honour killing, female
genital mutilation, female infanticide, femicide, forced abortion,
forced marriage, forced pregnancy, forced prostitution, genocidal
rape or rape in war, Gishiri cutting, human trafficking, infibulation,
marital rape, murder of pregnant women, rape (on campus, in prison,
in detention), sexual slavery, sexual violence, and violence against
prostitutes. Forced sex is now believed to be the main reason for the
continuing spread of HIV/AIDS.

A recent work, *Sex and World Peace*, which places itself in international relations and security studies, makes the case for a direct
causal relationship between violence against women at the micro level
(e.g. the home) and the macro level (the state and relations between
states). The authors show that the field of international relations is
gender-blind, and that the aetiology of a long list of human disasters
overlooks violence against, or the absence of, women as a cause. The
authors suggest that 'efforts to establish greater peace and security
throughout the world might be made more effective by also addressing the violence and exploitation that occur in personal relationships
between the two halves of humanity, men and women' (Hudson et al.
2012: 5). They recount many harrowing details of male violence on
women (too many to list here). In the course of their argument they
construct intermediate hypotheses, which are intended to answer the
question, 'How did male-dominated social structures develop throughout human cultures?' (Hudson et al. 2012: 69). They then provide a
thorough technical analysis, which concludes that any future 'clash of
civilizations' will be between those 'that treat women as equal members
of the human species and civilizations that cannot or will not do so'
(Hudson et al. 2012: 117).

Here are sixteen of the intermediate hypotheses, for all of which
evidence is provided:

Male dominance hierarchies organize male protection of the group, reduce in-group male conflict, and promote gender inequality. (72)
Female adaptive choices may help perpetuate violent patriarchy. (75)
Patriarchy uses power and violence to obtain resources. (76)
Male dominance is not inevitable in human society. (78)
The environment is critically involved in shaping male violence against women. (81)
Violence is used when it is functional and its rewards are immediate and frequent. (84)
Imitation of aggression against girls and women begins early in life. (86)
Male affiliation leads men to prefer male company and to associate with other men. (87)
As males group together they develop social identities that distinguish them from females. (88)
The male in-group views females as an inferior out-group. (89)
Where male groups condone violence against women, they perceive women as enemies and thus justify violence against them. (89)
Lack of female affiliation results in women's allegiance to male authorities. (91)
Norms of peaceful social relations are possible only where male–female relations have undergone fundamental transformation. (92)
Pervasive structural violence and systematic exploitation describe the means by which gender inequality is typically maintained within a society. (93)
Structural violence is based on cultural violence—that is, open or implicit violence in private spheres. (93)
Gendered hierarchies are thus at the root of structural inequality, group identities, and patriarchal nationalism. (94)

While these hypotheses operate at different levels, to different degrees, and are context dependent, the cumulative aetiological picture of SGBV emerges strongly, and religions are all complicit, to some extent, within it. The authors prescribe top-down and bottom-up activities for change. The former include rhetorical strategies, for example the renaming of 'previous accepted practices to reflect their true reality' (so that child or involuntary marriage is renamed 'a crime against humanity', 132, 136). It includes imperatives to 'make maternal mortality, access to contraception, and education of girls top priorities for state action' (140–1), and to 'make national family law equitable' (144–5), in particular by raising the minimum age of marriage to eighteen. Bottom-up activities include heroic examples of small steps with large consequences, such as the nine-year-old girl who escaped from her abusive Yemeni marriage by hailing a taxi and petitioning a judge (161). It is important, they say, to work within 'the grain of culture' instead of opposing it outright. Redefining honour as 'promoting progress for women' (171) is a prime example. Involving men in reforming activities is highly prudent (177–80).

Having examined several hundred anti-violence programmes across the world, the authors identify three critical areas for action:

> (1) preventing violence by making violence dysfunctional through creating laws, enforcing them, and modifying the power of traditions; (2) providing new patterns of thinking and acting that are more likely to keep gender conflicts from arising...and (3) helping all people to internalize gender-equity principles that are the basis of peaceful inter-action with the other sex. (Hudson et al. 2012: 180)

The authors have proposed a novel and very important thesis. Micro-violence and macro-violence are inextricably linked. The peace of the world will be hastened by the achievement of gender equity. The tone of the book is hopeful while remaining realistic about the huge tasks that remain. The extent to which some Islamic societies underwrite violence against women is truly shocking. While reform from within (states, universities; families and individuals) is advocated, one wonders whether the dark evil of gender violence worldwide can be dissipated by these means alone. Nothing less than a profound *metanoia* is needed.

8.4. GENDER AND MISSION

The subordination of women to men worldwide remains a scandalous, even a growing, problem. The United Nations Millennium Development Goal 3 was 'Promote gender equality and empower women.' It would be difficult for Christians *not* to support the conclusion of the United Nations Commission on the Status of Women (2013: para. 35)

> that ending violence against women and girls is imperative, including for the achievement of the internationally agreed development goals, including the Millennium Development Goals, and must be a priority for the eradication of poverty, the achievement of inclusive sustainable development, peace and security, human rights, health, gender equality and the empowerment of women, sustainable and inclusive economic

growth and social cohesion, and vice versa. The Commission strongly recommends that the realization of gender equality and the empowerment of women be considered as a priority in the elaboration of the post-2015 development agenda.

And herein lies the formidable theological problem. On the one hand the churches cannot but affirm the list of benefits for women that would flow from the end of discrimination and violence against them. Each benefit is a contribution to that 'fullness of life' that Jesus came to bring, for everyone (John 10:10). On the other hand many of the churches still maintain teachings which subordinate women to men and which continue to contribute to the stubborn legacy of oppression that is responsible for the many disadvantages women continue to suffer.

It may be the case that the record of world Christianity in matters of gender compares favourably with the record of some of the non-Christian religions. Would not the Christian faith be both more in tune with the mind of Christ and more *attractive* in the late modern global context, if it were to exorcize from its teachings all tendencies that 'otherize' half of the human race and, directly or indirectly, contribute to the violence against them? Writing about same-sex marriage Robert Song has drawn attention to 'exceptionally problematic, not to say disastrous, pastoral and missiological consequences of conservative positions' (Song 2014: 79). Quite. But perhaps an even greater missiological disaster is to be found in the equivocation of the churches with regard to gender. The reservation of priesthood to men is heavy with masculinist symbolism and patriarchal exclusion. These symbolics are actually well understood by people outside the churches (and many inside) as discriminatory, as having no place in a humanistic ethic, still less a Christian one.

The Christian faith will always be a missionary faith, not just because it is commanded to be, but also because faith is a gift from God which, having been received, cannot but be shared as the Good News that it is. But the work of God's Spirit (see section 8.1) is not confined to the making of Christian disciples. The work of the Holy Spirit is also to be discerned wherever there is a struggle for gender justice, or in the overcoming of violence by peace, or in the slow realization of any or all of the items listed in the intended post-2015 development agenda just discussed. Yes, such discernment is auto-interpretation intrinsic to the church's self-understanding, yet necessary for indicating the depth and breadth of God's redeeming power, whether or not God chooses Christian agencies for raising the poor, protecting the weak, feeding the hungry, achieving peace and security, advancing human rights, and so on. *Ubi caritas et amor, Deus ibi est* (Where charity and love are, God is there).

Sexism has intensified and exacerbated the fierce debates still going on in the churches about sex and gender. This is both unsurprising yet also mostly unremarked. Gender lies at the root of the churches' problems about sex! We noted (see section 4.5) that in a one-sex continuum of pliable bodies moving from men to women and from more perfect to less perfect, many men *preferred* friendships with men irrespective of any possible intimacies they may have shared with each other (and many still do, whether or not they identify as gay). The moral suspicion directed towards men having sex with men is probably best explained by two factors: the assumption that reproduction was the sole purpose of sex; and the belief that a penetrated man allowed himself to be feminized. A theological anthropology in which sexual similarity is emphasized over difference does not treat men and women as opposite sexes, but as similar instances of their common humanity in the image of God and made new in the image of God, which is Christ. A single common humanity is far more hospitable to all minorities who find it difficult or impossible to place themselves on one side or the other of a rigid binary which is culturally imposed upon them. Heterosexism makes individuals belonging to sexual minorities ill at ease with themselves (to say the least). It is time for the well-known proclamation 'there is no longer male and female' (albeit asserted first by Paul in a different context) to be believed and practised in the churches.

We have come a long way from the one-sex and two-sex theories of earlier chapters. The analyses in Part I were not merely historical but partly aetiological, offering an *explanation* for the extent of sexism that accompanies Christian faith and is still proving difficult to shake off. I hope the conclusion of the argument of this book has by now become clear. None of the three frameworks (one sex, two unequal sexes, two equal sexes) at which we arrived at the end of chapter 3 (section 3.3.1) is finally adequate either as a theological anthropology or as an ethical practice. All of them suffer from a theological deficit. Part II of the book has attempted to inject a healthy surplus of *theological* meaning into the space the deficit provides. Whereas there is some merit in thinking of men and women as a single continuum without the accompanying degrees of perfection, and some merit in thinking of two opposite and equal sexes, the theological contribution to the solution of the problem of gender lies elsewhere.

We noted several times that from alleged facts about bodies no prescription can be derived regarding the conduct of relations of gender. Secular narratives are by no means problem free (as the overinvestment in two sexes and the impasse in discourses about human rights indicate). Theology can enter this intellectual hiatus with prescriptions of its own. An alternative to each of the three frameworks has been suggested. This alternative draws on the rich resources of belief in God as Trinity, together with the Christian conviction that through the Incarnate Christ, God has redeemed humanity from the web of structural and corporate sin, and in particular from unjust gendered relationships. I described redemption as a participation in the fourfold reality—a new kingdom, a new creation, a new body, and a new humanity.

The invitation to share in the fourfold reality is of course more than intellectual assent to an alternative world view tinged with theological orthodoxy. Participation in redemption requires intellectual, existential, and practical commitment. Intellectually, attention must be given to the theology of gender in universities, theological societies, theological colleges, and training courses—attention which far exceeds a lecture or two on domestic violence. The dismantling of male hierarchies in the ancient churches has scarcely begun. Lame efforts at shoring up male power must continue to be countered. They include idolatrous appeals to a male God who is better imaged by and among men; to a male Jesus whose patriarchal accretions disqualify him from being represented by a woman; to an unchanging tradition which everyone knows has changed in innumerable ways; or to a brittle reading of the Bible's 'texts of terror' which are lacking in any sense of justice, context, or compassion. Existentially it requires an examination of congregational, liturgical, and family life. Practically it requires Christians globally to engage in the 'three critical areas for action' just described.

The book ends with a statement published by the male delegates to the World Council of Churches Women's and Men's Pre-Assembly in Busan, Korea, in 2013. Yes, the statement is about, and for, men. But it speaks about the radical change of heart and mind (in the theological lexicon the appropriate term is 'repentance') required for gender justice to be achieved within and beyond the churches. If this book contributes to the 'rethinking of theologies' that the statement advocates, the considerable effort in writing it will have proved worthwhile.

We the men in the first WCC Women's and Men's Pre-assembly express our immense gratitude to women who have enabled us to understand the pain and injustice of patriarchy and gender inequality. We have experienced transformation in our lives, by the grace of the God of Life, which has begun to open our hearts and minds to a shared struggle for gender justice. Yet, we are painfully aware that we men still have a long way to go on our journey toward a true community of women and men in the churches and in society at large.

The Spirit beckons us into a just community of equals. The Spirit is speaking to the churches and is calling us to listen. Today, as men committed to gender justice and a life affirming community of women and men, we listen and respond to the Spirit's call. We joyfully celebrate the advances of the women's movement, we appreciate the participation of men who have journeyed with the women and look forward to a full community of humans together.

As men, we are aware that almost every culture around the world accrues privilege to us. We acknowledge that this unequal allocation of privilege deprives many from living life in its fullness.

Unjust gender relations have not only disempowered women but also distorted us as men and limited the way we, as men, relate to others, nature and ourselves. Patriarchy as a social structure affects both women and men, it causes pain to both men and women.

Men have been the perpetrators of overt and covert violence against both women, children and other men. Many men continue to idolize violence at home, on the street or within communities. Militarization and the glorification of violence create a culture that endangers all of life. We acknowledge that we are socialized into aggression and have used culture, ideology, religion and theology to justify our violence.

There are many forms and practices of masculinity and we have not honoured the diversity of men. We express our solidarity with men who have been outcast because of their sexual orientation and suffer from the violence of homophobia.

Men have been absent from movements for gender justice within and outside of the church, even when we have claimed to be struggling for justice.

We pledge to stand in solidarity with movements for gender justice, by rethinking our theologies and our liturgies to be inclusive of gender concerns and to speak for justice. We will continue to reevaluate ourselves and our own understanding of masculinity. We heard the pain of women in the preassembly who find their gifts and calling to leadership rejected by patriarchal attitudes in the churches. We recognized the divided denominational views about ordination but still believe justice calls for the equal participation of women and men in the leadership of the churches.

We call on all the Churches to dare to work together towards just gender relations, promoting the life of peace and justice this will bring. Together as men and women we will play our part in being churches that are places of solidarity, affirmation and welcome of a new society of justice and life for all.   (World Council of Churches 2013)

Bibliography

Adams, Marilyn McCord (2015). 'Duns Scotus on the Female Gender'. In Adrian Thatcher (ed.), *The Oxford Handbook of Theology, Sexuality, and Gender*. Oxford: Oxford University Press, 255–70.

Aeschylus (458 BCE). *Eumenides*. Trans. E. D. A. Morshead (n/d). Internet Classics Archive. http://classics.mit.edu/Aeschylus/eumendides.html. Accessed 20 Aug. 2015.

Aghiorgoussis, Maximos (1976). *Women Priests?* Brookline, MA: Holy Cross Press.

Alcoff, Linda (2006). *Visible Identities: Race, Gender and the Self*. Oxford: Oxford University Press.

Alexander, Loveday (2013). 'Women as Leaders in the New Testament'. *Modern Believing*, 53.1, 14–22.

Allen, Diogenes and Eric O. Springsted (2007). *Philosophy for Understanding Theology*, 2nd edition. Louisville, KY: Westminster John Knox Press.

Alternative Service Book (1980). http://oremus.org/liturgy/asb/index.html. Accessed 20 Aug. 2015.

Amy-Chinn, Dee (2009). 'Is Queer Biology a Useful Tool for Queer Theology?', *Theology & Sexuality*, 15.1, 49–63.

Anderson, Elizabeth (2012). 'Equality'. In David Estlund (ed.), *The Oxford Handbook of Political Philosophy*. Oxford: Oxford University Press, 40–57.

Anderson, Pamela Sue (2012). *Re-visioning Gender in Philosophy of Religion: Reason, Love and Epistemic Locatedness*. Farnham, UK and Burlington, USA: Ashgate.

Anglican Consultative Council (2012). 'Resolution 15.07: Gender-based and Domestic Violence'. http://www.anglicancommunion.org/structures/instruments-of-communion/acc/acc-15/resolutions.aspx#s7. Accessed 20 Aug. 2015.

Aquinas (1889). *Textum Leoninum Romae 1889 editum*. http://www.corpusthomisticum.org/sth1090.html. Accessed 20 Aug. 2015.

Aquinas (1920). Trans. Fathers of the English Dominican Province. *The Summa Theologica of St. Thomas Aquinas*. http://www.newadvent.org/summa/. Accessed 20 Aug. 2015.

Aristotle (2013). *On the Generation of Animals*. Trans. Arthur Platt (n/d, updated 2013). eBook. University of Adelaide. Available at https://ebooks.adelaide.edu.au/a/aristotle/generation/book2.html. The licence to reproduce is at http://creativecommons.org/licenses/by-nc-sa/3.0/au/. Accessed 20 Aug. 2015.

Aristotle (n/d). *Politics*, trans. Benjamin Jowett. Internet Classics Archive. http://classics.mit.edu/Aristotle/politics.1.one.html. Accessed 20 Aug. 2015.

Armstrong, D. M. (1978). *Nominalism and Realism*. Cambridge: Cambridge University Press.

Augustine (1887). *De Trinitate*. http://www.newadvent.org/fathers/1301. htm. Accessed 20 Aug. 2015.

Balch, David L., Everett Ferguson, and Wayne A. Meeks (eds) (1990). *Greeks, Romans and Christians: Essays in Honour of Abraham J. Malherbe*. Minneapolis, MN: Fortress Press.

Balthasar, Hans Urs von (1988). 'The Marian Principle'. *Communio: International Catholic Review*, 15, 122–30.

Balthasar, Hans Urs von (1993). *Theo-Drama: Dramatis Personae*, vol. 2: *Theological Dramatic Theory*. San Francisco: Ignatius Press.

Barth, Karl (1958). *Church Dogmatics* III.1 (trans. J. W. Edwards et al.). Edinburgh: T. & T. Clark.

Bauckham, Richard (2002). *Gospel Women: Studies of the Named Women in the Gospels*. Grand Rapids, MI and Cambridge, UK: Eerdmans.

Beattie, Tina (2006). *New Catholic Feminism: Theology and Theory*. London and New York: Routledge.

Beattie, Tina (2015). 'The Theological Study of Gender'. In Adrian Thatcher (ed.), *The Oxford Handbook of Theology, Sexuality, and Gender*. Oxford: Oxford University Press, 32–52.

Bem, S. L. (1974). 'The Measurement of Psychological Androgyny'. *Journal of Consulting & Clinical Psychology*, 42, 155–62.

Berger, John (1972). *Ways of Seeing*. London: BBC Books.

Boberts, Robert A. and David Brakke (eds) (2002). *Reading in Christian Communities: Essays on Interpretation in the Early Church*. Notre Dame, IN: University of Notre Dame Press.

Book of Common Prayer (1662). http://www.eskimo.com/~lhowell/bcp1662/. Accessed 20 Aug. 2015.

Borsch, Frederick H. (1990). 'Jesus and Women Exemplars'. *Anglican Theological Review*, 11 March, Supplement Series, 29–40.

Boylan, Michael (1984). 'The Galenic and Hippocratic Challenges to Aristotle's Conception Theory'. *Journal of the History of Biology*, 17.1 (Spring), 83–112.

Bradley, Harriet (2007). *Gender*. Cambridge: Polity Press.

Brooke, Helkiah (1615). *Mikrokosmographia*. http://commons.wikimedia. org/wiki/File:Microcosmographia,_Crooke,_1615_-_0003.jpg. Accessed 20 Aug. 2015.

Brown, Peter (1988). *The Body and Society: Men, Women and Sexual Renunciation in Early Christianity*. London and Boston: Faber & Faber.

Bruce, F. F. (1984). 'Colossian Problems, Part 2: The "Christ Hymn" of Colossians 1:15–20'. *Bibliotheca Sacra*, 141, no. 562, April–June, 99–111.

Burrus, Virginia and Catherine Keller (eds) (2006). *Towards a Theology of Eros: Transfiguring Passion at the Limits of Discipline.* New York: Fordham University Press.

Cadden, Joan (1995). *The Meanings of Sex Difference in the Middle Ages: Medicine, Science, and Culture.* Cambridge: Cambridge University Press.

Cahill, Lisa Sowle (2011). 'Gender and Christian Ethics'. In Robin Gill (ed.), *The Cambridge Companion to Christian Ethics,* 2nd edition. Cambridge: Cambridge University Press, 103–16.

Catechism of the Catholic Church (1994). London: Geoffrey Chapman.

Cheng, Patrick (2015). 'Contributions from Queer Theory'. In Adrian Thatcher (ed.), *The Oxford Handbook of Theology, Sexuality, and Gender.* Oxford: Oxford University Press, 153–69.

Chitando, Ezra and Sophia Chirongoma (eds) (2013). *Justice Not Silence: Churches Facing Sexual and Gender-Based Violence.* Stellenbosch: EFSA.

Church of England (2006). *Promoting a Safe Church Policy for Safeguarding Adults in the Church of England.* London: Church House Publishing.

Clarke, Desmond M. and Catherine Wilson (eds) (2011). *The Oxford Handbook of Philosophy in Early Modern Europe.* Oxford: Oxford University Press.

Coakley, Sarah (2013). *God, Sexuality and the Self.* Cambridge: Cambridge University Press.

Colombo Realdo (1559 [1969]). *De re anatomica.* Venice: Nicolae Beuilacquae [Facsimile Culture et Civilisation, Bruxelles, 1969].

Common Worship (2000a). http://www.churchofengland.org/prayer-worship/worship/texts/principal-services/word/mornevesun.aspx. Accessed 20 Aug 2015.

Common Worship (2000b). https://www.churchofengland.org/prayer-worship/worship/texts/canticles/canticlesmv3.aspx. Accessed 20 Aug. 2015.

Common Worship (2000c). Holy Baptism text. Pastoral Introduction. https://www.churchofengland.org/prayer-worship/worship/texts/christian-initiation/baptism-and-confirmation/holy-baptism.aspx. Accessed 20 Aug. 2015.

Common Worship (2000d). Holy Communion. https://www.churchofengland.org/prayer-worship/worship/texts/principal-services/holy-communion/order2contemp.aspx. Accessed 20 Aug. 2015

Congregation for the Doctrine of the Faith (1976). *Inter Insigniores: On the Question of Admission of Women to the Ministerial Priesthood.* http://www.vatican.va/roman_curia/congregations/cfaith/documents/rc_con_cfaith_doc_19761015_inter-insigniores_en.html. Accessed 20 Aug. 2015.

Connell, R.W. (1987). *Gender and Power.* Stanford: Stanford University Press.

Connell, Raewyn and Rebecca Pearse (2015). *Gender in World Perspective,* 3rd edition. Cambridge: Polity Press.

Conway, Colleen (2015). 'The Construction of Gender in the New Testament'. In Adrian Thatcher (ed.), *The Oxford Handbook of Theology, Sexuality, and Gender*. Oxford: Oxford University Press, 222–38.

Conway, Colleen M. (2008). *Behold the Man: Jesus and Greco-Roman Masculinity*. Oxford: Oxford University Press.

Cornwall, Susannah (2010). *Sex and Uncertainty in the Body of Christ: Intersex Conditions and Christian Theology*. London: Equinox.

Cornwall, Susannah (2014). 'Sex Otherwise: Intersex, Christology, and the Maleness of Jesus'. *Journal of Feminist Studies in Religion*, 30.2, 23–39.

Cornwall, Susannah (2015). 'Intersex and Transgender People'. In Adrian Thatcher (ed.), *The Oxford Handbook of Theology, Sexuality, and Gender*. Oxford: Oxford University Press, 657–75.

Cotton, Hilary (2015). 'What Do We Need in Order to Flourish?' *Outlook*, 32, Summer.

Crammer, Corinne (2004). 'One Sex or Two? Balthasar's Theology of the Sexes'. In Edward T. Oakes, S. J. and David Moss (eds), *The Cambridge Companion to Hans Urs von Balthasar*. Cambridge: Cambridge University Press, 93–112.

Crawford, Katherine (2007). *European Sexualities, 1400–1800*. Cambridge: Cambridge University Press, 2007.

Croft, Steven and Paula Gooder (eds) (2013). *Women and Men in Scripture and the Church: A Guide to the Key Issues*. Norwich: Canterbury Press.

D'Angelo, Mary Rose (2002). 'Gender Refusers in the Early Christian Mission: Gal. 3:28 as an Interpretation of Gen. 1:27b'. In Robert A. Boberts and David Brakke (eds), *Reading in Christian Communities: Essays on Interpretation in the Early Church*. Notre Dame, IN: University of Notre Dame Press, 149–73.

D'Costa, Gavin (ed.) (1990). *Christian Uniqueness Reconsidered: The Myth of a Pluralistic Theology of Religions*. Maryknoll, NY: Orbis.

D'Costa, Gavin (2000a). *The Meeting of Religions and the Trinity*. Edinburgh: T & T Clark.

D'Costa, Gavin (2000b). *Sexing the Trinity: Gender, Culture and the Divine*. London: SCM Press.

Dabhoiwala, Faramerz (2013). *The Origins of Sex: A History of the First Sexual Revolution*. London: Penguin Books.

Dinter, Paul E. (1994). 'Christ's Body as Male and Female'. *Cross Currents*, 44.3, 390–9.

Dormor, Duncan (2013). 'Rebellious Bodies and Disordered Desires: The Challenge of Transsexuality to Influential Christian Theologies of Creation'. In Niamh Reilly and Stacey Scrivers (eds), *Religion, Gender and the Public Sphere*. New York and London: Routledge, 108–19.

Du Laurens, André (1639). *Les Oeuvres de Me André du Laurens*, ed. G. Sauvageon. Paris.

Dunning, Benjamin H. (2011). *Specters of Paul: Sexual Difference in Early Christian Thought*. Philadelphia, PA: University of Pennsylvania Press.

Elliott, Dyan (1999). *Fallen Bodies: Pollution, Sexuality, and Demonology in the Middle Ages*. Philadelphia, PA: Pennsylvania Press.

Ellison, Marvin (2012). *Making Love Just: Sexual Ethics for Perplexing Times*. Minneapolis, MN: Fortress Press.

Farley, Margaret (2006). *Just Love: A Framework for Christian Sexual Ethics*. New York and London: Continuum.

Fausto-Sterling, Anne (2000). *Sexing the Body: Gender Politics and the Construction of Sexuality*. New York: Basic Books.

Flew, Antony (1955). 'Theology and Falsification'. In Antony Flew and Alasdair MacIntyre (eds), *New Essays in Philosophical Theology*. London: SCM, 96–9.

Fulkerson, Mary McClintock and Sheila Briggs (eds) (2012). *The Oxford Handbook of Feminist Theology*. Oxford: Oxford University Press.

Furlong, Monica (ed.) (1998). *Act of Synod, Act of Folly?* London: SCM Press.

Galloway, Kathy and David Gamble (2002). *Time for Action*. London: CTBI.

Gorringe, T. J. (2004). *Furthering Humanity: A Theology of Culture*. Aldershot: Ashgate.

Green, Joel B. (ed.) (2010). *Hearing the New Testament: Strategies for Interpretation*, 2nd edition. Grand Rapids, MI and Cambridge, UK: Eerdmans.

Grenz, Stanley J. (1998). 'Theological Foundations for Male–Female Relationships'. *Journal of the Evangelical Theological Society*, 41.4, 615–30.

Grenz, Stanley J. (2001). *The Social God and the Relational Self: A Trinitarian Theology of the Imago Dei*. Louisville, KY: Westminster John Knox Press.

Harrison, Nonna Verna (1998). 'The Maleness of Christ', *St Vladimir's Theological Quarterly*, 42.2, 111–51.

Harrison, Nonna Verna (2002). 'Human Community as an Image of the Holy Trinity'. *St Vladimir's Theological Quarterly*, 46.4, 347–64.

Harrison, Nonna Verna (2011). 'The Trinity and Feminism'. In Gilles Emery and Matthew Levering (eds), *The Oxford Handbook of the Trinity*. Oxford: Oxford University Press, 519–29.

Harvey, Karen (2002). 'The Century of Sex? Gender, Bodies, and Sexuality in the Long Eighteenth Century'. *Historical Journal*, 45.4, 899–916.

Harvey, Karen (2004). *Reading Sex in the Eighteenth Century: Bodies and Gender in English Erotic Culture*. Cambridge: Cambridge University Press.

Hawkesworth, Mary (2013). 'Sex, Gender, and Sexuality: From Naturalized Presumption to Analytical Categories'. In Georgina Waylen et al. (eds), *The Oxford Handbook of Gender and Politics*. Oxford: Oxford University Press, 31–56.

Hegel, Georg Wilhelm Friedrich (1807 [1910]). *Phenomenology of Mind*. Trans. J. B. Baillie. London: S. Sonnenschein and New York: Macmillan. https://archive.org/details/phenomenologyofm02hege. Accessed 20 Aug. 2015.

Henderson, Suzanne Watts (2006). 'Taking Liberties with the Text: The Colossians Household Code as Hermeneutical Paradigm'. *Interpretation*, 60.4, 420–32.

Herdt, Gilbert (ed.) (1996). *Third Sex, Third Gender: Beyond Sexual Dimorphism in Culture and History*. New York: Zone Books.

Hillman, David and Mazzio Carla (eds) (1997). *The Body in Parts: Fantasies of Corporeality in Early Modern Europe*. London: Routledge.

Hines, Melissa (2004). *Brain Gender*. Oxford: Oxford University Press.

Hirschmann, Nancy J. (2014). 'Hobbes on the Family'. in AI. P. Martinich and Kinch Hoekstra (eds) (2014). *The Oxford Handbook of Hobbes*. Oxford: Oxford University Press. http://www.oxfordhandbooks.com/view/10.1093/oxfordhb/9780199791941.001.0001/oxfordhb-9780199791941-e-011?rskey=YD24YW&result-1. Accessed 3 Jan. 2016.

Hitchcock, Tim (1996). 'Redefining Sex in Eighteenth-Century England'. *History Workshop Journal*, 41 (Spring), 72–90.

Holmes, Brooke (2012). *Gender: Antiquity and its Legacy*. Oxford: Oxford University Press.

House of Bishops (1991). *Issues in Human Sexuality: A Statement by the House of Bishops*. London: Church House Publishing.

House of Bishops' Group on *Issues in Human Sexuality* (2003). *Some Issues in Human Sexuality: A Guide to the Debate*. London: Church House Publishing.

Hudson, Valerie M., Bonnie Ballif-Spanvill, Mary Caprioli, and Chad F. Emmett (2012). *Sex and World Peace*. New York: Columbia University Press.

Hunt, Lynn (2002). 'Against Presentism'. American Historical Association. http://www.historians.org/publications-and-directories/perspectives-on-history/may-2002/against-presentism. Accessed 20 Aug. 2015.

Illig, Jennifer (2007). 'Feminist Christology: Remembering Jesus, Re-envisioning Christ'. *Journal of Theta Alpha Kappa*, 31(1), 33–51.

Irshai, Ronit (2015). 'Judaism'. In Adrian Thatcher (ed.), *The Oxford Handbook of Theology, Sexuality, and Gender*. Oxford: Oxford University Press, 413–31.

Ivarsson, F. (2006). 'Vice Lists and Deviant Masculinity: The Rhetorical Function of 1 Corinthians 5:10–11 and 6:9–10'. In T. Penner and C. Vander Stichele (eds), *Mapping Gender in Ancient Religious Discourses*. Leiden and Boston: Brill, 163–84.

Jantzen, Grace M. (1998). *Becoming Divine: Towards a Feminist Philosophy of Religion*. Manchester: Manchester University Press.

Jay, Nancy (1992). *Throughout Your Generations Forever*. Chicago: University of Chicago Press.

Johnson, David H. (1992). 'The Image of God in Colossians'. *Didaskalia*, 3.2, April, 9–15.

Johnson, Jay Emerson (2011). 'Sodomy and Gendered Love: Reading Genesis 19 in the Anglican Communion'. In Michael Lieb et al. (eds), *The Oxford*

Handbook of the Reception History of the Bible. Oxford: Oxford University Press, 414–32.

Jones, Timothy Willem (2013). *Sexual Politics in the Church of England, 1857–1957*. Oxford: Oxford University Press.

Kant, Immanuel (1763 [1978]). *Observations on the Feeling of the Beautiful and Sublime*. Trans. John T. Goldthwait. Excerpt in Mary Mahowald (ed.), *Philosophy of Woman: Classical to Current Concepts*. Indianapolis, IN: Hackett, 116–27.

Karras, Ruth Mazo (2005). *Sexuality in Medieval Europe: Doing unto Others*. New York and London: Routledge.

Karras, Ruth Mazo (2015). 'Reproducing Medieval Christianity'. In Adrian Thatcher (ed.), *The Oxford Handbook of Theology, Sexuality, and Gender*. Oxford: Oxford University Press, 271–86.

Kartzow, Marianne Bjelland (2010). '"Asking the Other Question": An Intersectional Approach to Galatians 3:28 and the Colossian Household Codes'. *Biblical Interpretation*, 18/4–5, 364–89.

Katz, Jonathan Ned (2007). *The Invention of Heterosexuality*. Chicago and London: University of Chicago Press.

Kelly, J. N. D. (1965). *Early Christian Doctrines*. London: A. & C. Black.

Kessler, Suzanne and Wendy McKenna (1978). *Gender: An Ethnomethodological Approach*. New York: John Wiley.

King, Helen (1994). *Hippocrates' Woman: Reading the Female Body*. London and New York: Routledge.

King, Helen (2013). *The One-Sex Body on Trial: The Classical and Early Modern Evidence*. Farnham, UK and Burlington, USA: Ashgate.

Kinsey, Alfred et. al. (1948). *Sexual Behavior in the Human Male*. Philadelphia, PA: W. B. Saunders.

Kinsey, Alfred, et. al. (1953). *Sexual Behavior in the Human Female*. Philadelphia, PA: W. B. Saunders.

Knust, Jennifer (2011). *Unprotected Texts: The Bible's Surprising Contradictions about Sex and Desire*. New York: HarperOne.

Kraemer, Ross Shepard (2011). *Unreliable Witnesses: Religion, Gender, and History in the Greco-Roman Mediterranean*. Oxford: Oxford University Press.

Kraus, Norman (2012). *On Being Human: Sexual Orientation and the Image of God*. Eugene, OR: Cascade Books.

Kroeger, Catherine Clark (2011). '"Peace upon This House": Issues of Submission and Substance'. In Nancy Nason-Clark et al. (eds), *Responding to Abuse in Christian Homes: A Challenge to Churches and their Leaders*. Eugene, OR: Wipf & Stock, 76–86.

Kuefler, Mathew (2001). *The Manly Eunuch: Masculinity, Gender Ambiguity, and Christian Ideology in Late Antiquity*. Chicago and London: University of Chicago Press.

Kuefler, Mathew (2015). 'Desire and the Body in the Patristic Period'. In Adrian Thatcher (ed.), *The Oxford Handbook of Theology, Sexuality, and Gender*. Oxford: Oxford University Press, 241–54.

Lambeth Conference (1930). Resolution 15. http://www.anglicancommunion. org/media/127734/1930.pdf?language=English. Accessed 20 Nov. 2015.

Laqueur, Thomas (1986). 'Orgasm, Generation, and the Politics of Reproductive Biology'. *Representations*, 14, 1–41.

Laqueur, Thomas (1990). *Making Sex: Body and Gender from the Greeks to Freud*. Cambridge, MA and London: Harvard University Press.

Laqueur, Thomas (2003). 'Sex in the Flesh'. *Isis*, 94.2, 300–6.

Laqueur, Thomas (2012). 'The Rise of Sex in the Eighteenth Century: Historical Context and Historiographical Implications'. *Signs*, 37.4, 802–12.

Laqueur, Thomas W. (2000). 'Amor Veneris, vel Dulcedo Appeletur'. In Londa Schiebinger (ed.), *Feminism and the Body*. Oxford: Oxford University Press, 58–86.

Larsen, Timothy and Daniel J. Treier (eds) (2007). *The Cambridge Companion to Evangelical Theology*. Cambridge: Cambridge University Press.

Lawler, Michael and Todd Salzman (2015). 'People Beginning Sexual Experience'. In Adrian Thatcher (ed.), *The Oxford Handbook of Theology, Sexuality, and Gender*. Oxford: Oxford University Press, 557–72.

Leaper, Campbell (1995). 'The Use of Masculine and Feminine to Describe Women's and Men's Behavior'. *Journal of Social Psychology*, 135, 359–69.

Leaper, Campbell (2014). 'Gender Similarities and Differences in Language'. In Thomas M. Holtgraves (ed.), *The Oxford Handbook of Language and Social Psychology*. Oxford: Oxford University Press, 63–81.

Levine, Amy-Jill (1994). 'Second Temple Judaism, Jesus, and Women: Yeast of Eden'. *Biblical Interpretation* 2/1, 8–33.

Levinson, J. (2000). 'Cultural Androgyny in Rabbinic Literature'. In S. Kottek and M. Horstmanshoff (eds), *From Athens to Jerusalem: Medicine in Hellenized and Jewish Lore and Early Christian Literature*. Rotterdam: Erasmus, 119–40.

Lieb, Michael, Emma Mason, Jonathan Roberts, and Christopher Rowland (eds) (2011). *The Oxford Handbook of the Reception History of the Bible*. Oxford: Oxford University Press.

Loader, William (2010). *Sexuality in the New Testament: Understanding the Key Texts*. London: SPCK.

Loader, William (2013). *Making Sense of Sex: Attitudes towards Sexuality in Early Jewish and Christian Literature*. Grand Rapids, MI and Cambridge, UK: Eerdmans.

Lott, B. (1981). 'A Feminist Critique of Androgyny: Toward the Elimination of Gender Attributions for Learned Behavior'. In C. Mayo and N. M. Henley (eds), *Gender and Nonverbal Behavior*. New York: Springer-Verlag, 171–80.

Loughlin, Gerard (ed.) (2007). *Queer Theology: Rethinking the Western Body*. Malden, MA and Oxford: Blackwell Publishing.

Loughlin, Gerard (2015). 'Gay Affections'. In Adrian Thatcher (ed.), *The Oxford Handbook of Theology, Sexuality, and Gender*. Oxford: Oxford University Press, 608–23.

Ludlow, Morwenna (2007). *Gregory of Nyssa: Ancient and (Post-) Modern*. Oxford: Oxford University Press.

Luther, Martin (1958). *Lectures on Genesis*, trans. Jaroslav Pelikan. Saint Louis, MI: Concordia.

McClive, Cathy (n/d). 'The Body and Gender in Medical Writings c.1700–1830'. In *Defining Gender: 1450–1910*, 1–11. E-resource (restricted access).

Maccoby, Eleanor and Carol Jacklin (1974). *The Psychology of Sex Differences*. Stanford, CA: Stanford University Press.

MacCulloch, Diarmaid (2004). *Reformation: Europe's House Divided, 1490–1700*. London: Penguin Books.

McDermott, Gerald R. (ed.) (2010). *The Oxford Handbook of Evangelical Theology*. Oxford: Oxford University Press.

McKeon, Michael (2012). 'The Seventeenth- and Eighteenth-Century Sexuality Hypothesis'. *Signs*, 37.4, 791–801.

Mackey, James (1987). *Modern Theology: A Sense of Direction*. Oxford and New York: Oxford University Press.

Mahowald, Mary (ed.) (1978). *Philosophy of Woman: Classical to Current Concepts*. Indianapolis, IN: Hackett.

Malabou, Catherine (2011). *Changing Difference*. Cambridge: Polity Press.

Martin, Dale B. (2006). *Sex and the Single Savior*. Louisville, KY: Westminster John Knox Press.

Mauriceau, François (1683 [1st edition 1668]). *The Diseases of Women with Child, and in Child-Bed*, 2nd edition [translated and enlarged by Hugh Chamberlen]. London: John Darby.

Meeks, Wayne A. (1974). 'The Image of the Androgyne: Some Uses of a Symbol in Earliest Christianity'. *History of Religions*, 13.3, 165–208.

Messer, Neil (2015). 'Contributions from Biology'. In Adrian Thatcher (ed.), *The Oxford Handbook of Theology, Sexuality, and Gender*. Oxford: Oxford University Press, 69–87.

Milbank, John (1990). *Theology and Social Theory*. London: SCM Press.

Mill, John Stuart (1869). *The Subjection of Women*. London: Longmans.

Mill, John Stuart (1879). *Utilitarianism*. London: Longmans, Green, and Co. https://www.gutenberg.org/files/11224/11224-h/11224-h.htm#CHAPTER_II. Accessed 20 Aug. 2015.

Ministry Division [of the Church of England] (2014). 'The Five Guiding Principles: Guidance for Candidates for Ordination in the Church of England'. https://www.google.co.uk/#q=five+guiding+principles+church+of+england. Accessed 20 Aug. 2015.

Moltmann-Wendell, Elisabeth (1983). *The Women around Jesus*. New York: Crossroad.

Moore, Stephen D. and Janice Capel Anderson (eds) (2003). *New Testament Masculinities*. Atlanta, GA: Society of Biblical Literature.

Moss, David and Lucy Gardner (1998). 'Difference: The Immaculate Concept? The Laws of Sexual Difference in the Theology of Hans Urs von Balthasar'. *Modern Theology*, 14, 377–402.

Moule, C. F. D. (1962). *The Epistles of Paul the Apostle to the Colossians and to Philemon*. Cambridge: Cambridge University Press.

Nason-Clark, Nancy, Catherine Clark-Kroeger, and Barbara Fisher-Townsend (eds) (2011). *Responding to Abuse in Christian Homes: A Challenge to Churches and their Leaders*. Eugene, OR: Wipf & Stock.

Newsom, Carol Ann, Sharon H. Ringe, and Jacqueline E. Lapsley (eds) (1998). *Women's Bible Commentary*. Louisville, KY: Westminster John Knox Press.

Nielsen, Cynthia R. and Michael Barnes Norton (2015). 'Contributions from Philosophy'. In Adrian Thatcher (ed.), *The Oxford Handbook of Theology, Sexuality, and Gender*. Oxford: Oxford University Press, 137–52.

Nordling, Cherith Fee (2010). 'Gender'. In Gerald R. McDermott (ed.), *The Oxford Handbook of Evangelical Theology*. Oxford: Oxford University Press, 499–512.

Norris, R. A., Jr (1984). 'The Ordination of Women and the "Maleness" of the Christ'. In Monica Furlong (ed.), *Feminine in the Church*. London: SPCK, 71–85.

Oakes, Edward T., SJ and David Moss (eds) (2004). *The Cambridge Companion to Hans Urs von Balthasar*. Cambridge: Cambridge University Press.

O'Neill, Eileen (2011). 'The Equality of Men and Women'. In Desmond M. Clarke and Catherine Wilson (eds), *The Oxford Handbook of Philosophy in Early Modern Europe*. Oxford: Oxford University Press. Online, http://www.oxfordhandbooks.com/view/10.1093/oxfordhb/9780199556137.001.0001/oxfordhb-9780199556137-e-22?rskey=5qnKtp&result=1. Accessed 20 Aug. 2015.

Osborne, Grant R. (1989). 'Women in Jesus' Ministry'. *Westminster Theological Journal*, 51/2, 259–91.

Owens, Julie A. (2011). 'Notes from the Shelter'. In Nancy Nason-Clark et al. (eds), *Responding to Abuse in Christian Homes: A Challenge to Churches and their Leaders*. Eugene, OR: Wipf & Stock, 147–57.

Oxford Dictionaries Pro. http://english.oxforddictionaries.com. Accessed 20 Aug. 2015.

Park, Katharine (1997). 'The Rediscovery of the Clitoris'. In David Hillman and Mazzio Carla (eds), *The Body in Parts: Fantasies of Corporeality in Early Modern Europe*. London: Routledge, 170–93.

Park, Katharine and Robert A. Nye (1991). '"Destiny is Anatomy": Review of Thomas Laqueur, *Making Sex*'. *New Republic*, 18 Feb., 53–7.

Parsons, Stephen (2014). 'Understanding the Mind of the Conservative Christian: The Work of George Lakoff'. *Modern Believing*, 55.3, 271–82.

Penner, T. and C. Vander Stichele (eds) (2006). *Mapping Gender in Ancient Religious Discourses*. Leiden and Boston: Brill.

Phillips, Anne (2010). *Gender and Culture*. Cambridge, UK and Malden, MA: Polity Press.

Phillips, K. M. and B. Reay (eds) (2002). *Sexualities in History: A Reader*. New York: Psychology Press.

Phillips, Kim M. and Barry Reay (2011). *Sex before Sexuality: A Premodern History*. Cambridge: Polity Press.

Plaskow, Judith (1991). *Standing Again at Sinai: Judaism from a Feminist Perspective*. San Francisco, HarperSanFrancisco.

Pope Francis (2013). 'Address to Meeting on "Mulieris Dignitatem"'. In *Zenit: The World Seen from Rome*. http://www.zenit.org/en/articles/francis-address-to-meeting-on-mulieris-dignitatem, 14 Oct. Accessed 20 Aug. 2015.

Pope John Paul II (1981). *Familiaris consortio: On the Role of the Christian Family in the Modern World*. http://www.vatican.va/holy_father/john_paul_ii/apost_exhortations/documents/hf_jp-ii_exh_19811122_familiaris-consortio_en.html. Accessed 20 Aug. 2015.

Pope John Paul II (1988). *Mulieris dignitatem*. http://w2.vatican.va/content/john-paul-ii/en/apost_letters/1988/documents/hf_jp-ii_apl_19880815_mulieris-dignitatem.html. Accessed 17 Nov. 2015.

Pope John Paul II (1994). *Apostolic Letter, Ordinatio Sacerdotalis, to the Bishops of the Catholic Church on Reserving Priestly Ordination to Men Alone*. http://www.vatican.va/holy_father/john_paul_ii/apost_letters/1994/documents/hf_jp-ii_apl_19940522_ordinatio-sacerdotalis_en.html. Accessed 20 Aug. 2015.

Pope Leo XII (1880). *Arcanum divinae sapientiae*. http://w2.vatican.va/content/leo-xiii/en/encyclicals/documents/hf_l-xiii_enc_10021880_arcanum.html10%20Febr.%201880. Accessed 17 Nov. 2015.

Pope Pius XI (1930). *Casti connubii*. http://w2.vatican.va/content/pius-xi/en/encyclicals/documents/hf_p-xi_enc_31121930_casti-connubii.html. Accessed 17 Nov. 2015.

Porter, Muriel (2015). 'Doctrine of Headship Linked to Cases of Domestic Violence'. *Church Times*, 6 March.

Poullain de la Barre, François (1673). Trans. A. L. (1677). *The Woman as Good as the Man, or The Equallity of Both Sexes*. LSE Digital Library. http://digital.library.lse.ac.uk/objects/lse:zil223rij. Accessed 20 Aug. 2015.

Preus, Anthony (1977). 'Galen's Criticism of Aristotle's Conception Theory'. *Journal of the History of Biology*, 10/1 (Spring), 65–85.

Proposed Book of Common Prayer (1928). http://justus.anglican.org/resources/bcp/CofE1928/CofE1928.htm. Accessed 20 Aug. 2015.

Pseudo-Aristotle (1680). *Aristotle's Master Piece*. Ex-classics Project on-line edition, 2010. http://www.exclassics.com/arist/ariintro.htm. Accessed 20 Aug. 2015.

Rahman, Momin and Stevi Jackson (2010). *Gender and Sexuality: Sociological Approaches*. Cambridge: Polity Press.

Ratzinger, Joseph and Angelo Amato (2004). *Letter to the Bishops of the Catholic Church on the Collaboration of Men and Women in the Church and in the World*. http://www.vatican.va/roman_curia/congregations/cfaith/documents/rc_con_cfaith_doc_20040731_collaboration_en.html. Accessed 20 Aug. 2015.

Rawls, John (1973). *A Theory of Justice*. Oxford: Oxford University Press.

Richardson, Sarah S. (2012). 'Sexing the X: How the X Became the "Female Chromosome"'. *Signs*, 37/4, 909–33.

Ringe, Sharon (1985). 'A Gentile Woman's Story'. In Letty Russell (ed.), *Feminist Interpretation of the Bible*. Philadelphia: Westminster John Knox Press, 65–72.

Roberts, Christopher Chenault (2007). *Creation and Covenant: The Significance of Sexual Difference in the Moral Theology of Marriage*. New York and London: T & T Clark International.

Rogers, Eugene, Jr (1999). *Sexuality and the Christian Body*. Oxford, UK, and Malden, MA: Blackwell.

Rosario, V. (1997). 'Homosexual Bio-Histories: Genetic Nostalgias and the Quest for Paternity'. In V. A. Rosario (ed.), *Science and Homosexualities*. New York: Routledge, 89–107.

Rousseau, Jean-Jacques (1762 [in English 1763]). *Émile, or On Education*. Trans. Barbara Foxley. http://www.gutenberg.org/cache/epub/5427/pg5427.html. Accessed 20 Aug. 2015.

Ruether, Rosemary Radford (1992 [1st edition 1983]). *Sexism and God-Talk*. London: SCM Press.

Ruether, Rosemary Radford (1998). *Women and Redemption*. London: SCM Press.

Russell, Letty (ed.) (1985). *Feminist Interpretation of the Bible*. Philadelphia, PA: Westminster John Knox Press.

Salzman, Todd and Michael Lawler (2013). 'Usury and Homosexual Behaviour: Parallel Theological Tracks?' *Modern Believing*, 54/3, 193–200.

Sawyer, Deborah (1996). *Women and Religion in the First Christian Centuries*. London and New York: Routledge.

Schaberg, Jane D. (1998). 'Luke'. In Carol Ann Newsom et. al. (eds), *Women's Bible Commentary*. Louisville, KY: Westminster John Knox Press, 363–80.

Schiebinger, Londa (1989). *The Mind Has No Sex? Women in the Origins of Modern Science*. Cambridge, MA and London: Harvard University Press.

Schiebinger, Londa (1993). *Nature's Body: Gender in the Making of Modern Science*. Boston: Beacon Press.

Schultz, J. A. (2002). 'Bodies That Don't Matter: Heterosexuality before Heterosexuality in Gottfried's Tristan'. In K. M. Phillips and B. Reay (eds), *Sexualities in History: A Reader*. New York: Psychology Press, ch. 3.

Schüssler Fiorenza, Elisabeth (1983 [2nd edition 1994]). *In Memory of Her: A Feminist Theological Reconstruction of Christian Origins*. London: SCM Press.

Schüssler Fiorenza, Elisabeth (1995). *Jesus: Miriam's Child, Sophia's Prophet*. London: SCM Press.

Sevcik, Irene, Nancy Nason-Clark, Michael Rothery, and Robert Pynn (2011). 'Finding their Voices and Speaking Out: Research amongst Women of Faith in Western Canada'. In Nancy Nason-Clark, Catherine Clark-Kroeger, and Barbara Fisher-Townsend (eds), *Responding to Abuse in Christian Homes: A Challenge to Churches and their Leaders*. Eugene, OR: Wipf & Stock, 169–89.

Shanley, Mary Lyndon (1981). 'Marital Slavery and Friendship: John Stuart Mill's The Subjection of Women'. *Political Theory*, 9.2 (May), 229–47.

Shaw, Jane (1998). 'Gender and the Act of Synod'. In Monica Furlong (ed.), *Act of Synod, Act of Folly?* London: SCM Press, 14–26.

Shaw, Jane (2007). 'Reformed and Enlightened Church'. In Gerard Loughlin (ed.), *Queer Theology: Rethinking the Western Body*. Malden, MA and Oxford: Blackwell Publishing, 215–29.

Shepherd, John J. (1975). *Experience, Inference and God*. London and New York: Macmillan.

Shoemaker, Robert Brink (1998). *Gender in English Society, 1650–1850: The Emergence of Separate Spheres?* London: Longman.

Song, Robert (2014). *Covenant and Calling: Towards a Theology of Same-Sex Relationships*. London: SCM Press.

Stanton, Elizabeth Cady (1895). *The Woman's Bible*. On-line: *The Project Gutenberg EBook of The Woman's Bible, by Elizabeth Cady Stanton* (2006). https://archive.org/stream/thewomansbible09880gut/wbibl10.txt. Accessed 3 Jan. 2016. No pagination.

Storkey, Elaine (2007). 'Evangelical Theology and Gender'. In Timothy Larsen and Daniel J. Treier (eds), *The Cambridge Companion to Evangelical Theology*. Cambridge: Cambridge University Press, 161–76.

Stowers, Stanley, K. (1997). *A Rereading of Romans*. New Haven, CT: Yale University Press.

Stringer, Mark D. and Ines Becker (2010). 'Colombo and the Clitoris'. *European Journal of Obstetrics & Gynecology and Reproductive Biology*, 151, 130–3. http://intervalolibre.files.wordpress.com/2012/05/el-clitoris.pdf. Accessed 20 Aug. 2015.

Stuart, Elizabeth (2003). *Gay and Lesbian Theologies: Repetitions with Critical Difference.* Aldershot: Ashgate.

Stuart, Elizabeth (2015). 'The Theological Study of Sexuality'. In Adrian Thatcher (ed.), *The Oxford Handbook of Theology, Sexuality, and Gender.* Oxford: Oxford University Press, 18–31.

Swancutt, Diana (2003). '"The Disease of Effemination": The Charge of Effeminacy and the Verdict of God (Romans 1:18–26)'. In Stephen D. Moore and Janice Capel Anderson (eds), *New Testament Masculinities.* Atlanta, GA: Society of Biblical Literature, 193–234.

Swancutt, Diana (2006). 'Sexing the Pauline Body of Christ: Scriptural Sex in the Context of the American Christian Culture War'. In Virginia Burrus and Catherine Keller (eds), *Towards a Theology of Eros: Transfiguring Passion at the Limits of Discipline.* New York: Fordham University Press, 65–98.

Taylor, Charles (2007). *A Secular Age.* Cambridge, MA: Belknap Press of Harvard University Press.

Tertullian (n/d). *A Treatise on the Soul,* trans. Peter Holmes. Ante-Nicene Fathers, vol. 3. http://www.tertullian.org/anf/anf03/anf03-22.htm#P2560_840932. Accessed 20 Aug. 2015.

Thatcher, Adrian (1990). *Truly a Person, Truly God.* London: SPCK.

Thatcher, Adrian (1999). *Marriage after Modernity: Christian Marriage in Postmodern Times.* Sheffield: Sheffield Academic Press.

Thatcher, Adrian (2002). *Living Together and Christian Ethics.* Cambridge: Cambridge University Press.

Thatcher, Adrian (2007). *Theology and Families.* Malden, MA and Oxford, UK: Blackwell.

Thatcher, Adrian (2008a). *The Savage Text: The Use and Abuse of the Bible.* Chichester, UK: Wiley-Blackwell.

Thatcher, Adrian (2008b). 'Nuptial Imagery in Christian Doctrine and its Usefulness for a Marital Spirituality'. In Thomas Knieps-Port le Roi and Monica Sandor (eds), *Companion to Marital Spirituality,* Studies in Spirituality Supplement 18. Leuven: Peeters, 201–12.

Thatcher, Adrian (2011). *God, Sex and Gender: An Introduction.* Chichester: Wiley-Blackwell.

Thatcher, Adrian (2015a). 'Families'. In Adrian Thatcher (ed.), *The Oxford Handbook of Theology, Sexuality, and Gender.* Oxford: Oxford University Press, 590–607.

Thatcher, Adrian (ed.) (2015b). *The Oxford Handbook of Theology, Sexuality, and Gender.* Oxford: Oxford University Press.

Thurston, Bonnie (2004). *Women in the New Testament.* Eugene, OR: Wipf & Stock.

Tracy, Steven R. (2011). 'Calling the Evangelical Church to Truth: Domestic Violence and the Gospel'. In Nancy Nason-Clark, Catherine Clark-Kroeger, and Barbara Fisher-Townsend (eds), *Responding to Abuse in Christian Homes: A Challenge to Churches and their Leaders*. Eugene, OR: Wipf & Stock, 28–46.

Trumbach, Randolph (1978). *The Rise of the Egalitarian Family: Aristocratic Kinship and Domestic Relations in Eighteenth-Century England*. New York: Academic Press.

Trumbach, Randolph (1998). *Sex and the Gender Revolution*, vol. 1: *Heterosexuality and the Third Gender in Enlightenment London*. Chicago: University of Chicago Press.

Trumbach, Randolph (2012). 'The Transformation of Sodomy from the Renaissance to the Modern World and its General Sexual Consequences'. *Signs*, 37/4, 832–47.

Turner, Max (2000). 'Historical Criticism and Theological Hermeneutics of the New Testament'. In Joel B. Green and Max Turner (eds), *Between Two Horizons*. Grand Rapids, MI and Cambridge, UK: Eerdmans, 44–70.

United Nations Commission on the Status of Women (2013). http://www.un.org/womenwatch/daw/csw/csw57/CSW57_Agreed_Conclusions_(CSW_report_excerpt).pdf. Accessed 20 Aug. 2015.

Van der Horst, Peter (1990). 'Sarah's Seminal Emission: Hebrews 11:11 in the Light of Ancient Embryology'. In David L. Balch, Everett Ferguson, and Wayne A. Meeks (eds), *Greeks, Romans and Christians: Essays in Honour of Abraham J. Malherbe*. Minneapolis, MN: Fortress Press, 287–302.

van Klinken, Adriaan S. (2013). *Transforming Masculinities in African Christianity: Gender Controversies in Times of AIDS*. Surrey, UK and Burlington, VT: Ashgate.

Vanhoozer, Kevin J. (2003). 'Theology and the Condition of Postmodernity'. In Kevin J. Vanhoozer (ed.), *The Cambridge Companion to Postmodern Theology*. Cambridge: Cambridge University Press, 3–25.

Volf, Miroslav (2003). 'The Trinity and Gender Identity'. In D. A. Campbell (ed.), *Gospel and Gender: A Trinitarian Engagement with Being Male and Female in Christ*. London and New York: T&T Clark International, 155–78.

Wall, Alan (2009). *Myth, Metaphor and Science*. Chester: Chester Academic Press.

Ward, Graham (1998). 'The Erotics of Redemption: After Karl Barth'. *Theology and Sexuality*, 8, 52–72.

Warnke, Georgia (2011). *Debating Sex and Gender*. New York and Oxford: Oxford University Press.

Waweru, H. M. (2008). 'Jesus and Ordinary Women in the Gospel of John: An African Perspective'. *Svensk Missionstidskrift*, 96/2, 139–59.

Waylen, Georgina, Karen Celis, Johanna Kantola, and S. Laurel Weldon (eds) (2013). *The Oxford Handbook of Gender and Politics*. Oxford: Oxford University Press.

Wells, Jo Bailey (2013). 'Women and Men in the Creation and Fall Stories'. In Steven Croft and Paula Gooder (eds), *Women and Men in Scripture and the Church: A Guide to the Key Issues*. Norwich: Canterbury Press, 7–13.

Wikipedia (2015). 'Violence against Women'. https://en.wikipedia.org/wiki/Violence_against_women. Accessed 20 Aug. 2015.

Wiles, Maurice (1976). *Working Papers in Doctrine*. London: SCM Press.

Williams, Rowan (1990). 'Trinity and Pluralism'. In Gavin D'Costa (ed.), *Christian Uniqueness Reconsidered: The Myth of a Pluralistic Theology of Religions*. Maryknoll, NY: Orbis, 3–15.

Witte, John, Jr (1997). *From Sacrament to Contract: Marriage, Religion, and Law in the Western Tradition*. Louisville, KY: Westminster John Knox Press.

Witte, John, Jr (2009). *The Sins of the Fathers: The Law and Theology of Illegitimacy Reconsidered*. Cambridge: Cambridge University Press.

Witte, John, Jr (2015). 'Sex and Marriage in the Protestant Tradition, 1500–1900'. In Adrian Thatcher (ed.), *The Oxford Handbook of Theology, Sexuality, and Gender*. Oxford: Oxford University Press, 304–22.

Wollstonecraft, Mary (2004 [1792]). *A Vindication of the Rights of Woman*. London: Penguin Books.

Working Party Commissioned by the House of Bishops of the Church of England (2002). *Marriage in Church after Divorce*. London: Church House Publishing.

World Council of Churches (2013). Statement from the Men Gathered for the WCC Women's and Men's Pre-Assembly. https://www.oikoumene.org/en/resources/documents/assembly/2013-busan/pre-assembly-outcome-documents/statement-from-the-men-gathered-for-the-wcc-womens-and-mens-pre-assembly. Accessed 20 Aug. 2015.

Zamfir, Korinna (2007). 'The Quest for the "Eternal Feminine": An Essay on the Effective History of Genesis 1–3 with Respect to the Woman'. *Annali di storia dell'esegesi*, 24/2, 501–22.

Index